Jossey-Bass Teacher

Jossey-Bass Teacher provides educators with practical knowledge and tools to create a positive and lifelong impact on student learning. We offer classroom-tested and research-based teaching resources for a variety of grade levels and subject areas. Whether you are an aspiring, new, or veteran teacher, we want to help you make every teaching day your best.

From ready-to-use classroom activities to the latest teaching framework, our value-packed books provide insightful, practical, and comprehensive materials on the topics that matter most to K–12 teachers. We hope to become your trusted source for the best ideas from the most experienced and respected experts in the field.

The ESL/ELL Teacher's
BOOK OF LISTS
Second Edition

JACQUELINE E. KRESS, Ed.D.

JOSSEY-BASS
A Wiley Imprint
www.josseybass.com

Published by Jossey-Bass
A Wiley Imprint
989 Market Street, San Francisco, CA 94103-1741—www.josseybass.com

ISBN: 978-0-470-222-676

Library of Congress Cataloging-in-Publication Data

Kress, Jacqueline E.
  [ESL teacher's book of lists]
  The ESL : ELL teacher's book of lists / Jacqueline E. Kress.—2nd ed.
    p. cm.
  Rev. ed of: The ESL teacher's book of lists. 1st ed. 1993.
  Includes bibliographical references.
  ISBN 978-0-470-22267-6 (pbk.)
1. English language—Study and teaching—Foreign speakers. 2. Lists. I. Title.
  PE1128.A2K74 2008
  428.0071—dc22   2008036105

Printed in the United States of America

SECOND EDITION
PB Printing 10 9 8 7 6 5 4 3 2

About This Book

This unique resource and teacher time-saver includes scores of helpful, practical lists that may be reproduced for classroom use or referred to in the development of instructional materials and lessons for English Language Learners (ELLs). Written for general education teachers, specialists in English as a Second Language (ESL), special educators, English language arts instructors, reading and language tutors, and adult education instructors, this book was designed to help teachers reinforce and enhance the learning of grammar, vocabulary, pronunciation, and writing skills by ESL students of all ability levels. For easy use and quick access, the lists are organized into ten sections: "Getting Started," "Core English," "Pronunciation," "Vocabulary Builders," "Grammar," "Content Area Words," "Culture," "Teaching," "Assessment," and "Helpful Resources and References."

Educators will find this book to be a ready source of good examples, key words, teachable content, and teaching ideas that might otherwise take many years and much effort to compile. Also, the resources section includes a comprehensive glossary of ESL and education terms to provide readers with an indispensable guide to the specialized language of ESL instruction.

The Author

Jacqueline E. Kress is dean and professor of education at Georgian Court University in Lakewood, New Jersey, where she works with college and school faculty to prepare classroom teachers, ESL teachers, reading specialists, special education teachers, school counselors, and school administrators. Prior to her tenure at Georgian Court she served as dean at New York Institute of Technology and at Fordham University. She earned a doctorate in Reading from Rutgers University, where she was honored with the Evelyn Headley Award for her research in children's reading comprehension.

Before becoming a dean, Kress taught reading skills and methods courses at colleges in New York and New Jersey. She also worked with native and nonnative speakers of English as a language arts classroom teacher and reading specialist in urban schools in New Jersey.

Kress's work on behalf of at-risk students has resulted in the development of numerous education programs to improve literacy and school achievement. She is also recognized for her work in assessment and accreditation. She is coauthor of *The Reading Teacher's Book of Lists* (Fifth Edition, Jossey-Bass, 2006) and *The Readability Machine* (Prentice Hall, 1986).

Contents

Section 2 Core English 29

Section 3 Pronunciation 63

Section 6   Content Area Words   213

Section 7   Culture   233

Section 8 Teaching   273

Preface to the Second Edition

Because you have picked up this book, you are probably aware of the growing number of students in our schools for whom English is a second, or even third, language. When the first edition of *The ESL Teacher's Book of Lists* was published in 1993, about 13 percent of the school population spoke a language other than English at home. As of 2007, according to the National Center for Education Statistics, this proportion had risen to more than 20 percent. That's about 10.6 million school-aged children. As the number of English language learners has increased, so has the need for materials that teachers can use to support their developing language skills.

That's where this book comes in. Like the first edition of *The ESL Teacher's Book of Lists*, the goal of this book is to put practical, classroom-tested content into the hands of ESL and regular classroom teachers, like you, to help provide effective instruction to ELLs. Much has changed in language, education, and testing since the first edition was written. In response, *The ESL/ELL Teacher's Book of Lists* presents updated and expanded versions of the original lists, and forty completely new ones. As was the previous volume, *The ESL/ELL Teacher's Book of Lists* is a convenient repository of easy-to-find teaching content, not a manual for implementing a particular approach to language teaching and learning.

The ten sections of *The ESL/ELL Teacher's Book of Lists* cover all the bases: getting started, core English vocabulary, pronunciation, vocabulary builders, grammar, content area words, culture, teaching, assessment, and helpful resources and references. Each list begins with a brief introduction that provides background and teaching suggestions.

Section 1, "Getting Started," includes teaching tips and a taxonomy to help organize instruction, must-know classroom vocabulary for typical directions and learning activities, one hundred ways to acknowledge good work, and templates for making active-response cards for whole-class participation. Tips for working with response cards are also included.

Section 2, "Core English," provides lists of English words that are essential in daily life, including the five hundred most frequently used English words, and lists that focus on numbers, weather, time, health, family and relationships, money, transportation, safety, and more. This section is especially helpful to students in newcomer programs.

Section 3, "Pronunciation," has fifteen lists to help you pinpoint potential pronunciation problems and provide practice. Yes, there is a list of tongue twisters! Practice words for mastering English stress and intonation patterns are included as well.

Sections 4 and 6, "Vocabulary Builders" and "Content Area Words," offer twenty-one lists ranging from synonyms, American idioms, cognates, and collocations to basic and intermediate vocabulary in math, social studies, geography, and science. The content area words are more important than ever given the increasing emphasis on academic English and standardized testing. The content area word lists were drawn from the vocabulary of current popular textbooks in each discipline.

In Section 5, "Grammar," more than twenty lists present the parts of speech and sentence patterns, including patterns for negation, for questions and answers, and for active and passive sentences. Common grammatical errors and spelling rules are also included in this section.

Section 7, "Culture," is new. Use the Month-by-Month Commemorative Dates and the Seasons and Holidays lists to plan themed units throughout the year and as a foundation for current events and newspaper reading. Other lists in this section use proverbs and idioms to discuss similarities and differences in world cultures. The "Common Names" list introduces students to the most common first and last names in the United States. The "Government and States" list and the "Flag Pledge and Patriotic Songs" list are musts for civics units.

Sections 8 and 9, "Teaching" and "Assessment," go hand in hand and provide suggestions and ideas to support lesson planning all year. Lists include ideas for thematic language units, word walls, conversation and discussion starters, and targeted activities to improve listening, speaking, reading, and writing skills. In addition, there are templates for common activities such as bingo, calendars, and advance organizers. Assessment activities are organized by target area (for example, auditory skills and reading comprehension) to make it easy to match an activity to your instructional needs. An annotated list of commonly used standardized tests and their publishers rounds out Section 9.

Finally, in Section 10, "Helpful Resources and References," you will find a comprehensive list of Web sites for ESL/ELL teachers and the URLs for a virtual ESL/ELL reference library. Plan to spend time online visiting the Web sites listed. Bookmark those you find most useful, and introduce students to those that have special features (such as audio pronunciation guides). Section 10 also includes an extensive glossary of ESL/ELL language learning terms, an indispensable guide to the specialized language of ESL instruction.

Other than "Getting Started," the sections are not meant to be used in a particular order. Instead, I invite you to spend some time scanning the table of contents and browsing through the pages of *The ESL/ELL Teacher's Book of Lists*. I am confident that you will find many new and effective strategies to address the range of needs of your ELL students and to keep your classes interesting.

JACQUELINE E. KRESS

Section One

Getting Started

List 1.1. Tips for Teaching ESL/ELLs

Language development research tells us that second-language acquisition follows the same natural order as first-language learning. The initial stage is a silent period in which individuals develop the ability to hear the sounds, rhythms, and patterns of the language and match some words to actions, ideas, and things. It is often a frustrating time for English language learners (ELLs) because they cannot communicate their needs or ideas and they feel isolated from others in the classroom.

In the second stage, ELLs begin to put their knowledge of words and syntax together to speak in simple sentences. They augment their productive communication with gestures, pointing, and simple diagrams or pantomimes.

As listening and speaking competence continues to develop, ELLs' readiness for reading and writing emerges. Although we think of these stages as coming one after another, it is more accurate to think of them as a progression of starting points for three stages that continue along an increasingly integrated pathway toward proficiency. Here are some tips to help you support ELLs' transition to proficiency.

- Welcome students every day with a smile, a greeting, and their given names.
- Speak clearly and slowly, and use short, simple sentences.
- Face students when speaking to them; communicate with facial expressions and gestures.
- Watch students' body language and facial expressions for signs of comprehension.
- Pause between sentences to give students processing time.
- Praise students' efforts and successes appropriately; use "One Hundred Ways to Praise" (List 1.3).
- Use the same language for repeated tasks and routines.
- Demonstrate or pantomime responses to directions until all students understand and can perform them.
- Introduce yes/no active response cards immediately to enable active participation; frame questions for yes/no responses.
- Use choral response and whole-group active response cards to limit individual students' anxiety.

- Use realia, labels, and pictures to name objects and show actions.
- Establish routines for attendance, calendar review, assignments, homework review, and so on.
- Read to students daily using high-interest controlled vocabulary materials with lots of pictures.
- Present information in more than one modality: words and graphics plus spoken language.
- Provide computer-aided practice for individual students to give opportunities for self-paced work, including self-selected topics.
- Construct word walls to prompt students' memories and help them to be independent.
- Provide bilingual dictionaries at appropriate grade levels and encourage students to use them.
- Plan nonverbal ways for students to show they have understood stories, directions, and so on; for example, have them select appropriate pictures or draw diagrams.
- Write page numbers and other information on the board after giving directions to *"turn to page . . ."* or *"underline the answer. . . ."*
- Post homework assignments in the same place every day.
- Establish assessment systems that enable students to record and monitor their own progress in at least one or two areas.
- Have students keep word books and journals and add to them frequently.
- Post a world map (or regional map as needed) and have students identify their countries of origin.
- Provide opportunities for students to share cultural and linguistic information; for example, have them label a family tree with family relationships in both English and their first language; or have them list each language's greeting or its words for *excellence, student, learning,* and so on.
- Plan music and art exhibits to showcase cultures represented in the class.
- Remember that students know much more than they can say—don't water down content; do simplify the language.
- Gather content reading materials on several grade levels.
- Use cognates to help connect new learning with prior knowledge.
- Establish class rules with brief commands and gestures: *Sit. No talking. Show me the answer. Go to page___.*
- Post the names of students in groups and point to each group's list of names when calling students to a learning station or table. Seeing and hearing group members' names helps ELLs learn the names and eases communication within the group.
- Start portfolios of students' work at the beginning of the term and add to them as they progress throughout the year.

List 1.2. Teaching Taxonomy for Beginning ELLs

A taxonomy is an ordered list that categorizes many elements. The following teaching taxonomy organizes essential English language objectives to provide ideas and guidance for lesson planning. It is not meant to be followed in sequence. The taxonomy includes elements that are also part of an English Language Arts (ELA) curriculum, but it does not replace your reading, spelling, or writing objectives. ELLs need both ELA and English as a Second Language (ESL) instruction to succeed. Copy the list and put a check or date next to the elements needed by your current ELL students to plan a month, term, or year at a time.

Personal and Family Information

❏ Personal identity information: name, address, phone number, parents' names, guardian's name, country of origin, age, nationality, birth date, Social Security number
❏ Spelling of first and last names
❏ Responses to questions about grade, school, teacher
❏ Responses to and requests for personal information, for example, *Where do you . . . ? Who are . . . ? When did . . . ? What is . . . ?*
❏ Completing an information card, including providing a signature
❏ Responses to questions about parents, siblings, sponsors
❏ Family members and relations
❏ Pets and other animals

Social Interaction and Self-Expression

❏ Greetings and good-byes
❏ Asking and thanking
❏ Introductions to peers, nonpeers; shaking hands; kissing
❏ Expressing like/dislike, agreement/disagreement
❏ Manners and customary phrases for events: birthdays, anniversaries, holidays, illness, giving compliments and congratulations, and so on
❏ Beginning and ending conversations
❏ Asking for assistance or services; offering help
❏ Small talk about family, friends
❏ Expressing emotions and feelings: anger, frustration, love, affection, fears, needs, concerns, hopes, wishes
❏ Asking for clarification
❏ Expressing lack of understanding or lack of English skills
❏ Polite and impolite language
❏ Making eye contact
❏ Manners as a guest and host
❏ Invitations: making, accepting, and refusing
❏ Apologizing and expressing regret
❏ Using the phone: answering, making a call, leaving messages
❏ Writing a letter, addressing an envelope
❏ Post office: types of mail, cost of postage
❏ Writing e-mail and text messages

Class and School

❏ Classroom elements: books, desks, screen, whiteboard, chalk, pens, blackboard, learning center, overhead projector, computer, table, pencil sharpener, closet, and so on

❏ Class directions, such as *point to, show, circle, print, copy, color, put an X through, sit down, line up, take out your___ book, turn to page___, stop talking, raise your hand, turn to your neighbor*

❏ Class procedures: flag salute, announcements, calendar, weather, class schedule, morning exercises, attendance, permission form, bathroom pass, hall pass

❏ School locations: classroom, library, principal's office, cafeteria, gym, locker room, nurse's office, and so on

❏ School personnel: teacher, secretary, custodian, principal, librarian, and so on

❏ School activities: learning, subjects, assembly, clubs, field trips, home room, sports teams, newsletter, school home page, permission forms, medical exam, testing program, guidance counselor, resource room

❏ School assessments: homework, directions, grades and report cards, cheating, independent and group work

❏ Test-taking skills

Calendar, Time, and Weather

❏ Calendar: days of the week, dates, months, seasons

❏ Read, write, and say the current date

❏ Holidays, birthdays, anniversaries, school holidays, vacations

❏ Writing and reading dates in alternate forms

❏ Concepts of yesterday, today, and tomorrow

❏ Difference between weekday and weekend

❏ Telling time: digital and analog clocks, watches

❏ Concepts of day, noon, midnight, dawn, morning, evening, and so on

❏ Telling time with Roman numerals

❏ Concepts of starting and ending time, beginning and end, opening and closing time, class periods, terms, semesters, school year

❏ Weather conditions: hot, cold, cool, sunny, cloudy, rainy, snowing

❏ Weather phrases and related vocabulary: *What's it like out? How will it be later? What's the temperature? Hazy, hot, and humid. Winds will die down later. Weather vane, meteorologist, weather report, tracking the storm,* and so on

Health and Safety

❏ Vocabulary for body parts

❏ Vocabulary for health problems and illnesses: *Does your head hurt? I have a headache.*

❏ Making and keeping appointments with doctors, nurses, dentists

❏ Medical-related vocabulary: *illnesses, clinic, hospital, procedures*

❏ Medical insurance-related vocabulary needed for applications and claims

❏ Emergencies: calling 911, describing the emergency, giving the location

❏ Symbols and vocabulary for *poison, emergency, no smoking, flammable, danger, caution,* and so on

❏ Staying safe at home: locking doors, fire safety, dangerous objects, child safety, bathtubs, leaving children, seasonal issues, firecrackers
❏ Recognizing and following directions and symbols for walking to school and crossing streets
❏ Reporting incidences of bullying, abuse, or assault

Life and Living

❏ Recognizing and using color names
❏ Recognizing and using shape names
❏ Recognizing and using names for foods
❏ Recognizing and using food-related vocabulary: *breakfast, lunch, dinner, supper, snack, beverage, drink, buying lunch, bringing lunch, packing lunch, eating lunch, nutrition,* and so on
❏ Working with recipes and food measurements
❏ Understanding the food pyramid and nutrition
❏ Making a shopping list, using coupons, shopping
❏ Setting the table
❏ Using table manners
❏ Reading prices using dollars and cents
❏ Selecting clothing: types, sizes, colors, fabrics, parts
❏ Shopping for clothes: store types, prices, sales, ads, trying on/fitting room
❏ Doing laundry: how, when, and why
❏ Recognizing, reciting, and writing numbers 1–10, 1–100, beyond 100
❏ Counting by 2, 5, and 10
❏ Recognizing odd and even numbers
❏ Recognizing and writing number words one to ten, one to one hundred, beyond one hundred
❏ Recognizing and using ordinal numbers
❏ Recognizing and understanding the use of a comma in numbers
❏ Recognizing and using money: coins, bills, counting, making change
❏ Reading prices and currency amounts
❏ Understanding decimal and comma use in currency
❏ Counting money and making change
❏ Setting up bank accounts (savings, checking), writing checks, using the ATM
❏ Making and using a budget
❏ Recognizing and using measurements: *cup, quart, gallon, ounce, pound*

Home and Community

❏ Names for rooms in house and related vocabulary
❏ Names for types of housing: *house, apartment, condo, mobile home, attached, ranch, split level, co-op, rooming house,* and so on
❏ Names for furniture and furnishings
❏ Locations in community: churches, theaters, shopping mall, library, schools, government buildings, supermarkets, hospitals
❏ Signs and symbols for restrooms, entrance, exit, accessible route, parking

❏ Community workers and their jobs
❏ Government: local, state, federal
❏ U.S. flag, Pledge of Allegiance, patriotic songs
❏ Names of mayor, governor, and president
❏ Names and associated words for common jobs
❏ Employment vocabulary: *getting a job, earning a living*
❏ Types of entertainment and sports and related vocabulary
❏ Common games, rules, and related vocabulary

Transportation and Directions

❏ Directions: left, right; ahead, behind; up, down
❏ Directions: north, south, east, west; compass; compass rose
❏ Using directions to find a location, giving directions to a location
❏ Using a map to locate a city, state, the United States, birthplace, country of origin
❏ Asking for clarification of directions
❏ Using online direction service to find directions to important places in city
❏ Transportation words
❏ Highway and travel words and symbols
❏ Travel safety: child safety seats, leaving children or pets in cars, speed limits, parking zones, calling for help, emergency equipment for car

Beginning Literacy

❏ Alphabet: recognize, recite, alphabet song, print upper- and lowercase
❏ Understanding alphabetical order
❏ Writing upper and lower letters in cursive and to form words
❏ Recognizing book parts
❏ Directionality for print: left to right, top to bottom
❏ Copying words (print) in correct order and direction
❏ Labeling pictures
❏ Matching words and pictures
❏ Discriminating between rhyming and nonrhyming words
❏ Discriminating individual words in sentences
❏ Phonemic awareness
❏ Following one-, two-, and three-step verbal directions
❏ Giving one- and two-step verbal directions
❏ Rhymes and chants
❏ Singing along with repetitive songs
❏ Recognizing word order in sentences
❏ Listening to and getting the gist of a story read aloud
❏ Sequencing pictures
❏ Relating sounds to beginning and ending phonemes
❏ Segmenting words into individual syllables and sounds
❏ Recognizing and using rhyming words and word families
❏ Recognizing and using short vowels
❏ Recognizing and using long vowels

❏ Blending sounds
❏ Recognizing and using diphthongs and digraphs
❏ Discriminating minimal pairs
❏ Recognizing sight vocabulary in frequency lists, word walls, labels
❏ Recognizing and using sound clusters
❏ Recognizing silent letters
❏ Recognizing and using root words
❏ Recognizing and using prefixes and affixes
❏ Accent reduction

Nouns, Pronouns, and Modifiers

❏ Articles: *a, an, the, some*
❏ Singular and plural regular nouns
❏ More than one noun as subject (*and,* series)
❏ Compound nouns
❏ Countable and noncountable nouns
❏ Personal pronouns
❏ Object pronouns
❏ Possessive pronouns
❏ Demonstrative pronouns
❏ Adjectives of color, size, age
❏ Other descriptive adjectives
❏ Comparison of adjectives
❏ Adverbs of frequency
❏ Adverbs of manner
❏ Adverbs of time and place
❏ Comparison of adverbs
❏ Using *many* and *much*

Verbs

❏ Verb: *to be*
❏ Verb: *be + not*
❏ Verb: *have/don't have*
❏ Simple present tense: affirmative
❏ Simple present tense: negative
❏ Simple present tense: questions
❏ Simple past tense: affirmative
❏ Simple past tense: negative
❏ Simple past tense: questions
❏ Simple past tense: irregular verbs
❏ Common verbs in present tense
❏ Future tense: *will* + verb
❏ Future tense: *going to*
❏ Verbs: command forms
❏ Verbs: negative commands

❑ Common two-word verbs
❑ Past continuous tense: *was* + verb + *ing*
❑ Verb pattern: Verb + *to* + verb
❑ Passive voice

Sentence Patterns

❑ Distinguishing nouns and verbs
❑ Sentence pattern: noun + verb
❑ Sentence pattern: subject + *be* + verb + *ing*
❑ Sentence pattern: subject + *be* + verb + *ing* + noun
❑ Sentence pattern: questions using *who, what, where, when, how, why*
❑ Compound sentences
❑ Sentence pattern: tag questions
❑ Sentences beginning with *there is, there are*
❑ Sentences using nonspecific *it:* It's time to go. It's raining.
❑ Subject-verb agreement
❑ Sentence pattern: subject + *be* + verb + prepositional phrase
❑ Sentences using transitions : *however, therefore,* and so forth
❑ Sentences using *if* clauses

Reading and Learning from Text

❑ Using a picture dictionary
❑ Using a bilingual dictionary
❑ Using a chart or graph to answer questions
❑ Using an index to find information
❑ Using a table of contents to find information
❑ Recognizing and using sequence and chronology markers
❑ Using context clues to aid comprehension
❑ Choral reading
❑ Reading and understanding poetry
❑ Reading and understanding expository text
❑ Reading and understanding narrative text
❑ Finding information through key word searches on the Internet
❑ Fluency
❑ Sentence rhythms

Spelling, Capitalization, Punctuation, and Writing

❑ Using objects, drawings, charts, and other media to support spoken message
❑ Irregularly spelled but frequently used words
❑ Spelling rules
❑ Punctuation marks and sentence types
❑ Capitalization rules and proper nouns and adjectives
❑ Language registers and writing for the audience
❑ Writing a description

❏ Writing a paragraph with time sequence
❏ Writing directions using numbered steps
❏ Writing a story
❏ Writing dialogue
❏ Keeping a journal
❏ Writing a book report

Other Instructional Targets

❏ Antonyms
❏ Contractions
❏ Conjunctions
❏ Homographs and homonyms
❏ Idioms
❏ Prepositions: *to, in, on, under, near*
❏ Prepositions: *at, from, for, with, next to, between, behind, over*
❏ Synonyms

List 1.3. One Hundred Ways to Praise

Learning to speak another language is not easy. It takes motivation, courage, perseverance, attention, and work. Recognizing students' efforts and gains builds confidence, motivates, confirms, shows respect, acknowledges, rewards, and sets standards for accomplishment. Use words of praise often—even for small successes; it will encourage greater ones. Be genuine and specific about what was praiseworthy. Remember, your smile and tone convey a lot, even with a limited vocabulary.

Excellent!

Good work!

You did well today.

Impressive!

Wow!

A+

Fantastic!

Good thinking.

This is great!

Very good!

This is clever.

Much better.

Keep it up.

Interesting!

Good job!

This is well done.

Very nice!

I like the words you chose.

You are creative.

Superb!

Beautiful work.

What neat work!

Congratulations!

Very interesting!

You have improved a lot.

Terrific!

Good point!

You made a great start.

Super!

I like your idea.

This is excellent.

Well done!

★ ★ ★ ★

GR 8!

Awesome!

Fantastic!

I like your topic.

Great style!

This is well organized.

Very convincing!

Good use of details.

You've really mastered this.

Excellent beginning!

Good observation.

You've got it!

Your family will be proud of this.

This shows your talent.

That's really nice.

★ quality!

You're on target.

Expert work.

You know this well.

Thank you!

You've made my day.

Very creative.

Very interesting.

I like the way you're working.

That's an interesting way of looking at it.

Now you've figured it out.

Keep up the good work.

You're on the ball today.

This is something special.

Excellent work.

That's the right answer.

Exactly right.

I like your choice of words.

I can tell you were very careful with this.

You made me smile.

You're quite an expert.

Very informative.

You really caught on!

Be sure to share this—it's great!

You're a Rising Star!

You're on the right track.

This is quite an accomplishment.

I like the way you handled this.

This is coming along nicely.
You have been paying attention.
You've put in a full day today.
This is prize-winning work.
Bravo!
I like your style.
Hurray!
Clear, concise, and complete!
A well-developed theme!
You're right on the mark.
Good reasoning.
Dynamite!

Outstanding!
This is a winner!
Great going!
I knew you could do it!
What neat work!
You really outdid yourself today.
That's a good point.
That's a very good observation.
You've got it now.
This shows you've been thinking.
Very fine work.
That's quite an improvement.

List 1.4. Meeting and Greeting

Meeting people, making new friends, and finding their way around in school and in the neighborhood are priorities for new ESL/ELL students. Many students will have some knowledge of the spoken forms of the following frequently used words and phrases but may not have adequate pronunciation and visual recognition skills, fluency, or natural intonation or accent patterns to be understood or to understand others. Use these words and phrases to develop appropriate dialogues for role-playing in class.

Hello.
Hi.
Good morning.
Good afternoon.
Good evening.
Hi, there.

How are you?
How're you doing?
How's it going?
How have you been?

Fine, thanks. And you?
Good, thanks. And you?
I can't complain. And you?
Fine, thank you. And you?

What's your name?
My name is _____.
Your name, please.
I'm [name]_____.
May I have your name?

Where do you live?
I live on _____ Avenue.
What's your address?
I'm at 34 Locust Drive, Montville.
My address is 612 Second Avenue, Allenhurst.

Street   Avenue   Road   Drive   Circle
Court   Place   Boulevard   Lane   Way

Do you go to school?
Where do you go to school?
What school do you attend?
What school are you in?

Are you in high school?
Do you go to the high school?
Do you go to [name of school]?
What grade are you in?
What class are you in?
What are you taking this year?
What classes do you have this year?
What do you have fourth period?

I'm a freshman [sophomore, junior, senior].
I'm a student at _____.
I go to _____ School.
I attend _____.
I'm in third grade.
I'm in middle school.
I'm in Mr. Cox's class.
I'm taking algebra.
I'm in the ESL class.
I have math fourth period.
I have math fourth period with Mr. Bix.

Where's the cafeteria?
Where is the library?

Principal's office, school nurse, book room, attendance office, boys' locker room, girls' room, Coach's office, home room, assembly hall, theater, auditorium, stage, hockey field, gym, chemistry lab, IT office, multimedia center, AV storeroom, visitors' entrance, teachers' room, teachers' lounge, staff room, custodian's office

Do we have practice?
Is there a game tonight?
Would you like to go to the game?
Do you like to dance?

Do you like music?
Would you like to listen to some
    music?
What kind of music do you like?
What's your favorite group?
Do you like to go to concerts?

I'm hungry.
Are you hungry?
Do you want to get some lunch?
Do you want lunch?
Do you want to eat now?
I'm starved.
I'm famished.
I'm thirsty.
I need something to drink.
I'm dry. I'd like some water.
Would you like a bottle of water?
Where can I get a bottle of water?
Where can I get something to eat?
Where can I buy a snack?

Would you like a cup of coffee? Tea?
I'd like a cup of coffee, please.
May I have a cup of coffee,
    please?
What can I get you?
Can I get you something?
What would you like to have?
A burger and large fries, please.
Just an iced tea, please.

Thank you.
Thanks a lot.
Call me tonight.
What's your phone number?
I've got to go now.
I have to run.
Have a nice day.
See you later.
See you tomorrow.
Bye now.
Bye-bye.
Good-bye.
So long.
Good night.

Are you new here?
When did you move here?
Where did you live before?
Where are you from?
Are you from _____?
Where are you going?
What's the matter?
Is something the matter?

Excuse me.
I'm sorry.
Pardon me.
I apologize.
That's all right.
No problem.

Go ahead.
Come on, let's go.
Come on in.
I appreciate it.
You're very kind.
No, thank you.
Yes, please.
May I help you?
Would you help me, please?
Of course.
It would be a pleasure.
My pleasure.

Who is that?
That's Alex.
Would you introduce us?
Philip, this is Alex.
Nice to meet you.
Please join us.
Thanks for calling.

Congratulations!
Happy Birthday!
What's that?
I don't know.
Who knows?
I'm sorry for your loss.
I was sorry to hear about your _____.
Is there anything I can do to help?
Can you use some help?

I'm sorry, I don't understand English.

Would you repeat that more slowly, please?

What does _____ mean?

Please say that again.

I'm sorry, I don't understand.

Pardon?

How do you say _____ in English?

How do you pronounce this word?

How do you spell _____?

Is this the correct word?

Is this the correct spelling?

I don't understand the directions.

Please repeat the directions.

What should I do next?

I'm finished with the assignment.

List 1.5. Realia and Manipulatives

Realia—objects used to illustrate and teach vocabulary—are now commonplace in ESL/ELL classrooms. These artifacts provide multisensory experiences with words that express some facet of American life and, in addition to providing a natural context for learning, they facilitate students' cultural experiences. Manipulatives—objects that can be manipulated or changed during problem solving—have long been used in mathematics, and they add active learning to any classroom.

action figures
bingo tokens
blocks
brochures from states, cities
buttons
catalogs
checks
clothing
costumes
counting rods
coupons
dental floss, toothbrush, toothpaste
digitized audio files of sounds, conversations
dollhouse with furniture
empty food packages
fruit
games
globe
greeting cards for many occasions
holiday decorations and figures
jars and containers
keys
leaf collection
magazines of all types
maps
measuring cups
measuring spoons
menus
miniature houses
miniature tools
movie or concert tickets

newspaper want ads
phone books
plastic flowers
plastic fruit
play jewelry
play money
postcard collection
puppets
receipts
recipes and cookbooks
rock collection
rulers
seeds, flowerpot, watering can
shell collection
shoe collection
small dolls with clothes
small flags from around the world
supermarket circulars
top or other spinning toy
touch panel (with different textures)
toy animals (plastic or stuffed)
toy boats
toy cars
toy dish set
toy doctor's kit
toy musical instruments
toy phones
toy pots
train and bus schedules
travel and tourism brochures
vegetables (real or plastic)

List 1.6. Predictable School Routines

Getting off to a good start in any teaching and learning setting is important. One effective strategy is to establish routines from the very first meeting. For ESL/ELL classes the routines should engage the students, review core vocabulary, and use as many senses as possible. Write the class agenda on the board, post it on a bulletin board, or give it to students on a handout. The following list contains typical class activities and vocabulary.

Class Commands

Use gestures and demonstrations to show students what the commands mean. Begin with four commands and practice them until all students respond easily. Then add a few more commands and mix up the order. Review daily until students follow the directions without hesitation.

Sit down.
Stand up.
Raise your hand.
Put your hand down.
Raise both hands.
Put both hands down.
Take out a piece of paper.
Take out a pencil.
Give me your paper.
Give me your pencil.
Take out your language notebook.
Put your language notebook away.
Open your language notebook.
Close your notebook.

Look at me.
Look at the door.
Look at the window.
Look at the flag.
Look at your desk.
Look at the calendar.
Look at the blackboard.

Point to the door.
Point to the window.
Point to the flag.
Point to your desk.
Point to your chair.
Point to the calendar.
Point to the blackboard.

Stand up and walk to the door.
Walk to your desk.

Sit down.
Stand up and walk to the blackboard.
Walk to your desk.
Sit down.
Stand up and walk to the window.
Walk to your desk.
Sit down.
Stand up and push your chair in.
Pull out your chair and sit down.

Take out your language notebook.
Open your notebook.
Write your name on the top line.
Write the word *class* in your notebook.
Copy the word *class* two times.
Underline the word *class*.
Copy the word *class* again.
Circle the word *class*.
Close your book.
Put your book away.

Get your language notebook.
Open to a new page.
Take out your language book.
Open to page _____.
Close your book.
Put your book away.

[Student's name], please hand out the paper.
[Student's name], please hand out the pencils.
[Student's name], please collect the paper.
[Student's name], please collect the pencils.

Calendar Routines

Most teachers include a calendar routine at the beginning of the day or class. Start with the name of the day and the date. Later add birthdays and special events. In addition to oral recitation, have students write the day and date in their language notebook.

> This is the calendar.
> Today is [weekday name].
> This month is _____.
> Today's date is [month, date].
> Today is _____'s birthday.
> Happy Birthday, _____.

Weather and Season Routines

Weather routines often follow the calendar exercise. Below the calendar place a row of pictures of different sky and weather conditions with the descriptions captioned. Have students pick the sky and weather conditions that match the day's weather and pin them to the calendar in the appropriate spaces. Also have a digital thermometer nearby so students can read the temperature and post it on the calendar.

> Today's sky is [blue, gray, cloudy, foggy, dark].
> Today's weather is [sunny, rainy, snowy, windy].
> Today's temperature is _____ degrees.
> It is [cold, cool, mild, warm, hot].
> We are in the _____ season.
> Colors of [season] are [use pointer to point to the list on the word wall for seasons].
> Special days in [season] are [use pointer to point to list on word wall for seasons].
> Things we do in [season] are [use pointer to point to list on word wall for seasons].

Flag Salute

Teachers often end their opening exercises with the flag salute. On the bulletin board closest to the flag have the Pledge of Allegiance written out and point to the words as they are said.

> Please stand up.
> Face the flag.
> Put your hand over your heart.
> Say the Pledge of Allegiance with me.
> I pledge. . . .

List 1.7. Active Response Activities

Active response activities allow all students to participate throughout an exercise, greatly increasing time on task for every student. In addition, during ELLs' silent period, before they are able and confident enough to respond orally, students can practice and demonstrate their acquisition of target vocabulary, idioms, structures, and more. The following exercises are examples of activities that can be used with response cards for letters, numbers, yes/no, true/false, 1-2-3-4, A-B-C-D, same/different, and before/after answers. See List 1.8, on active response cards, for additional information on their use.

Distribute the appropriate set of cards to students and have them place the cards face up on their desks. Demonstrate how to select and show the answer. For "strip" cards, which have more than one answer (numbers, letters), show how to hold the card with fingers on the correct answer. Begin slowly and wait until everyone has responded, picking up the pace when everyone has understood the question-response pattern. Repeat challenging items to allow students to correct an earlier incorrect response. Do the drill silently as a quiz or have students vocalize their answers as they show them.

Yes/No Response Cards

Is Hector a boy? Is Anna a boy?
Do birds fly? Do cats bark?
Are baby lions called kittens?
Can you use a paddle to write?
Do you see with your ears?
Is this blue? [Show card or object.]
Is this California? [Point to state on map.]
Is this breakfast? [Show picture of a meal.]
Is this a sweater? [Show picture of clothing.]

Same/Different Response Cards

The sounds at the beginning of *pit/pen*
The sounds at the beginning of *sigh/slight*
The sounds at the beginning of *big/pig*
The sounds at the end of *pat/pad*
The sounds at the end of *bang/bank*
The sounds at the end of *hit/hid*

Before/After Response Cards

Study: before or after a test?
Practice: before or after a performance?
Pay: before or after picking a sandwich?
Wet: before or after the rain?
Sleepy: before or after a nap?

True/False Response Cards

Ms. Polk is the science teacher.
It is raining today.
It snowed yesterday.
The custodian cleans the school.
Rene has red hair.
The U.S. flag has twenty-five stars.
George Washington is president.
New York City is the capital of New York.

Letter Response Cards

Show me an *M* [any letter].
Show me the letter for [make a specific sound].
Show me the letter at the beginning of _____.
Show me the letter at the end of _____.
Show me the silent letter in _____.

Number Response Cards

Show me a 7 [any number].
Show me 2 + 6 [any addition fact].
Show me 10 − 4 [any subtraction fact].
If plums cost twenty-five cents each, how many can I buy with one dollar?
How many sides does a triangle have?
How many shoes are in seven pairs?

1, 2, 3, 4 or A, B, C, D Response Cards

Where do you sleep? 1. table; 2. desk; 3. bed; 4. lamp
Which one goes with parties? 1, 2, 3, or 4 [show pictures]
I have a toothache. Call: A. the nurse; B. the dentist; C. the clerk; D. the minister
The boy in the story had: A. a dog; B. a cat; C. a monkey; D. a pony

Note: To minimize memory problems and focus language, show images one at a time using presentation software.

List 1.8. Active Response Cards

Response cards may be used with ESL/ELL students of any age and for both simple and complex exercises. See List 1.7, on active response activities, for exercises that work well with whole-class active response techniques. Photocopy a set of active response cards (letters, numbers, yes/no, true/false, 1-2-3-4, A-B-C-D, same/different, before/after) on heavy index stock for each student in the class. Cut the cards apart and distribute to the students. Demonstrate how to show the answer.

Yes/No Example

Ask, *Is Hector a boy?* Show the yes card to the class. Say, *Yes, Hector's a boy.* Then return the card to the desk and ask the next question: *Is Anna a boy?* Show the no card. Say, *No, Anna's not a boy.* Tell the class it is their turn to answer the questions, and begin a drill. Begin slowly and wait until everyone has responded, picking up the pace when everyone has understood the question-response pattern. Repeat challenging items to allow students to correct an earlier incorrect response.

Variations: Model the response and vocalization and have students show and say with you. Have them show the answer while you vocalize the correct answer. Do the drill silently as a quiz.

For letters and numbers: cut one-line strips, not individual letters or numbers. Have students show the correct answer by holding it between their thumbs and forefingers.

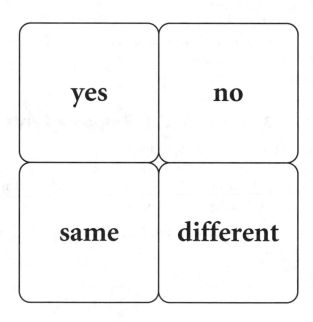

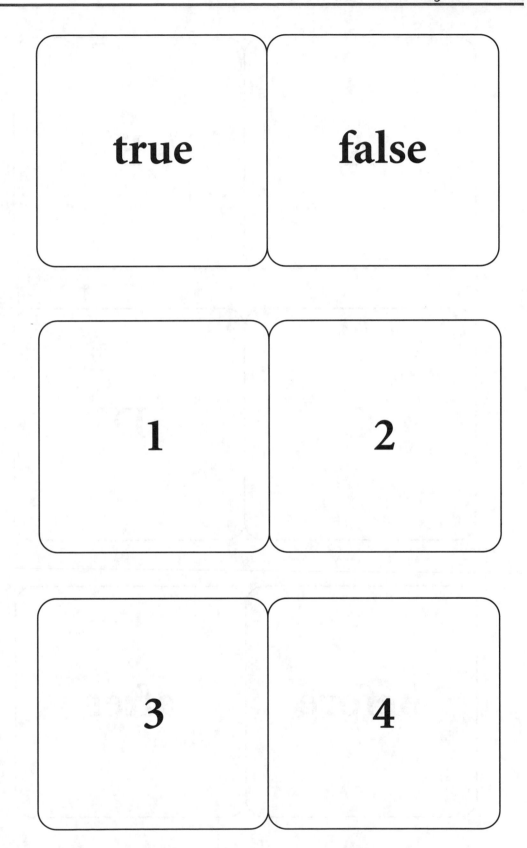

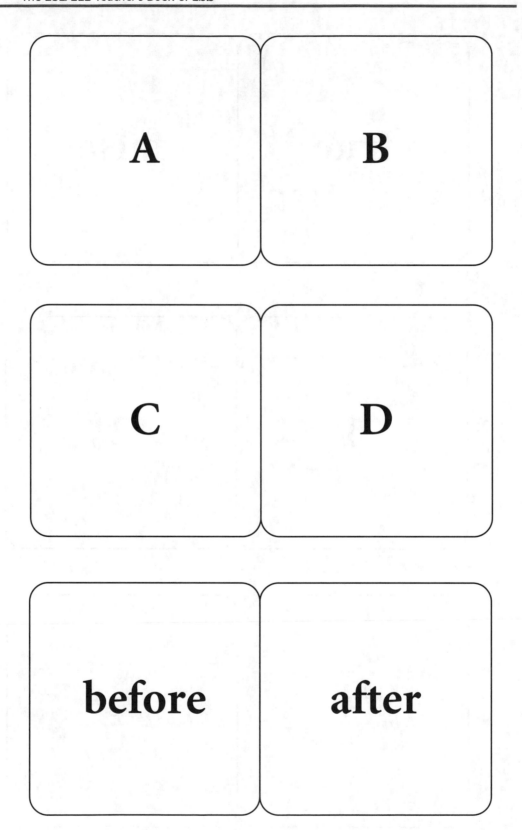

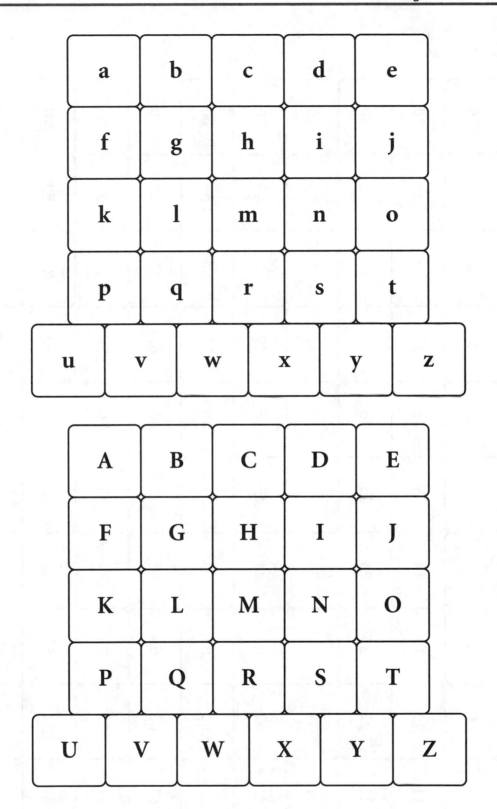

1	2	3	4	5	6	7	8	9	10
11	12	13	14	15	16	17	18	19	20
21	22	23	24	25	26	27	28	29	30
31	32	33	34	35	36	37	38	39	40
41	42	43	44	45	46	47	48	49	50
51	52	53	54	55	56	57	58	59	60
61	62	63	64	65	66	67	68	69	70
71	72	73	74	75	76	77	78	79	80
81	82	83	84	85	86	87	88	89	90
91	92	93	94	95	96	97	98	99	100

List 1.9. Class and School Vocabulary

One way to help newcomers become comfortable in their new surroundings is to help them learn the names of things they say, see, and do in school. Labels on objects and a word wall about "our classroom" or "our school" are useful aids in mastering this important category of vocabulary. Using the same idioms and vocabulary in daily routines will also make learning them easier.

Assignment Directions

Ask your neighbor	Hand in your _____	Raise your hand
Check your work	Next one	Show me the _____
Circle	No talking	Skip one
Cross out	Pass out the _____	Take turns
Draw a line	Point to _____	Write your name on your
Fill in the answer	Put an X on the _____	paper
Fill in the blank	Put the date on your paper	
Finger-width margin	Quiet, please	

General Class and School Words

absent	co-ed	flunk
achievement test	combination lock	game
administration	computer lab	girls' room
advanced placement	crayons	grades
advisor	dance	graduate
aide	data projector	graduation
assembly	dean	guidance counselor
assignment	desk	guidance office
attendance	desktop	gym
auditorium	detention	gymnasium
backpack	dictionary	half-day
ballpoint	dismissal	hall pass
bathroom	education	headphone
bell	ELL (English Language	headset
blackboard	Learner)	highlighter
book	enroll	holiday
book room	ESL (English as a Second	homeroom
bookstore	Language)	homework
boys' room	exam	honor roll
bus pass	examples	honors class
cafeteria	exercises	instructor
campus	extracurricular activity	janitor
cassette tape	faculty	lab
class discussion	fail	laboratory
classroom	file	language lab
club	finals	language proficiency test
coach	fire drill	laptop

lavatory	pen	school secretary
learn	pencil	scores
learning group	pencil sharpener	seat
lecture	period	security guard
librarian	permission slip	snow day
library	photocopy	software
locker	placement test	stage
locker room	playground	state tests
looseleaf paper	portfolio	student
lunch	present	study hall
lunch box	principal	superintendent
map	probation	tardy
marker	professor	teach
marking period	program	teacher
media center	prom	teachers' lounge
midterms	PTA	teachers' room
note	pupil	team
notebook	quiz	term
nurse	reading group	test
nurse's office	recess	textbook
online	remedial	theater
open house	report card	truant
orientation	resource room	tutor
pad	ruler	vacation
parent conference	safety glasses	vice principal
party	schedule	warning notice
pass	school	whiteboard
PC	school bus	workbook

Course Titles

Algebra	Data Processing	History
American Government	Drama	Home Economics
Art	Driver's Education	Industrial Education
Basic Math	Earth Science	Italian
Bilingual _____	English	Latin
Biology	ESL (English as a Second	Literature
Black Studies	Language)	Mathematics
Bookkeeping	European History	Music
Business English	Foreign Language	Philosophy
Business Math	Forensic Science	Phys. Ed.
Calculus	French	Physical Education
Chemistry	General Math	Physical Science
Civics	Geography	Physics
Composition	Geometry	Precalculus
Computer Science	German	Psychology
Cooperative Education	Gym	Science
Dance	Health	Shop

Social Studies
Sociology
Spanish
Spelling

Stenography
Technical Education
Technology
Trigonometry

Typing
U.S. History
Vocational Education
World History

Types of Schools

private school
public school
day care center
nursery school
kindergarten
preschool
elementary school

middle school
intermediate school
junior high school
secondary school
senior high school
regional high school
vocational school

technical school
trade school
junior college
community college
college
university

Common School Idioms

as easy as ABC
back to basics
bookworm
cap and gown
handouts
higher education
honor roll
in ink
in pen
in pencil
in single file
Ivy League
on campus
school of thought
show of hands
show-and-tell
teacher's pet
the three R's
to be absent
to be present
to be tardy
to brainstorm something
to call the roll
to collect homework
to collect the papers
to copy
to cover a lot of ground
to crack a book
to cram
to cut class
to daydream
to demonstrate
to dictate

to discuss
to do an assignment
to do an example
to do homework
to do math
to do research
to draw a blank
to drop out of school
to erase the board
to fill in the blanks
to flunk out
to get credit for
to get partial credit
to get through a course
to go off campus
to goof off
to hand out
to have one's nose in a
    book
to hit the books
to know one's ABC's
to learn
to learn by heart
to learn by rote
to lecture
to line up
to listen carefully
to make the grade
to meet the requirements
to memorize
to pass
to pass the papers out
to pass with flying colors

to pay attention
to play a tape
to play hooky
to print
to put on one's thinking
    cap
to read
to read out loud
to read through something
to read to oneself
to report to the office
to salute the flag
to sharpen a pencil
to sign
to sign in
to sign up
to skim the chapter
to study
to take [name of course]
to take a course
to take a test
to take an exam
to take attendance
to take notes
to take the roll
to talk about
to type
to work one's way through
    college
to write
to write a paper

List 1.10. ESL/ELL Students' Language Background

According to the U.S. Census Bureau's 2006 American Community Survey, 19.7 percent of the U.S. population over the age of five—some 54.9 million people—speak a language other than English at home. This may seem surprisingly high. However, more than half (55.8 percent) of these individuals not only speak their native language but also speak English very well. Children in many of these households develop competence in both languages as they grow up. In contrast, more than 24.2 million people in the United States are non-English or limited English speaking. Census data for 2006 indicate that nearly 5 percent of all U.S. households are linguistically isolated. That is, no member of the household aged fourteen or older speaks English very well.

Data submitted by states to the U.S. Department of Education identified four hundred languages spoken by students who are limited English proficient (LEP). The first of the following tables shows the languages, other than English, spoken most frequently in U.S. homes. The second table shows the most common language groups of LEP students. Spanish is by far the most frequently spoken other language in either category, accounting for 61 percent of non-English home language use and 79 percent of the language backgrounds of LEP students.

Languages Spoken at Home

1. Spanish	7. Other Germanic	13. Other Slavic	19. Other Indic
2. French	8. Scandinavian	14. Armenian	20. Other Indo-European
3. Italian	9. Greek	15. Persian	21. Chinese
4. Portuguese	10. Russian	16. Gujarathi	22. Japanese
5. German	11. Polish	17. Hindi	23. Korean
6. Yiddish	12. Serbo-Croatian	18. Urdu	24. Khmer

Language Groups of LEP Students

1. Spanish	7. Arabic	13. Portuguese	19. Chinese (other)
2. Vietnamese	8. Russian	14. Urdu	20. Chamorro
3. Hmong	9. Tagalog	15. Serbo-Croatian	21. Marshallese
4. Cantonese	10. Navajo	16. Lao	22. Punjabi
5. Korean	11. Khmer	17. Japanese	23. Armenian
6. Haitian Creole	12. Mandarin	18. Chuukese	24. Polish

For additional information visit the U.S. Census Bureau at http://www.census.gov or the National Clearinghouse for English Language Acquisition at http://www.ncela.gwu.edu.

Section Two

Core English

List 2.1. Five Hundred Most Frequently Used English Words

Some word lists are graded and reflect the typical school-based development of young children's reading skills. The following list is different. It provides, in ranked order, the English words most frequently encountered in newspapers, magazines, textbooks, children's books, and novels. The first one hundred words account for approximately 50 percent of the words in a given piece of prose. The first three hundred make up approximately 65 percent. For ESL/ELL students of any age to become fluent listeners, speakers, readers, and writers of English, they need to recognize these words both aurally and in print, be able to pronounce them alone and in phrasal units, and be able to read and write them.

1–50

the	in	he	as	at
of	is	was	with	be
and	you	for	his	this
a	that	on	they	have
to	it	are	I	from

or	but	we	there	she
one	not	when	use	do
had	what	your	an	how
by	all	can	each	their
word	were	said	which	if

51–100

will	many	some	him	two
up	then	her	into	more
other	them	would	time	write
about	these	make	has	go
out	so	like	look	see

51–100 (*continued*)

number	my	call	find	get
no	than	who	long	come
way	first	oil	down	made
could	water	its	day	may
people	been	now	did	part

101–200

over	little	live	very	name
new	work	me	after	good
sound	know	back	thing	sentence
take	place	give	our	man
only	year	most	just	think

say	much	mean	boy	also
great	before	old	follow	around
where	line	any	came	form
help	right	same	want	three
through	too	tell	show	small

set	well	such	ask	land
put	large	because	went	different
end	must	turn	men	home
does	big	here	read	us
another	even	why	need	move

try	change	away	letter	still
kind	off	animal	mother	learn
hand	play	house	answer	should
picture	spell	point	found	American
again	air	page	study	world

201–300

high	between	last	never	light
every	own	school	start	thought
near	below	father	city	head
add	country	keep	earth	under
food	plant	tree	eye	story

saw	along	next	life	together
left	might	hard	always	got
don't	close	open	those	group
few	something	example	both	often
while	seem	begin	paper	run

important	car	sea	four	hear
until	mile	began	carry	stop
children	night	grow	state	without
side	walk	took	once	second
feet	white	river	book	later

miss	watch	let	cut	song
idea	far	above	young	being
enough	Indian	girl	talk	leave
eat	real	sometimes	soon	family
face	almost	mountain	list	it's

301–400

body	questions	horse	knew	usually
music	fish	birds	since	didn't
color	area	problem	ever	friends
stand	mark	complete	piece	easy
sun	dog	room	told	heard

order	top	short	hours	measure
red	ship	better	black	remember
door	across	best	products	early
sure	today	however	happened	waves
become	during	how	whole	reached

listen	fast	five	true	table
wind	several	step	hundred	north
rock	hold	morning	against	slowly
space	himself	passed	pattern	money
covered	toward	vowel	numeral	map

farm	cold	sing	town	field
pulled	cried	war	I'll	travel
draw	plan	ground	unit	wood
voice	notice	fall	figure	fire
seen	south	king	certain	upon

401–500

done	fly	correct	shown	front
English	gave	of	minutes	feel
road	box	quickly	strong	fact
half	finally	person	verb	inches
ten	wait	became	stars	street

401–500 (*continued*)

decided	building	rest	stay	less
contain	ocean	carefully	green	machine
course	class	scientists	known	base
surface	note	inside	island	ago
produce	nothing	wheels	week	stood

plane	boat	warm	though	yes
system	game	common	language	clear
behind	force	bring	shape	equation
ran	brought	explain	deep	yet
round	understand	dry	thousands	government

filled	object	power	dark	fine
heat	am	cannot	ball	pair
full	rule	able	material	circle
hot	among	six	special	include
check	noun	size	heavy	built

List 2.2. Fluency Practice for Most Frequently Used Words

Practice in reading and speaking the most frequently used words helps all students to develop their sight-reading and natural speaking abilities and their reading rhythms. The sentences in group 1 use only the first one hundred most frequently occurring words in American English. The sentences in group 2 use the three hundred most frequently occurring words. Use these phrases and sentences for choral reading exercises and as dictation for listening and writing practice.

Group 1

Be on time.
They will do it.
Come down from there.
Go with him.
He and I will write the numbers.
Come get some water.
We were all there.
Now is the time.
Who called?
Write the first word.
When can you find more time?
Go see them now.
How are they?
Which one is it?
How do you do it?
No way! He *cannot* do it.
She has been to the water.
Did you get it all?
People write one word at a time.
Is this all there is?
Some of the time I write numbers.
Will we go out now?
Look up the word.
Look at me.
I have this other oil to use.
I have to see him now.
Look for some water in there.
She said I could go there.
What would make her find some more?
It was all I had.
Did you like it?
Who called her about it?
I could see him with her.
They were with other people.
Go, but do not call him.

They will write about each other.
There were many people.
Call me first.
Did you have a long day?
You said you could do it.
He made part of it.
Is that water?
Many people could do it.
Your day is long.
These days are not all long.
That one is for you.
This one is for me.
You and I will go now.
She will write to him.
Use this first.
We were all there.
First, oil it.
There were many more people than at first.
May I have these?
Part of the time I write words.
I write about many people.
There are two more days to go.
People could see the many parts.
I like many parts.
People like water.
What are these?
Many of them see the other part first.
When will they find us?
I will go see her in two more days.
Write it down.
Write about the other day.
She said you can do it.
In time, we will look at them.
Go into it with all you have.
Call him now.

This is the way to look at it.
Each of you will use one.
Which one is his?
Come and get some water.
She could find some over there.
He or she will find the way to do it.
Do you see it?
Many more people went into the water.
Have you some time to talk?
I had many calls to make.
Each one had a number.
I had no more time to look for him.
Look at what time it is!
Other people look up to him.

Did you see her come and get it?
Would you go now?
Write the numbers as you see them.
See how he does it?
This has to be number one.
Look down there.
My number is one.
Is that all there is?
So, this is where you are!
There is oil on the water.
Which part was his?
Which way is it to the water?
I like many other people.
More water will find its way down there.

Group 2

I know his name.
That is a good sentence.
She is an American now.
Ask her where she lives.
I will take over the work.
Ask where I could find them.
I want to learn to read.
I know the answer.
It's a good list.
I miss my family.
I like being in a new state.
I have a good idea.
It is almost time to go.
Turn around and look this way.
Soon I will see my family.
I want to leave this place.
Turn here to go to the sea.
Show me where it is.
Tell me what you want.
Turn it off now.
There was enough to eat.
We play, spell, and read in school.
Close it up so no water gets in.
My home was in a different country.
After a long time I saw a new plant.
They have a white car.
It was more than four miles away.
A few children left the school.
Mother had a letter from the school.

It is just what I want.
Did you mean that?
Can you help me?
Point to the first word on the page.
Point to the first sentence.
I study every day.
Father read the letter.
I can tell my own story.
It is a very big tree.
I saw the light before he did.
This is a hard example.
Let her cut it now.
Young boys sometimes watch men work.
I have many books in school.
The river water came up high.
Move over, so I can see.
I found the answer before he did.
Think a little, work a little.
Try another answer.
Hand mother the letter.
I could hear the sound of the sea.
A second later I could see it.
Sometimes we go to the mountains.
I found the answer on the page.
He likes to study about the world.
The plant began to grow.
The plant cannot grow without water.
First, we talk; second, we walk.
The young girl grew up in the city.

Give the school book back to mother.
Most of us like to eat good food.
Old men still learn new things.
Every year we grow more food.
First we start, then we stop.
Between us we have four feet.
I need a picture of a different animal.
Three small boys came to my home.
Think about one very good thing.
This year we will give the most help.
In the new country we will start over.
The mother took her children to the sea.
The girl brought the papers to school.
I saw the picture of a face.
He gave the most back to his people.
The man came to show us the house.

They planted every tree in the city.
Men thought about the hard work.
What does it mean?
When does school end this year?
The light was in our eyes.
Show me what you want.
Keep the animals away from the house.
We need to read to see where to turn.
Three old men were kind to father.
We never start something new at night.
The tree began to grow in the earth.
It is just a picture of an animal.
We could always hear the sound.
Good works gave him a good name.
The letter was still in the house.
The boys and girls came to play together.

We could hear the sounds of many people's songs.
Sometimes my mother lets me carry important papers.
Because of the water, we had to go to a new place.
Open it now and let the children come into the school.
Mother likes to keep three small plants around the tree.
It took a long time for the animal to walk around the tree.
The sound of all the children was like a song.
Before father had a car he would walk to the city.
One book can make a big difference in your life.
Change is important if you want to grow.
Every year the show came to the city for us to see.
Because the animal was so large, it had to live in the country.
I like to write letters to my family and take pictures of them.
He is in high school now, but she is not.
Tell me the same story again, because I like it.
Father had a good example of an answer.
The group likes to see pictures of mountains.
I have a list of work I have to do for school.
The group often got together to eat good food.
Mother said she still likes to learn new things.
We also took three boys to the country with our family.
We like to eat too much once in a while.
I walked around the house to see every side.
There is a story to tell about every life.
There are always enough new ideas to think about.
Stop to hear what father will say, then start on your way again.
In school we study about the rivers and the lands of the world.
I thought about the sea and the sound of the water.
Don't be mean to other people; they will not like you.
I learn how to spell many new words while I am in school.

The boy's feet are little; the father's feet are very large.

First, I saw the light. Then, a second later, I could hear the sound.

I like being in high school; it's a good change.

There is something on the list that is far more important than play.

I saw the time and, because it might close soon, I began to run to the school.

I had to study hard to learn to spell all the new words and numbers.

After high school I will work hard and do many good things.

Just before night I like to take a two-mile walk near the river.

Once I read the book I could see why the animals are in the country and not in the city.

I want to write a story about a mountain in my old country.

Your ideas are important but not enough; you need to learn how to make them real.

Work hard in school and later you will not have to work as hard as some others.

Change does not end, but because of it we can always grow.

List 2.3. Calendar Words

Calendar words are part of early ESL/ELL instruction and are incorporated into the daily routines of the classroom. Many teachers begin the day with a recitation of the day and date, a brief weather report, the Pledge of Allegiance, and the announcement of students' birthdays. See Section 7 for lists of holidays and other commemorative dates and their origins.

Days of the Week	Abbreviations	
Monday	Mon.	M
Tuesday	Tues.	T
Wednesday	Wed.	W
Thursday	Thurs.	TH
Friday	Fri.	F
Saturday	Sat.	S
Sunday	Sun.	SU

Months	Abbreviations	Months	Abbreviations
January	Jan.	July	July
February	Feb.	August	Aug.
March	Mar.	September	Sept.
April	Apr.	October	Oct.
May	May	November	Nov.
June	June	December	Dec.

Seasons	Months
spring	March, April, May
summer	June, July, August
fall (autumn)	September, October, November
winter	December, January, February

Related Vocabulary

celebrate	holiday	semester break
celebration	month	snow day
commemorate	national holiday	spring break
commemoration	observance	symbol
date	parade	vacation
day	patriotic	week
decorate	remembrance	weekday
decoration	school closing	weekend
eve	season	winter break

Ways to Write a Date

In American English we speak and write the month first, followed by the day and year. However, in most other languages the customary order is day, month, and then year. As a result, in Europe and other parts of the world, September 11, 2001, is remembered as 11/09/01. This change in the order can be a problem when students or guardians are filling out forms, making appointments, or reading notices from school. To eliminate miscommunication, be sure to write out the dates and indicate the order preferred on forms using "mm/dd/yy" or another indicator.

March 28, 1972	3/28/72	03/28/72
3.28.72	3-28-72	03/28/1972

List 2.4. Number Words

Counting numbers, also called cardinal numbers, show how much or how many. Ordinal numbers show rank or the order of things in a series. The symbols we use to show number are often called *Arabic numerals*. The term is somewhat misleading because the symbols were developed in India but spread through Europe and the rest of the world through the work of Arab and Persian mathematicians. The symbols used for numbers in the Arabic language are as follows:

٠	١	٢	٣	٤	٥	٦	٧	٨	٩	١٠
0	1	2	3	4	5	6	7	8	9	10

Many languages use a full stop or period instead of a comma as the separator for thousands. In English we write 52,876 but in other languages it would be written 52.876. The written form for decimals also differs between English and other languages. In English, a decimal number uses a period, which when spoken is called "point," as in "eighty-seven point five" (87.5). In other languages it would be written 87,5 and read "87 virgule 5."

Counting (Cardinal) Numbers		**Ranking (Ordinal) Numbers**	
0	zero		
1	one	1st	first
2	two	2nd	second
3	three	3rd	third
4	four	4th	fourth
5	five	5th	fifth
6	six	6th	sixth
7	seven	7th	seventh
8	eight	8th	eighth
9	nine	9th	ninth
10	ten	10th	tenth
11	eleven	11th	eleventh
12	twelve	12th	twelfth
13	thirteen	13th	thirteenth
14	fourteen	14th	fourteenth
15	fifteen	15th	fifteenth
16	sixteen	16th	sixteenth
17	seventeen	17th	seventeenth
18	eighteen	18th	eighteenth
19	nineteen	19th	nineteenth
20	twenty	20th	twentieth
21	twenty-one	21st	twenty-first
22	twenty-two	22nd	twenty-second
23	twenty-three	23rd	twenty-third
24	twenty-four	24th	twenty-fourth

Counting (Cardinal) Numbers		Ranking (Ordinal) Numbers	
25	twenty-five	25th	twenty-fifth
26	twenty-six	26th	twenty-sixth
27	twenty-seven	27th	twenty-seventh
28	twenty-eight	28th	twenty-eighth
29	twenty-nine	29th	twenty-ninth
30	thirty	30th	thirtieth
31	thirty-one	31st	thirty-first
40	forty	40th	fortieth
50	fifty	50th	fiftieth
60	sixty	60th	sixtieth
70	seventy	70th	seventieth
80	eighty	80th	eightieth
90	ninety	90th	ninetieth
100	one hundred	100th	one hundredth
150	one hundred and fifty	150th	one hundred and fiftieth
151	one hundred and fifty-one	151st	one hundred and fifty-first
200	two hundred	200th	two hundredth
500	five hundred	500th	five hundredth
1,000	one thousand	1000th	one thousandth
1,100	one thousand one hundred	1,100th	one thousand one hundredth
1,100	eleven hundred	1,100th	eleven hundredth
1,500	one thousand five hundred	1,500th	one thousand five hundredth
1,500	fifteen hundred	1,500th	fifteen hundredth
2,000	two thousand	2,000th	two thousandth
2009	two thousand nine	2009th	two thousand ninth
2009	two thousand and nine	2009th	two thousand and ninth
1,000,000	one million	1,000,000th	one millionth
1,000,000,000	one billion	1,000,000,000th	one billionth

List 2.5. Weather Words

A daily review of the weather is a good way to start the school day and to talk about weather words. Students enjoy taking turns as the class meteorologist, reading the day's forecast like their favorite TV personality.

Adjectives

arctic	damp	misty
balmy	dreary	overcast
breezy	drizzly	rainy
bright	dry	snowy
brisk	foggy	stormy
calm	freezing	sunny
chilly	frigid	sweltering
clear	hazy	tropical
clearing	hot	warm
cloudy	humid	wet
cold	icy	windy
cool	mild	

Nouns and Verbs

barometer	gust	snowfall
blizzard	hail	snowflake
blow	hailstone	squall
breeze	heat wave	storm
climate	humidity	sun
cloud	hurricane	sunshine
crest	ice	surge
cyclone	lightning	temperature
degrees	meteorologist	thunder
dew	overflow	thunderstorm
Doppler radar	precipitation	tornado
downpour	rain	torrent
drizzle	raindrop	tropical storm
flood	rainfall	weather
fog	shower	weather forecast
forecast	sleet	weather map
frost	snow	weather report
gale	snowstorm	weather vane
gathering	snowdrifts	wind

List 2.6. Color Words

Coloring is a favorite childhood pastime worldwide. You probably learned the names of colors by reading the labels on your very own box of crayons. According to Binney and Smith, their famous Crayola® Crayons now come in 120 colors. The words in Group 1 are a little less challenging to new ESL/ELL students than the words in Group 2.

Group I

black	green	violet
blue	orange	white
brown	red	yellow

Group II

apricot	green	pink
aquamarine	ivory	plum
beige	khaki	purple
black	lavender	red
blue	lemon yellow	rose
brick red	magenta	salmon
bronze	mahogany	sea green
brown	maize	sepia
carnation pink	maroon	silver
cerulean	melon	sky blue
chartreuse	mint green	spring green
copper	mulberry	tan
cornflower	navy blue	taupe
cream	off-white	teal
eggplant	olive green	turquoise
forest green	orange	violet
fuchsia	orchid	white
gold	peach	yellow
goldenrod	periwinkle	
gray	pine green	

List 2.7. Time Words

The Egyptians and Babylonians divided daylight and nighttime into twelve-hour periods, creating a twenty-four-period sun cycle. The length of the periods, however, changed on the basis of the length of daylight during each season. As a result, summer daylight hours were longer than daylight hours in winter. In 725, an English monk named Bede wrote a persuasive argument for twenty-four equal hours at all times, but the standard sixty-minute hour was not set until clocks were widely used in the 1300s.

Check out Time for Time at http://www.time-for-time.com/swf/myclox.swf and the time lesson and clocks at http://arcytech.org/java/clock/clock.html.

What Time Is It?

It is one o'clock.		It's four thirty.
It's 6 A.M.		It's six in the morning.
It's 6 P.M.		It's six in the afternoon.
It's 6:30 P.M.		It's midnight.
It's noon.		It's twelve o'clock.

It's a quarter to nine.	It's 8:45.	It's eight forty-five.
It's a quarter after nine.	It's 9:15.	It's nine fifteen.
It's half past three.	It's 3:30.	It's three thirty.
It's ten after eight.	It's 8:10.	It's eight ten.
It's five of seven.	It's 6:55.	It's six fifty-five.
It's around seven.	It's 7-ish.	It's about seven.

Time Words

sunrise	noon	sunset
dawn	high noon	dusk
sunup	midday	twilight
daybreak	afternoon	sundown
morning		evening
daytime		night
daylight		midnight

A.M. (after midnight, but before noon)
P.M. (after noon, but before midnight)

second	watch	digital clock
minute	wristwatch	analog clock
quarter hour	calendar	watch battery
half hour	stopwatch	hour-hand
hour	timer	minute-hand
day	clock radio	second-hand
clock	alarm clock	

Time-Related Idioms

a matter of time

ahead of time

all the time

at one time

be before your time

be in the right place at the right time

be only a matter of time

before your time

bide your time

big time

buy time

do time

Do you have the time?

find the time to do something

from time to time

give someone a hard time

have a hard time

have the time

in no time

in the nick of time

keep time

kill time

lose time

mark time

on time

pass time

punch in

serve time

set the clock

set your watch

synchronize your watches

take time out

take your time

tell time

time flies

time's up

two-time someone

wind your watch

Analog and Digital Clocks for Showing the Time

List 2.8. Health Words

Being able to communicate about health is key to staying healthy and to receiving appropriate care when ill. These lists provide core vocabulary and phrases for seeking medical and dental care, naming illnesses and complaints, identifying body parts, and following care instructions. Many limited-English speakers can receive translation assistance from local agencies or volunteers, and hospitals in most states have some interpreter services available. But waiting for an interpreter can cost time and delay treatment. Role-play multiple scenarios, including an accident, asthma attack, making appointments for an office visit, getting admitted to a hospital, and receiving outpatient care.

Basic Phrases

How are you?

Are you okay?

Are you sick?

Are you ill?

You don't look too well.

Do you need a doctor?

I am fine.

I don't feel well.

I am sick.

I feel dizzy.

I need a doctor.

I need help.

Please, call an ambulance.

Take me to a hospital.

Where is the nurse's office?

Where is the doctor's office?

This is an emergency.

She fell off her bike.

He took many pills.

I think she ate poison.

He is choking.

He was hurt on the job.

He's having an asthma attack.

I think she's having a heart attack.

I think she's had a stroke.

I think he had a drug overdose.

She is allergic to _____.

He is diabetic.

She fainted.

He is not conscious.

He's having a seizure.

I think he has broken bones.

He's bleeding.

He's in shock.

Complaints

I have a cold.	burn	injury
I have the flu.	chest pains	My chest hurts.
I have a sore throat.	chills	nausea
I have a backache.	constipation	pain
I have a cough.	cramps	rash
I have a fever.	cut	runny nose
I have a headache.	diarrhea	sore
I have something in my eye.	dizzy	sore throat
I sprained my ankle.	feel faint	stiffness
I broke my arm.	fever	swollen
My arm hurts. (My arms hurt.)	have an ache in	tender
My leg hurts. (My legs hurt.)	have an allergy	vomiting
be allergic to	head cold	wound
be in an accident	headache	
bleeding	hurt	

People

ambulance driver	lab technician	pharmacist
care coordinator	next of kin	physical therapist
dietician	nurse	physician
doctor	optician	police officer
emergency squad	optometrist	psychiatrist
EMT	orthopedic surgeon	psychologist
eye doctor	outpatient	school nurse
firefighter	patient	specialist
gynecologist	pediatrician	surgeon

Getting Care

admitting	examination room	nuclear medicine
ambulance	hospital	outpatient clinic
burn unit	injection	pharmacy
cardiac care unit	insurance card	physical therapy
claim form	insurance carrier	recovery room
clinic	insurance form	sleep center
CT scan	intensive care unit	surgical suite
delivery room	isolation	thermometer
drug store	labor room	treatment room
EEG	laboratory	waiting room
EKG	MRI	X-ray
emergency room	needle	

Diagnoses and Doctor's Orders

Ace bandage	coma	fluids
anesthesia	concussion	follow-up visit
antibiotics	condom	fracture
aspirin	contagious	gargle
asthma	contraceptive	gauze
Band-Aid	cough syrup	German measles
bandage	crutches	heal
bed rest	deaf	heart attack
birth control	decongestant	heating pad
blind	diabetes	hepatitis
blister	diagnostic tests	blood pressure
blood test	diet	ice pack
broken	dislocated	infected
bronchitis	drugs	infection
cancer	examination	infectious
cast	examine	inflammation
chicken pox	flu	inhaler
cholesterol	flu shot	injection

insulin
isolation
lab tests
laxative
liquid
measles
medication
medicine
mono
mononucleosis
mumps
nasal spray
operation
over the counter

oxygen
period
pills
pneumonia
pregnant
prescription
pulse
recuperate
rest
rubella
sanitary napkins
scrape
shot
sinusitis

soak
sprain
stitches
stroke
surgery
tablet
tampon
tetanus
ulcer
urinalysis
virus
vitamins
X-ray

External Parts of the Body

abdomen
Adam's apple
ankle(s)
arm(s)
back
breast(s)
buttocks
calf (calves)
cheek(s)
chest
chin
collarbone
dimple(s)
ear lobe(s)
ear(s)
elbow(s)
eye(s)
eyebrow(s)
eyelash(es)
eyelid(s)

face
finger(s)
fingernail(s)
fist(s)
foot (feet)
forearm(s)
forehead
genitals
hair
hand(s)
head
heel(s)
hip(s)
jaw
knee(s)
leg(s)
lip(s)
mouth
neck
nose

palm(s)
penis
rectum
scalp
shin(s)
shoulder(s)
skin
sole(s)
spine
temple(s)
testicles
thigh(s)
throat
thumb(s)
toe(s)
tongue
tooth (teeth)
vagina
waist
wrist(s)

Internal Parts of the Body

appendix
bladder
blood
bone(s)
brain

heart
intestines
kidney(s)
liver
lung(s)

muscle(s)
nerve(s)
rib(s)
spleen

Dental Health

bite
braces
cap
cavity
checkup
chin
cleaning
crown
dentures
drill

false teeth
filling
floss
gargle
gums
jaw
molar
mouthwash
nerve
novocaine

plaque
porcelain
root canal
toothache
toothbrush
toothpaste
whitening
wisdom tooth
X-ray

Health Idioms

back on one's feet
blackout
breakout
bring to
catch a cold
checkup
clean bill of health
come down with
draw blood
feel like a million bucks
feel on top of the world
flare-up
have a physical (exam)
make an appointment
out cold

pull through
run a temperature
run down
run some tests
splitting headache
take a turn for the worse
take someone's temperature
the picture of health
throw up
under the weather
if symptoms persist . . .
keep out of reach of children
pre-op tests
refer you to a specialist
take only as directed

List 2.9. Family and Relationship Words

According to French linguists Pierre Bancel and Alain de l'Etang, many of the world's six thousand spoken languages have common words and meanings for family members or kin, including the words *mama* and *papa*. In fact, they believe that these two words have been part of spoken language across the globe for at least fifty thousand years. Why? Perhaps it's because early parents were just as happy as today's modern moms and dads to respond to babies' first babbling sounds.

Use Adam's Family Relationships to practice identifying and speaking about core members of a family. Creating their own family tree helps students to master family relationship words by personalizing the learning. Several free family tree templates are available on the Web for you and your students to use.

Adam's Family Relationships

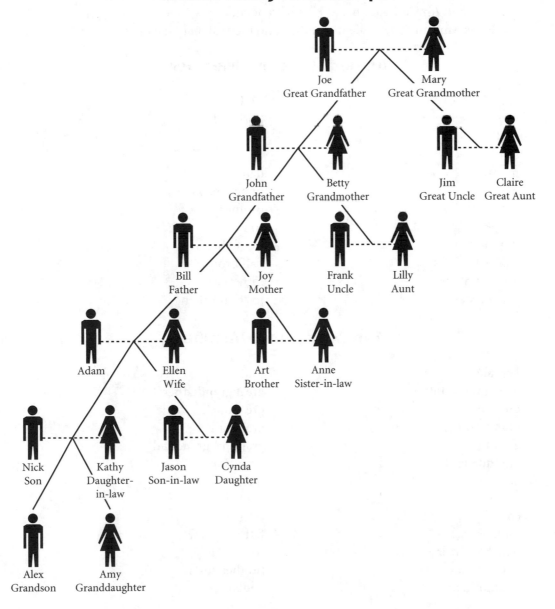

1. Adam's great grandparents Joe and Mary married shortly after they came to the United States.
2. They had two children, John and Claire.
3. John is Adam's grandfather and Claire is his great aunt.
4. Grandpa John married Grandma Betty the same year that great aunt Claire married Jim.
5. Adam's grandparents John and Betty had two sons, Bill and Frank.
6. Frank's grandfather Joe taught him how to drive a car.
7. Bill married Joy and is Adam's dad.
8. Adam is married to Ellen.
9. Adam's brother Art is married to Anne.
10. Art plays golf with his dad, Bill, and his grandfather John.
11. Ellen and her mother-in-law, Joy, like to garden, but her sister-in-law Anne doesn't.
12. Adam and Ellen have two children, Nick and Cynda.
13. Nick married Kathy and they also have two children, Alex and Amy.
14. Alex and Amy are Adam and Ellen's grandchildren.
15. Joy is Amy and Alex's great grandma and they call her Nana Joy.

Immediate Family Members

Female	**Male**
wife	husband
mother	father
mom	dad, pop
mommy	daddy
mama	poppa, papa
sister	brother
daughter	son
stepmother	stepfather
half sister	half brother
foster mother	foster father
foster sister	foster brother

Extended Family Members

Female	**Male**
great grandmother	great grandfather
great aunt	great uncle
grandmother	grandfather
grandma	grandpa, granddad
granddaughter	grandson
aunt	uncle
niece	nephew
cousin	cousin
mother-in-law	father-in-law
daughter-in-law	son-in-law
sister-in-law	brother-in-law
godmother	godfather

Other Relationships Words

adopted
adoptive
baby
boyfriend
bride
bridegroom
child
children
dependent
dependents
divorcée
family
fiancé
fiancée
folks
girlfriend

godchild
goddaughter
godson
grandchild
grandchildren
groom
guardian
immediate family
infant
in-laws
kids
kin
maternal relatives
nana
next of kin
orphan

parent
parents
partner
paternal relatives
relations
relatives
siblings
sponsor
spouse
teenager
toddler
triplets
twins
widow
widower

Family Event Words

adopt
be pregnant
expect a baby
have a baby
give birth to
born
birthday
birth certificate

baptize
raise a child
live together
get engaged
be engaged
marry
get married
be married to

anniversary
separated
get divorced
divorce
be widowed
lose someone
pass away
reunion

List 2.10. Money Words

Economists and others who watch the interaction of money, technology, and people predict that we are heading toward the end of cash. Instead of the now-familiar printed paper, we will be using only debit cards, online bill paying, and other electronic transfers. In the meantime, it's nice to know that annually the U.S. Treasury's Bureau of Engraving and Printing prints about 38 million notes a day, with a face value of approximately $750 million, most of which replace old and damaged bills.

U.S. Currency

$0.01	1 cent	one penny	1/100 of a dollar
$0.02	2 cents	two pennies	1/50 of a dollar
$0.05	5 cents	one nickel	1/20 of a dollar
$0.10	10 cents	one dime	1/10 of a dollar
$0.25	25 cents	one quarter	1/4 of a dollar
$0.50	50 cents	one half dollar	1/2 of a dollar
$1.00	100 cents	one dollar bill	1 dollar
$5.00		five dollar bill	5 dollars
$10.00		ten dollar bill	10 dollars
$20.00		twenty dollar bill	20 dollars
$50.00		fifty dollar bill	50 dollars
$100.00		one hundred dollar bill	100 dollars

Money-Related Words

ATM	credit limit	interest rate
authentication	credit rating	investments
balance	credit union	invoice
bank	currency	lend
bank account	debit card	loan
bills	debit payments	millionaire
borrow	default	money
cash	deposit	money order
change	direct debit	net worth
charge	direct deposit	notes
check	discount	on sale
check card	dollar bill	online banking
checking account	e-check	overdraft protection
cleared	e-commerce	overdrawn
coin	e-payment	paycheck
consumer	exchange rate	PayPal
cost	for sale	personal code
credit card	fortune	PIN
credit history	interest	price

receipt
refinance
sales tax
save
savings account

sign
spend
teller
tip
total

traveler's check
wealthy
withdrawal

Common Idioms

a run for the money
be broke
be loaded
be minting it
be tightfisted
bet your bottom dollar
blank check
bounce a check
cash a check
change a bill
cost an arm and a leg
easy money
endorse a check
for my money
funny money
get a loan
get change
get your money's worth
have money to burn
hit the ATM
hush money
in the money

made of money
make a deposit
make a withdrawal
Money doesn't grow on trees.
Money is no object.
money talks
money to burn
Monopoly money
pin money
on the money
pots of money
put money away
put money in the bank
put money on something
Put your money where your mouth is.
seed money
spend money like water
take money out of the bank
the smart money
throw good money after bad
throw money around
throw money at something

List 2.11. Practice Checks

Students enjoy practicing bill paying with these checks, especially if the purchases include hot cars, trips to Disney World, cell phones, or other fantasy purchases. Use the newspaper or other advertising to determine the costs.

Ima Newcomer
612 Lincoln Street, Apt. K
Old Town, NY 12345

No. 901

Date _____

Pay to the
Order of _____ $ _____

_____ Dollars

Memo _____   _____

Old Town Bank, Old Town, NY 12345

⑆1234556789 0⑆23456789 0901⑈

Ima Newcomer
612 Lincoln Street, Apt. K
Old Town, NY 12345

No. 902

Date _____

Pay to the
Order of _____ $ _____

_____ Dollars

Memo _____   _____

Old Town Bank, Old Town, NY 12345

⑆1234556789 0⑆23456789 0902⑈

Ima Newcomer
612 Lincoln Street, Apt. K
Old Town, NY 12345

No. 903

Date _____

Pay to the
Order of _____ $ _____

_____ Dollars

Memo _____   _____

Old Town Bank, Old Town, NY 12345

⑆1234556789 0⑆23456789 0903⑈

List 2.12. Safety Words

In times of unexpected events, natural or manmade disasters, the safety of our students and schools requires knowledge of specialized vocabulary. Viewing short videos on staying safe during natural disasters or dangerous events is an effective way to introduce the following terms.

accident	evacuate	lockdown
alarm	evacuation	medical condition
alert	evacuation route	medicine
allergic reaction	exit	next of kin
allergy	explosion	no admittance
ambulance	explosive	no smoking
arson	FBI	no trespassing
asthma attack	fire	odor
blast	fire drill	perpetrator
blind	fire exit	poison
blockade	fire extinguisher	police
bomb	fire fighter	police report
bomb threat	first aid	policeman
break glass	flammable	polluted
burn	flood	portable toilet
caution	fumes	predator
collapse	gang	quarantine
combustible	gas	relief station
contagious	glass	robbery
contaminated	guard	sanitation
cop	gun	security office
crash	hall monitor	security officer
crime scene	handle with care	shelter
danger	hard hat area	siren
deaf	harmful if swallowed	smell
disabled	hazard	smoke
disaster	hazardous material	smoke detector
do not cross	heart attack	stroke
do not drink	Homeland Security	suspicious
do not enter	hospital	terrorism
doctor	hostage	terrorist
don't walk	hurricane	threat
down	hurt	tornado
drill	identification	twister
drinking water	incident	up
drugs	infectious	walk
early dismissal	injured	warning
earthquake	injury	weapon
emergency	insurance card	wear eye protection
emergency contact	keep out	wheelchair
entrance	knife	

Common Idioms

to be assaulted

to be hurt

to be in an accident

to be injured

to be lost

to be raped

to be abused

to be threatened

to be frightened

to be afraid

to be mugged

to be robbed

to fall

to go for help

to look for

to lose a _____

to need a policeman

to need an ambulance

to need help

to stay calm

to report a threat

to make a threat

to take a hostage

List 2.13. Transportation and Travel Words

Travel is an important part of life and knowing how to get to a destination, whether local or distant, is a critical life skill. The following transportation and travel words are organized into four lists. The first list includes words related to getting to school, shopping areas, and other local destinations. The second list includes words for travel by car and train. Next is a list of words needed for distant travel, and finally is a list of common travel and transport idioms.

Local Travel Words

bike	bus stop	gate	sign
bike lock	crossing guard	green	stop
bike rack	crossing signal	guest(s)	subway
bridge	crosswalk	intersection	ticket
bus	don't walk	pick up	token
bus driver	drop off	red	traffic
bus monitor	elevator	route	traffic light
bus pass	entrance	schedule	walk
bus station	exit	school bus	yellow

Car and Train Travel

airbag	impound	seat belt
auto	insurance	service station
car	insurance card	slow
car keys	interstate	south
car seat	junction	speed limit
child seat	keep right	speeding
curve	lane	speeding ticket
dead battery	left lane ends	thruway
dead end	left turn on signal only	tire
detour	license	toll
directions	map	toll booth
divided highway	merge	tow-away zone
do not enter	no left turn	traffic jam
drive	no right turn	train
driver's test	no right turn on red	train station
driver's permit	no turns	trunk (of a car)
driving under the influence	north	turnpike
drunk driving	oil	use alternate route
DUI	one way	valid
east	parking lot	vehicle
E-ZPass	parking meter	violation
fire hydrant	parkway	west
flat tire	reduce speed	wheel
freeway	registration	winding road
gas	restaurant	wrong way
gas station	restroom	yield
gasoline	right lane ends	
identification	road test	

Distant Travel

airplane	checkout	helicopter	pilot
airport	checkpoint	hotel	plane
airsick	claim ticket	hotel van	receipt
aisle	compartment	identification	register
arrival	conductor	immigration	reservation
arrivals	confirm	inn	ship
arrivals hall	confirmation	itinerary	stow
baggage	connection	kiosk	taxi
baggage claim	credentials	life jacket	tram
birth certificate	currency	luggage	travel agent
boarding pass	currency exchange	monorail	traveler's aid
border	delay	motel	traveler's checks
border patrol	departing	observation deck	visa
cabin attendant	departure	overhead	window
captain	e-ticket	passport	
check-in	ferry	pickup	

Transportation and Travel Idioms

back up (the car)	go through security
baggage claim	hail a taxi
board	have an accident
book a flight	hit the road
buy a ticket	land
call a cab	landing
call ahead	layover
circle	nonstop
confirm a reservation	onboard
crash	park the car
fasten your seat belt	pick up your baggage
frequent flyer	see you off
get a parking ticket	start the car
get away	stopover
get in at	takeoff
get in the car	taxi (a plane)
get on	touch down
go through customs	travel light

List 2.14. Traffic Signs

ESL/ELL students of all ages need to recognize traffic signs and understand their meanings in order to safely walk, bike, or drive in our communities. Traffic signs in the United States use shapes, symbols, and words to warn or give information. Begin with shape recognition; next add the international symbols and English words. Your state's motor vehicle agency and department of transportation will have information about many additional local signs and their meanings. Most have materials online that can be downloaded for student use.

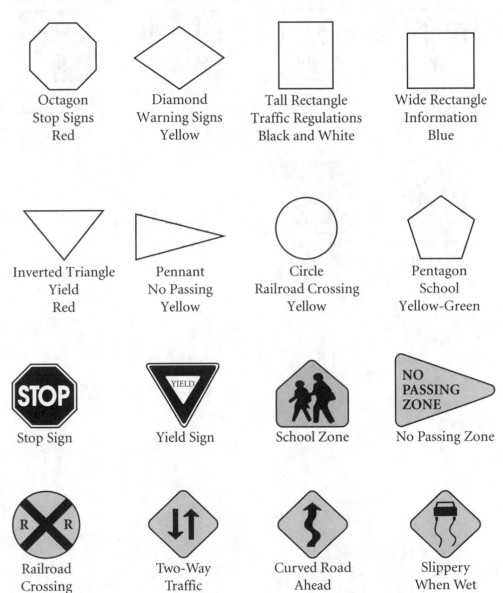

Octagon
Stop Signs
Red

Diamond
Warning Signs
Yellow

Tall Rectangle
Traffic Regulations
Black and White

Wide Rectangle
Information
Blue

Inverted Triangle
Yield
Red

Pennant
No Passing
Yellow

Circle
Railroad Crossing
Yellow

Pentagon
School
Yellow-Green

Stop Sign

Yield Sign

School Zone

No Passing Zone

Railroad
Crossing

Two-Way
Traffic

Curved Road
Ahead

Slippery
When Wet

Deer Crossing—
Use Caution

One Way Traffic—
This Direction

Left Lane Must
Turn Left

No Left Turn

Divided Road—
Keep Right

No Turn
on Red

Wheelchair-
Accessible Services

Service Station—
Fuel Available

Lodging Available
This Exit

Hospital
Nearby

List 2.15. Application and Form Words

Filling out forms and applications is a necessary part of living in a community. The words in this list are commonly used to register for school, get a bank account or credit card, apply for a job, get help from the government, or rent an apartment. Practice filling out applications as a class before having students complete one on their own. Applying for a library card is a good place to start for ESL/ELL students of any age.

Group 1

name	province	date of birth
first name	state	school
last name	ZIP code	grade
family name	ZIP + four	teacher's name
surname	e-mail address	parent's name
middle name	phone number	emergency contact
address	home phone	relationship
apartment (apt.)	cell phone	sign here
street	mobile phone	print
avenue	age	guardian's name
city	male	
county	female	

Group 2

accepted	birth certificate	day
account	blank	debit card
account owner	business phone	deduction
advisor	cancelled check	department
agency	car	dependent
alien	certificate	deposit
alien registration card	check	disability
allowance	check the box	divorced
amount	checking account	dotted line
annual	claim	driver's license
applicant	college	each
application	company	education
assistance	complete	electronic statements
attached	consent	elementary school
authorized	counselor	eligible
available	country of origin	employer
balance	credit	employment
bank account	credit card	enrolled
baptismal certificate	credit check	ethnic group
beneficiary	creditors	ethnicity
benefits	date	ever

exempt
felony
fill in
fill out
first
gender
green card
health insurance
high school
HMO
home owner
immigrant
immigration office
impairment
income
income tax return
independent
insurance
insurance card
interest rate
landlady
landlord
lease
license
list
mailing address
marital status
married
matriculated
middle initial
military
money order
monthly
mortgage

mother's maiden name
nationality
next of kin
nonrelative
notarized
notary public
online banking
own or rent
passbook
passport
permit
personnel
phone number
photo ID
physician
policy
post office box
previous
primary owner
proficiency test
qualifications
race
receipt
references
referred
registration
relative
religion
renewal
rent
requirements
resources
revoked
schedule

school records
secondary owner
secondary school
section
separated
service charge
sign
signature
single
smoker/nonsmoker
Social Security number
spouse
statement
student
student visa
tax
temporary
tenant
total
town
transcript
type
university
utilities
valid
vehicle registration
verification
widow/widower
withdrawal
witness
write
year
years at this address
zone

Section Three

Pronunciation

List 3.1. Speech Sound Production

Human language uses about one hundred sounds, or *phonemes*. Each language uses a subset of these sounds. Speakers become sensitized to the particular set used in their native language by hearing the sounds repeatedly and linking them to information and meaning. As infants develop, they imitate the language sounds they hear and ignore other sounds that don't appear to be important. By eight years of age, children have learned to recognize and to utter clearly all the sounds of their native language. When learning English as a Second Language, students must learn to recognize and produce sounds that may not be used in their native language.

Before students can produce a specific sound, they have to be aware of and able to discriminate it from other sounds. This is not as easy as it may seem. There are variations of sounds, called *allophones*, that, although they are not exactly the same, don't count as different sounds. Think of the sound variations that happen when someone has a head cold, or of differences attributable to regional dialects. They are not new sounds but variations of recognized English sounds. Linguists define *allophones* as variations that do not affect the meaning of the utterance.

Knowing which English sounds are not in a student's native language allows you to introduce them systematically through discrimination practice. (See Lists 3.7 through 3.11.) Once students are aware of a target speech sound, they must learn to articulate it, that is, to produce it. Speech sounds are produced using air flow and the muscles and chambers of the mouth, throat, and nose. They are commonly categorized according to their features.

Air flow during articulation:

- *Stops*—stopping air, then releasing
- *Continuants*—releasing air in a continuous stream
- *Nasals*—sending air through the nose instead of the mouth
- *Orals*—sending air through the mouth instead of the nose

Parts used during articulation:

- *Dental*—using the teeth
- *Lingual*—using the tongue
- *Labial*—using the lips

Whether the vocal chords are used:

- *Voiced*—the buzzing sound made by the vocal cords; put your fingers over your Adam's apple and say *the;* the vibration felt is the voiced quality of /<u>th</u>/
- *Unvoiced*—put your fingers over your Adam's apple and say *thin;* there is no vibration of the vocal chords when pronouncing the /th/ in thin

Whether the facial muscles are tensed:

- *Tensed*—say *whoa*
- *Relaxed*—say *bat*

List 3.2. Consonant Production Chart

Knowing how individual consonant sounds are made helps you teach new speakers of English how to pronounce the sounds correctly. Sounds are generally categorized according to their production features: whether air flow is stopped or continues, whether the vocal chords are used, which part or parts of the mouth are used, whether the air flow is nasal or oral, and sometimes whether the facial muscles are tensed or relaxed. The following chart shows these features for consonants. Pronounce each sound and notice its production elements.

	Flow of Air		Use of Vocal Chords		Articulation			Air Passage	
	Stop	*Continuant*	*Voiced*	*Unvoiced*	*Dental*	*Lingual*	*Labial*	*Nasal*	*Oral*
b	x		x				x		x
d	x		x			x			x
f		x		x	x		x		x
g	x		x			x			x
h		x		x					x
k	x			x		x			x
l		x	x			x			x
m		x	x				x	x	
n		x	x			x		x	
ng		x	x			x		x	
p				x			x		x
r		x	x				x		x
s		x		x		x			x
sh		x		x			x		x
t	x		x			x			x
th		x		x	x	x			x
th		x	x		x	x			x
v		x	x		x	x			x
w		x	x				x		x
y		x	x			x			x
z		x	x			x			x
s		x	x				x		x
ch	x			x			x		x
dg	x		x				x		x

Note: *th* is voiced.

When helping others learn to produce specific sounds, we need the preceding information, and we need to know the position and action of the tongue and the use of friction during sound production. Thus, in addition to being *dental* (using the teeth), *lingual* (using the tongue), and *labial* (using the lips), consonant production may also be *bilabial* (using both lips), *labio-dental* (using lips and teeth), *interdental* (occurring between the teeth), *alveolar* (placing the tongue at the ridge just behind the teeth), *palatal* (raising the tongue to the hard palate or roof of the mouth), *velar* (raising the tongue to the soft palate or back of the roof of the mouth), or *glottal* (using the middle part of the voice box, where the vocal chords are located). The following chart explains how consonants are produced. Practice the sounds in front of a mirror before demonstrating them to others or explaining what to do to make the sounds.

p	Put lips together to stop air, then part lips, expelling air in a burst. Vocal cords do not vibrate.
b	Put lips together to stop air, then part lips, expelling air in a burst. Air travels up from the throat and vibrates the vocal cords.
t	Put teeth together, then place front of tongue at ridge behind upper central teeth to stop air flow; lower tongue and part teeth, allowing built-up air to be expelled in a burst. Vocal cords do not vibrate.
d	Put teeth together, then place front of tongue at ridge behind upper central teeth to stop air flow; lower tongue and part teeth, allowing built-up air to be expelled in a burst. Air travels up from the throat and vibrates the vocal cords.
k	Raise back of tongue to roof of mouth to stop air, then lower tongue, expelling air in a burst. Vocal cords do not vibrate.
g	Raise back of tongue to roof of mouth to stop air, then lower tongue, expelling air in a burst. Air travels up from the throat and vibrates the vocal cords.
f	Put top teeth on lower lip to block air, then push air out through the blocked opening, causing audible friction. Vocal cords do not vibrate.
v	Put top teeth on lower lip to block air, then push air out through the blocked opening, causing audible friction Air travels up from the throat and vibrates the vocal cords.
th	Put tip of tongue on lower edge of top teeth to block air, then force air over surface of tongue while pulling tongue back. Vocal cords do not vibrate.
th	Put tip of tongue on lower edge of top teeth to block air, then force air over surface of tongue while pulling tongue back. Air travels up from the throat and vibrates the vocal cords.
s	Raise middle and sides of tongue to roof of mouth, forming a central channel, then force air through the channel, causing audible friction as air moves and is expelled through the space between tongue and teeth. Vocal cords do not vibrate.
z	Raise middle and sides of tongue to roof of mouth, forming a central channel, then force air through the channel, causing audible friction as air moves and is expelled through the space between tongue and teeth. Air travels up from the throat and vibrates the vocal cords.
sh	Tense lips and push them forward, then raise sides of tongue to roof of mouth, forming a central channel, and push air through channel and lips. Vocal cords do not vibrate.
dg (j)	Tense lips and push them forward, then raise sides of tongue to roof of mouth, forming a central channel; push air through channel and lips as you lower the tongue. Air travels up from the throat and vibrates the vocal cords.

h	Open mouth and push air up from throat. Vocal cords do not vibrate.
m	Put lips together to stop air, then push air up from throat and expel through nose. Vocal cords vibrate.
n	Put tongue at ridge behind top teeth to stop air, then push air up from throat and out through nose. Vocal cords vibrate.
ng	Raise back of tongue to roof of mouth to stop air, then push air up from throat and out through nose. Vocal cords vibrate.
l	Put tongue at ridge behind center top teeth, then push air up from throat and out through nose, vibrating the vocal cords.
r	Round lips, raise middle of tongue to roof of mouth to stop air, then push air up from throat and out through mouth, vibrating the vocal cords.
w	Round lips and push them forward while raising back of tongue toward roof of mouth, then glide tongue and lips back and push air up from throat and out through mouth, vibrating the vocal cords.
y	Raise middle of tongue to roof of mouth, then push air up from throat and out through mouth while lowering tongue. Vocal cords vibrate.
ch	Tense lips and push them forward while bringing teeth together, put tip and sides of tongue to roof of mouth to block air, then lower tongue and open mouth, expelling air. Vocal cords do not vibrate.

Visit http://www.uiowa.edu/~acadtech/phonetics for an excellent interactive articulatory diagram that shows how each phoneme in English is produced.

List 3.3. Vowel Production Chart

Unlike consonants, which have more descriptive features, vowels are usually voiced and usually allow air to flow through the mouth unless stopped by the action of a consonant. To experience this, say *see*, then say *set*. When a vowel is not stopped by a consonant, the sound and air flow continue. The most important features of vowel production are the positions of the tongue and the lips, and the tension of the facial muscles. Tongue position (height and location), lip position (*rounded* or *unrounded*), and facial muscles (*tensed* or *relaxed*) are key factors in vowel production. The height of the tongue may be *high, middle,* or *low,* and the position may be *front, center,* or *back.*

Knowing how individual vowel sounds are made helps you teach new speakers of English how to pronounce them correctly.

Read the following vowel progression list to experience how your tongue, lips, and facial muscles change from vowel sound to vowel sound.

Vowel Sound	Key Word	Tongue Position	Lip Position	Facial Muscles
ē	me	high-front	unrounded	tensed
i	hit	high-front	unrounded	relaxed
ā	ate	mid- to high-front	unrounded	tensed
e	let	mid-front	unrounded	relaxed
a	sat	low-front	unrounded	relaxed
o	hot	low-center	unrounded	relaxed
u	hut	mid-center	unrounded	relaxed
aw	saw	low-back	slightly rounded	tensed
ō	so	mid- to high-back	round to more round	tensed
oo	look	high-back	rounded	relaxed
ōō	cool	high-back	very rounded	tensed
ī	kite	low/high-center/front	unrounded	tensed
ow	cow	low/high-center/back	unrounded to round	tensed
oy	boy	low/high-back/front	round to unrounded	tensed

To experience the impact of changing lip and tongue positions, try this vowel progression practice list:

Pete, pit, pate, pet, pat, pot, putt, Paul, pole, pull, pool.

Note: Linguists consider long ī a *diphthong,* or two quickly blended sounds, not a stand-alone sound.

Visit http://www.uiowa.edu/~acadtech/phonetics for an excellent interactive articulatory diagram that shows how each phoneme in English is produced.

List 3.4. English Sounds
Not Used in Other Languages

Not all languages use the same set of speech sounds. The number of distinct speech sounds—phonemes—also varies across languages. English has about forty-one, depending on the dialect, and this number is greater than the average for modern spoken languages.

Children are physically capable of learning any of the phonemes. However, from birth they sort out and recognize those that are part of the language they hear. As a result, ESL/ELL students have difficulty recognizing, or "hearing," the unfamiliar English sounds and therefore have difficulty pronouncing words that use them. Notice in the following chart that the sound /*th*/ (voiced th), a common English sound, is not part of all languages. This makes pronouncing *the*, the most common English word, a challenge for many ESL/ELL students.

To master the pronunciation of sounds not used in their native languages, students need to practice recognizing the sounds, then producing them. Practice with *minimal pairs*—words that differ by one sound—to isolate the sound of interest. Example: *pit/bit* and *pit/spit*.

Language	English Sounds Not Used in the Language						
Spanish	dg	j	sh	th	z		
Chinese	b	ch	d	dg	g	oa	sh
	s	th	*th*	v	z		
French	ch	ee	j	ng	oo	th	*th*
Greek	aw	ee	*i*	oo	ə		
Italian	a	ar	dg	h	i	ng	th
	th	ə					
Japanese	dg	f	*i*	th	*th*	oo	v
	ə						

List 3.5. Problem English Sounds for ESL/ELL Students

In addition to having a different set of phonemes, each language has patterns of sound use that make different sounds more or less frequently heard and used. The following sounds can be a challenge to ESL/ELL students. Auditory and articulation training and lots of practice will help students recognize these challenging sounds and correctly pronounce English words that include them.

Native Language	**Problem English Sounds**
Chinese	b ch d dg f g j l m n ng ō sh s̲ th *th* v z l-clusters r-clusters
French	ā ch ē h j ng oo oy s th *th* *s* ə
Greek	aw b d ē g i j m n ng oo r *s* w y z ə end clusters
Italian	a ar dg h i ng th *th* v ə l-clusters end clusters
Japanese	dg f h i l th *th* oo r sh *s* v w ə l-clusters r-clusters
Korean	b l ō ow p r sh t *th* l-clusters r-clusters
Spanish	b d dg h j m n ng r sh t th v w y z s-clusters end clusters
Urdu	ā a d ē e f n ng *s* sh t th *th*
Vietnamese	ā ē k l ng p r sh *s* y l-clusters r-clusters

List 3.6. Problem English Contrasts for ESL/ELL Students

Before ESL/ELL students can produce certain English sounds, they have to be able to perceive them. It is often difficult for new English speakers to discriminate among sounds when one is not considered a separate sound in their native language. Many adult English Language Learners continue to have difficulty pronouncing some English sounds long after they have developed competent reading, writing, and speaking skills. The following chart shows the most common contrast problems for native speakers of other languages. Use minimal pair contrasts at the initial, final, and then medial position to develop students' auditory discrimination for the sounds, then practice pronouncing them using the same pattern.

Problem Contrast	Chinese	French	Greek	Italian	Japanese	Korean	Spanish	Urdu	Vietnamese
ā/a			x	x	x	x		x	
ā/e			x	x	x	x	x	x	x
a/e	x		x	x	x	x	x	x	x
a/o	x	x	x	x	x	x	x	x	x
a/u	x		x	x	x		x	x	
ē/i	x	x	x	x	x	x	x	x	x
e/u	x		x	x			x	x	
ō/o	x		x	x	x		x	x	x
o/aw	x		x		x	x	x	x	x
o/u	x		x	x	x		x		x
u/ōō	x	x	x	x			x	x	x
u/oo	x		x		x		x		x
u/aw	x		x	x	x	x	x	x	
ōō/oo	x	x		x		x	x	x	
b/p	x					x	x		x
b/v			x		x	x	x		x
ch/j				x		x	x		x
ch/sh	x	x	x		x	x	x		x
d/*th*	x			x	x	x	x	x	x
f/th				x		x	x	x	x
l/r	x				x	x	x		x
n/ng	x	x	x	x	x		x	x	
s/sh			x	x	x	x	x		x
s/th	x	x		x	x	x	x	x	x
s/z	x		x	x		x	x		x
sh/th				x	x	x	x	x	x
t/th	x			x	x	x	x	x	x
th/*th*	x	x		x	x	x	x	x	x
th/z	x	x	x	x	x	x	x	x	x

List 3.7. Practice for Phonemes in the Initial Position

Sounds that are high frequency and high contrast are the easiest to learn for all students. On the basis of research, the suggested teaching order for consonants is *t, n, r, m, d, s, l, c, p, b, f, v.* The suggested teaching order for vowels is short vowels, long vowels using the final *-e* rule, *-y* vowels, long vowel digraphs, *-r* vowels, and other vowels.

Consonants

b	bat	bay	boy	bit	bug
	bee	bun	belt	bike	box
	bake	bail	boar	bath	bow
	boat	bone	bar	beat	bough
c, k	can	cane	corn	cub	cone
	connect	cube	code	cot	call
	country	come	car	cash	cool
	cater	coast	cause	curl	cat
	kit	kite	key	kind	kiss
	kick	keep	kettle	kale	keel
	kennel	kidney	kilt	king	kink
	kin	kill	kindle	kitchen	kitty
ch	check	chair	chin	cheat	chum
	chess	chap	chime	choose	chill
	child	choice	chomp	chick	chat
	chuck	chain	char	chose	charm
d	dad	dare	door	daze	day
	deep	dell	do	dough	die
	dirt	dim	doll	deer	dune
	dot	dust	dean	dump	dash
f	fat	for	fir	fine	fast
	feet	find	fun	food	foot
	fed	fate	fall	fence	faint
	feather	foil	fear	fire	foe
g	got	get	gold	good	game
	girl	gum	gather	geese	goal
	gauge	gall	gore	gutter	gash
	gain	gape	gone	gave	gift
h	hat	head	heed	hug	his
	hate	herd	hurt	have	hope
	hive	hilt	hero	hag	harm
	hire	high	howl	horse	hoe

j, g	jam	jet	joy	jetty	joke
	jaw	January	juice	jute	jaunt
	jeans	jolly	jeep	jail	jig
	jack	junk	jelly	Jew	jury
	gem	gym	gentle	ginger	germ
	gypsy	gin	gene	giant	geode
	general	gender	generous	gerbil	gent
	gist	giraffe	gyrate	genius	gyp
l	lit	late	lost	load	light
	low	loose	lime	library	let
	lease	lead	lack	limb	law
	lay	loom	lush	lug	lock
m	mat	meet	made	music	metal
	more	mitten	much	might	most
	moth	mink	mine	mix	mute
	mood	mourn	mere	malt	myth
n, gn, kn	net	nice	nature	north	not
	neat	neither	now	new	nag
	numb	notice	nick	never	naked
	near	noose	nine	node	nurse
	gnash	gnarl	gnome	gnaw	gnat
	knit	knee	knot	knock	known
	kneel	knight	knack	knob	knave
	knead	know	knoll	knuckle	knew
	knowledge	knife	knapsack	knickers	knell
p	path	pain	peat	pen	pit
	pine	pose	point	power	Paul
	paw	pallor	purse	port	poem
	pot	paste	pass	perk	pun
qu	quick	queen	quasar	quest	queer
	quack	quaint	quite	qualify	quote
	quadrant	quantum	queasy	quart	quiz
	quilt	question	quiet	quality	quit
r, wr	rest	rose	rain	rattle	rib
	ride	rein	reach	report	ruin
	run	room	rob	rabbit	rape
	right	route	row	raw	roar

write	wring	wrestle	wren	wreck
wrap	wrath	wreath	wrench	wry
wrong	writer	wriggle	wretch	wrist

s, c				
set	soft	south	sane	seek
seat	sow	sand	sable	said
say	sign	sight	sick	saw
symbol	sore	suds	sure	sue

city	circle	celery	celebrate	cell
cement	century	cemetery	center	cent
cyclone	certain	citrus	cirrus	civil
cite	circulate	circuit	circus	cycle

sh				
show	share	sheet	shame	ship
shop	shape	Shetland	shine	shear
shed	sheep	shepherd	shy	shell
shoal	shin	shackle	shrimp	shark

t				
teeth	tone	tether	tons	table
tan	tame	tune	tunnel	tax
tooth	touch	tow	two	tide
toe	tire	tied	talk	took

th				
think	thistle	thief	thieves	thin
thatch	thank	thaw	theater	theme
theory	theology	theorem	thermal	thick
thesis	thimble	thigh	thicket	thorn

th				
these	they	those	this	then
the	than	their	thence	that
there	thine	thou	thy	thus

v				
vain	vegetable	violet	visor	vet
verb	veer	view	vex	verse
vote	voice	vow	vat	vigor
volt	vying	vein	vent	vapor

w				
wish	want	wane	wax	wet
we	wire	wore	won	would
wood	worry	war	wall	woe
win	woman	wail	wine	worse

y				
yet	yam	yeast	yore	Yale
yak	yard	yawn	yellow	yea
you	yolk	yacht	yowl	yell
year	young	youth	yodel	yen

z	zoo	zero	zip	zest	zebra
	zipper	zenith	zinc	zoom	zany
	zeal	zing	zone	zodiac	zip
	Zen	zephyr	zither	zinnia	Zeus

Vowels

a, ai, a__e	able	aim	ate	acre	Asia
	age	ache	ailment	aid	ace
	acorn	acreage	aorta	agency	ain't
	angel	ancient	amen	Amish	ale

a	apple	accident	advice	alcove	add
	actress	acrobat	animal	attic	as
	activity	adhere	afghan	aggravate	after
	album	alto	amble	anarchy	apt

au, aw, al	auto	awful	autumn	automatic	awe
	always	awning	awkward	author	all
	audience	audit	audible	authentic	also
	almost	almanac	audition	augment	alter

e, ee, ea	equal	ego	easy	eel	each
	even	evil	east	eagle	ear
	easel	evenly	edict	equinox	eaten
	either	eerie	ether	evening	ethos

e	exit	edit	epic	empty	elk
	elbow	edge	elder	emphasis	else
	enemy	educate	embalm	empathy	ebb
	endive	essay	ethnic	every	etch

i, i__e	ice	icy	icing	idle	ideal
	identify	idea	island	iodine	idol
	ion	irate	iris	iron	ivory
	ivy	item	isotope	isle	ire

i	ignite	itch	idiom	ignore	ill
	image	imagine	impact	improve	ink
	inch	indeed	Indian	index	inept
	induct	invest	install	insure	if

o, oa, o__e, ow	oasis	oats	opus	over	obey
	open	own	ocean	oboe	okra
	odor	omit	owe	oak	oath
	owner	old	opium	ode	opal

o	otter	opera	option	observe	odd
	opt	optical	opposite	oxygen	oxide
	Oscar	osprey	osmosis	opulent	oxen
	operate	ominous	octopus	onto	olive

or	orchid	orchestra	orate	orator	orb
	order	orange	ordeal	orderly	orbit
	ornate	oregano	organ	organize	ore

u, u__e	unit	uniform	union	united	usual
	universe	utilize	unique	unicorn	unity
	unanimous	unify	unison	universal	uses
	uranium	Uranus	Utopia	utility	use

u	ugly	ulna	ugh	udder	uncle
	ulcer	ultra	umbrella	umpire	under
	upper	uphold	upward	upset	upon
	utter	usher	uprising	ultimate	until

ə a	about	affront	afford	amend	adapt
o,u	abuse	amuse	among	apart	apply
	appear	assist	astound	address	aside
	assault	attest	astute	avoid	away
	object	opossum	oblige	observe	occur
	occult	oppress	oppose	obsession	obtain
	umbrella	unarmed	upon	unwise	untie

List 3.8. Practice for Phonemes in the Medial Position

The medial position is the most difficult for auditory recognition and pronunciation. Work on discrimination of difference for medial sounds before working on improving medial sound production.

Consonants

b	pebble	number	rubber	object	Bobby
	bribe	problem	probably	rabbit	robe
	babble	bible	embryo	terrible	ruby
	robbery	acrobat	hobbled	treble	table

c, k	picture	pucker	decree	backer	uncap
	preclude	because	second	attacker	acorn
	package	sticky	spackle	speckle	picky
	pocket	picket	parking	tractor	liked

ch	purchase	merchant	preacher	teacher	achoo
	hunches	trenches	benches	beaches	inches
	bleacher	exchange	recharge	unchain	itchy

d	daddy	bleeding	siding	ladder	tidal
	trader	bidder	garden	pudding	codes
	fading	buddy	under	undress	hides
	muddy	wedding	cuddle	seedling	raids

f	offer	after	effort	effect	oft
	infidel	infest	afford	differ	rifle
	refuse	safety	sniffle	refine	unfed
	crafty	leftist	sifter	shifty	lofty

g	giggle	logger	regress	English	anger
	region	danger	origin	ogre	rigor
	juggle	baggage	digger	rigging	wagon
	piggy	stagger	argon	organ	muggy

h	behave	inhale	unhinge	unhappy	ahead
	adhere	rehire	behold	inhabit	ahoy
	inherent	rehash	behalf	behead	unhook
	beholden	behind	unhealthy	perhaps	unholy

j, g, dg	wager	aging	ranger	merger	ajar
	adjourn	adjacent	adjust	adjunct	agent
	larger	margin	badger	fragile	angel
	agile	agitate	agenda	paging	fudgy

l	million	fellow	follow	mallard	silly
	gallon	felon	melody	stellar	melon
	feeling	teller	bailer	ballot	oily
	ballast	bowler	crawling	wallet	jelly
m	hammer	steamer	amend	stammer	homey
	steamy	clammy	number	example	mommy
	chemical	tremor	calmer	stampede	army
	cramming	trample	sample	stamina	armor
n, gn, kn	minute	winning	chinning	ground	any
	frown	sinner	banner	thinner	tiny
	handy	window	winter	banana	tenor
	dinner	slander	calendar	lender	dense
ng	singing	wings	bangs	clanged	fangs
	single	finger	winged	mingle	tongs
	bringing	languor	languish	tingle	pings
	springy	spangled	language	linguist	anger
p	paper	dapper	zipper	competent	opera
	depend	caption	happy	impress	apple
	preppy	upper	helpless	puppy	super
	pepper	copper	sweeper	important	caper
qu	acquaint	acquire	acquit	inquire	
	require	request	aqua	inquiry	
r	mirror	earring	warrior	warts	party
	jarring	berry	furry	prying	fury
	correct	error	sherry	sorry	worry
	curry	bury	carry	boring	barn
s, c	assent	acid	fussy	sissy	also
	assist	aside	mossy	sister	list
	mister	slicer	absent	abscissa	nicer
	racer	accent	twisted	brisk	ask
sh	lashes	worship	kinship	crashed	wishes
	bushy	crushed	finishing	fresher	mashed
	freshman	fashion	marshes	cashes	mushy
	ashore	seashore	wishing	leashed	washer
s	measure	treasure	pleasure	vision	fissure
t	chatter	matter	pattern	little	actor
	faster	mortar	mitten	tomato	motor
	sitting	gifted	mountain	attend	meter
	catalog	notebook	cottage	lettuce	altar

th	author	authentic	athlete	rethink	ether
	nothing	python	faithful	bathroom	Kathy
	moths	something	Ethan	anthem	ethic
th	either	bathers	lather	father	mother
	clothing	brother	weather	other	bother
v	invade	invoice	evolution	evolve	evade
	evening	event	eventual	evergreen	even
	every	ever	Everest	avarice	aver
	adverse	adversary	invert	covert	cover
w	reward	rewind	forward	awaken	
	inward	halfway	sidewalk	midway	
	Darwin	dogwood	Edward	coward	
	bewilder	beeswax	aware	away	
y	lawyer	beyond	canyon	vineyard	
	mayor	sawyer	payee	backyard	
z, s	lazy	busy	puzzle	pretzel	
	embezzle	jazzy	quizzical	fizzy	
	wizard	fuzzy	wisdom	wizen	
	buzzard	citizen	scissors	dozen	

Vowels

a, ai, a__e	table	rain	fame	bathe	gable
	baby	save	place	trade	grave
	dame	face	slain	matron	lake
	grain	brace	shade	slate	fade
a	crab	glad	grand	scrap	flat
	span	bran	rack	stack	drab
	captive	tractor	cabin	flag	pass
	Patty	jacket	spackle	class	snag
au, aw, al	drawn	lawn	pawn	stalled	salt
	brawn	yawn	clawed	called	malt
	halted	fault	vault	cauldron	Walt
e, ee, ea	behold	beef	veer	meat	keep
	teach	wheat	squeal	speak	rerun
	redeem	greeting	steeple	really	deal
	sweet	streak	speed	spear	leaky

e	best	spend	smell	letter	send
	better	lesson	pedal	federal	shred
	vest	sled	text	quest	then
	strength	stench	crest	fender	fret
i, i__e, igh	tripod	bicycle	dime	shrine	wide
	spicy	rice	crime	diner	tiny
	mind	prime	bright	might	fighter
	sight	size	drive	quite	five
i	sit	trip	grip	knit	skit
	skid	sick	skinny	bitter	kick
	timid	victim	vigor	wicker	gin
	mitten	mist	middle	mixture	kiss
o, oa, o__e	gold	zone	phone	boat	moldy
	goat	clone	joke	coke	cone
	stolen	bolt	broke	coat	bone
	gross	toast	bloat	hope	home
o	crop	frog	bottle	copper	body
	rocky	Bobby	robber	jogger	jock
	jolly	shot	drop	blotter	shop
	box	stock	snob	block	copy
oi, oy	royal	boil	soil	cloister	toil
oo	book	foot	brook	took	good
	hood	crook	wool	good-bye	hoof
oo	soon	balloon	school	noon	tool
	cool	smooth	goose	mood	choose
u, u__e	June	flume	usual	suing	tune
	flute	dues	glued	prunes	nude
	rude	bluish	truth	crude	jute
	bugle	prude	fluid	glucose	clues
u	numb	mustard	lunch	hunter	rusty
	trust	number	putter	butter	just
	thunder	hundred	punch	crust	bust
	budget	thumb	fudge	judge	lust
ə a, e, o	cadet	thousand	balance	banana	balloon
	item	chapel	shovel	mitten	open
	beacon	honey	method	octopus	atom

List 3.9. Practice for Phonemes in the Final Position

Backwards buildup is an effective method for teaching ESL/ELL students to pronounce phonemes in the final position, because it isolates the target sound and provides iterative practice with it as the word is built up. For example: /b/ → /ab/ → /tab/ → /stab/.

Consonants

b	stab	verb	carob	bulb	tub
	crib	nib	suburb	orb	bib
	drab	robe	bribe	globe	swab
	babe	slab	cob	cube	tube
c, k	back	crack	stack	stick	thick
	block	book	cake	hike	trick
	croak	smoke	coke	Mike	tack
	spike	truck	tuck	speak	trek
ch, tch	touch	breach	reach	clutch	catch
	ditch	pitch	much	inch	cinch
	punch	ranch	stench	stitch	itch
	couch	grouch	such	branch	ouch
d	dad	dead	deed	did	died
	dude	dud	wood	could	blood
	scold	around	code	shod	hound
	bland	brood	blade	dyed	breed
f	leaf	chief	off	brief	half
	proof	relief	safe	life	thief
	roof	laugh	fife	self	wolf
	muff	staff	rough	graph	goof
g	stag	flag	fig	sprig	bag
	log	hug	drug	brig	slag
	frog	slug	fatigue	grog	fog
	beg	drag	league	flog	peg
j, g, dg	badge	sludge	fudge	cringe	rage
	large	surge	singe	edge	lunge
	bridge	hedge	pledge	wedge	barge
	lodge	purge	page	stage	ridge
l	keel	doll	pole	school	mile
	style	mole	dill	goal	shoal
	still	shale	smile	trill	tile
	kale	kennel	tunnel	title	trial

m	scream	drum	prom	swim	trim
	room	broom	loam	storm	some
	problem	cram	cream	crime	crumb
	stem	deem	inform	dome	slum
n	learn	turn	tan	tine	torn
	corn	nine	stone	mine	moan
	grown	drown	sane	drain	tune
	spoon	dragon	plankton	mourn	from
ng	sing	bang	tong	sung	bring
	sting	stung	song	lung	gang
p	scoop	drop	whip	swipe	drape
	ripe	limp	flip	crop	rope
	trap	lump	loop	pup	crape
	grape	pipe	ship	thump	troupe
r	mirror	warrior	washer	flyer	error
	dear	over	editor	mayor	roar
	beer	fire	inspire	October	water
	stir	star	sire	sir	smear
s, c	trace	use	class	coarse	race
	juice	miss	abuse	bus	mice
	twice	boss	abyss	lass	loss
	truce	hearse	worse	curse	ice
sh	wish	cash	stash	gosh	blush
	mush	crush	dish	fish	frosh
	flash	trash	swish	posh	lush
	slush	flush	fresh	finish	mesh
t	habit	treat	skit	crate	write
	blot	foot	bunt	coat	quart
	stint	vote	flute	suit	shot
	fleet	edit	state	about	riot
th	tooth	twelfth	truth	booth	sleuth
v	sleeve	gave	give	slave	glove
	dove	cave	eve	Steve	love
	believe	twelve	stove	drive	move
	have	leave	wave	prove	five
z, s	clothes	froze	doze	shows	toes
	rose	graze	dresses	maze	farms
	firs	praise	eyes	years	hers
	flaws	dens	prize	rise	fleas

Vowels

a, ay	ray	stray	clay	bay	quay
aw	saw	straw	claw	flaw	squaw
e, ee	me	bee	tree	knee	he
ea, y	tiny	busy	flea	plea	silly
i, ie	tie	lie	quasi	alumni	pie
igh, y	sty	sigh	sky	high	thigh
o, oe, ow	stow	go	snow	toe	mow
	blow	slow	hoe	hello	jello
oy	toy	boy	soy	coy	joy
u, ue, ew	mew	true	flue	clue	renew
	new	gnu	emu	crew	stew

List 3.10. Practice for Beginning and End Clusters

Practice with beginning and end clusters improves students' pronunciation and reading fluency. For pronunciation practice, work with individual students or small groups. For fluency practice, work with the whole class or reading group.

L-Clusters

bl	cl	fl	gl	pl	sl	spl
blast	class	flask	glass	place	slice	splash
blue	clue	flew	glue	plum	slave	splat
blood	claim	flame	gleam	please	sleeve	splice
black	clear	fled	glum	plight	slight	spleen
bliss	clinic	flicker	lade	plain	slow	splint
blouse	cloth	float	glow	plow	slim	splendor
blind	climate	flight	glider	plant	slam	split
blur	cloak	flood	glove	pledge	sled	splurge
bleed	clef	flock	glitter	plant	slew	splendid
blade	club	flea	gloom	plod	slope	splinter

R-Clusters

br	cr	dr	fr	gr	pr
brat	cram	drive	free	great	prize
brick	crock	dream	frost	green	praise
broom	creek	drain	friend	grass	practice
brave	crib	drew	frame	grow	pretty
break	cross	drape	from	groom	prune
breed	creed	dread	freak	Greek	princess
brother	crane	drip	fruit	gray	pray
brisk	crumb	drove	frozen	grown	produce
bright	cry	drum	fright	grime	prime
broad	crude	dragon	fret	gradual	prepare

scr	spr	str	thr	tr
scream	spring	street	through	train
screech	sprig	stream	throat	trade
scrimp	sprung	string	thrive	trim
scram	sprang	struggle	throne	treat
scrape	spree	straight	thread	treadle
scrounge	sprawl	strive	three	trust
scroll	sprinkle	strum	thrash	try
scratch	sprite	stretch	throw	trial
screw	spray	strain	thrift	true
script	sprout	straw	thrill	trap

S-Clusters

sc/sk	scr	sh	sl	sm	sn	sp/spr
scar	screen	shell	slip	small	sneeze	spite
scare	scratch	ship	slap	smell	snack	space
score	scrub	shape	slept	smack	snow	spice
scorn	scrape	shimmer	slum	smear	snip	speak
scout	screw	shout	slump	smile	snob	spend
skate	scram	sheep	sleep	smooth	sniff	spring
skid	scrap	shine	slay	smother	snake	sprint
ski	scrambled	shadow	slick	smoke	snap	spry
skill	screech	shoot	slouch	smash	sneak	spray
skunk	scribble	show	slim	smurk	snoop	sprain

squ	st/str	sw
squeeze	stick	sweet
squid	stuck	swim
squeak	stone	sweat
squash	steak	swagger
square	stare	sway
squint	street	swipe
squire	stream	sworn
squad	stray	swear
squaw	stride	swat
squeal	strove	swell

End Clusters

mp	nch	nd	ng	nk	nt	st
lamp	inch	land	sang	sank	saint	list
damp	hunch	sand	sung	bank	pint	mist
champ	lunch	brand	hang	blank	pant	lost
tramp	pinch	grand	bang	thank	ant	mast
stamp	cinch	send	sing	crank	bent	crust
clamp	bunch	blend	sting	dank	sent	least
dump	crunch	tend	among	trunk	splint	host
jump	ranch	round	song	pink	lint	ghost
bump	branch	kind	bring	think	flint	just
crimp	staunch	mind	hung	bunk	hunt	must

List 3.11. Practice for Problem Sounds and Contrasts

Practice with word pairs helps contrast sounds and improve pronunciation. To be effective, work with individuals or very small groups of students. Pronounce the word pair and then have the student echo your pronunciation. Repeat up to three times before moving on to the next pair. The repetition helps students correct their auditory discrimination before altering their sound production. You may find it helpful to record practice sessions biweekly to track progress, and to make a recording of your part so that students can practice independently. Focus on each student's unique problem contrasts.

ā/a	bake back	fade fad	cape cap
	base bass	rain ran	haze has
	played plaid	rake rack	shame sham
	brain bran	mate mat	slate slat
	gale gal	lace lass	aid add
ā/e	bait bet	late let	gate get
	aid Ed	raid red	rake wreck
	paper pepper	fade fed	wait wet
	Yale yell	sale sell	lace less
	taste test	wade wed	waist west
a/e	pack peck	mass mess	dad dead
	sat set	lad led	vary very
	mat met	land lend	bag beg
	dance dense	pat pet	land lend
	pan pen	laughed left	past pest
a/ī	cat kite	mat might	fat fight
	dam dime	fan fine	Dan dine
	bran brine	dad died	flat flight
	clam climb	back bike	grand grind
	lack like	Mack Mike	man mine
a/i	pan pin	ban pin	knack Nick
	sat sit	fat fit	cat kit
	stack stick	pack pick	cast kissed
	draft drift	wax wicks	track trick
	slam slim	drank drink	dad did
a/o	hat hot	pat pot	cat cot
	hag hog	mass moss	lack lock
	rat rot	bag bog	flack flock
	rack rock	cad cod	axe ox
	black block	racket rocket	chap chop

a/u	rag rug	calf cuff	ankle uncle
	back buck	branch brunch	gal gull
	lag lug	track truck	slam slum
	patter putter	dance dunce	rang rung
	badge budge	rash rush	bank bunk
ē/i	Pete pit	meat mitt	read rid
	feet fit	deep dip	seen sin
	sleep slip	seek sick	seat sit
	week wick	teen tin	wheeze whiz
	sleek slick	bean bin	fleet flit
e/i	let lit	pet pit	set sit
	check chick	ten tin	spell spill
	hell hill	peg pig	etch itch
	weather wither	left lift	mess miss
	better bitter	bell bill	lest list
e/o	pep pop	den Don	get got
	check chock	net not	deck dock
	said sod	penned pond	pet pot
	yet yacht	debt dot	fleck flock
	leg log	keg cog	bend bond
e/u	bed bud	pep pup	best bust
	meddle muddle	pen pun	pedal puddle
	desk dusk	dell dull	flesh flush
	dead dud	dense dunce	bench bunch
	check chuck	deck duck	bet but
i/o	pit pot	tip top	clip clop
	nib knob	kid cod	Sid sod
	flick flock	tick tock	lick lock
	click clock	Nick knock	picket pocket
	rickets rockets	spit spot	slit slot
i/u	pin pun	bin bun	rim rum
	sin sun	din done	biddy buddy
	bid bud	tin ton	fin fun
	lick luck	trick truck	stick stuck
	miss muss	tress truss	mitt mutt
ō/o	road rod	hope hop	goat got
	folks fox	holy holly	note not
	slope slop	smoke smock	soak sock
	robe rob	cloak clock	cone con
	coat cot	mope mop	tote tot

o/aw			
	odd awed	Don dawn	not naught
	tot taught	cot caught	sod sawed
	hock hawk	stock stalk	knotty naughty
	fond fawned	clod clawed	collar caller
	body bawdy	pod pawed	pond pawned

o/u			
	pot put	lost lust	lock luck
	boss bus	model muddle	rot rut
	dog dug	hot hut	gosh gush
	pop pup	shot shut	robbed rubbed
	cot cut	dock duck	smog smug

u/ōō			
	pull pool	full fool	soot suit
	look Luke	hood who'd	could cooed
	but boot	stood stewed	should shoed

u/oo			
	tuck took	luck look	buck book
	stud stood	putt put	Huck's hooks
	cud could	huff hoof	shuck shook

u/aw			
	done dawn	dug dog	sun sawn
	cull call	gull gall	fun fawn
	cruller crawler	bus boss	flood flawed
	bud baud	thud thawed	bubble bauble
	hunch haunch	lunch launch	punch paunch

ōō/oo			
	wooed would	cooed could	shoed should
	pool pull	stewed stood	Luke look

b/p			
	bade paid	bin pin	big pig
	cub cup	back pack	bet pet
	by pie	beat Pete	mob mop
	bale pale	boast post	bony pony
	beach peach	batter patter	bee pea

b/v			
	boat vote	bet vet	robe rove
	berry very	bend vend	cabs calves
	bat vat	ban van	best vest
	bolt volt	curb curve	bane vane
	saber savor	bicker vicar	lobes loaves

ch/j			
	chin gin	chain Jane	chest jest
	choke joke	cheap jeep	etch edge
	chill Jill	cheer jeer	chip gyp
	char jar	chunk junk	searches surges
	cinch singe	choice Joyce	chug jug

ch/sh	chew shoe	chop shop	chip ship
	witch wish	cheap sheep	match mash
	choose shoes	much mush	chair share
	chore shore	cheer sheer	chin shin
	cherry sherry	chew shoe	watch wash
d/*th*	den then	dine thine	day they
	dough though	dare their	ladder lather
	bade bathe	seed seethe	breed breathe
	Dan than	dense thence	die thy
	loads loathes	wordy worthy	ride writhe
f/th	fin thin	free three	frill thrill
	fret threat	fought thought	fresh thresh
	Fred thread	first thirst	miff myth
	oaf oath	reef wreath	roof Ruth
	deaf death	half hath	laughs laths
l/r	loyal royal	lay ray	law raw
	led red	low row	lax racks
	list wrist	lake rake	sill sir
	lap wrap	goal gore	load road
	late rate	lung rung	tile tire
s/sh	same shame	sack shack	seat sheet
	sign shine	self shelf	sealed shield
	sock shock	sift shift	sake shake
	save shave	seer sheer	sore shore
	sigh shy	sell shell	sail shale
s/th	sigh thigh	sick thick	seem theme
	sank thank	saw thaw	sin thin
	sink think	sought thought	some thumb
	sump thump	face faith	pass path
	mass math	mouse mouth	moss moth
s/z	bus buzz	sip zip	peace peas
	hiss his	close clothes	face phase
	sue zoo	dice dies	sink zinc
	seal zeal	sewn zone	price prize
	since sins	fuss fuzz	rice rise
sh/th	shy thigh	shred thread	shrill thrill
	shin thin	sheaf thief	shank thank
	shrew through	frosh froth	harsh hearth
	lash lath	mash math	rash wrath

t/th	tin thin	tick thick	taught thought
	true threw	tinker thinker	teem theme
	tank thank	tie thigh	ticket thicket
	tong thong	timbale thimble	trash thrash
	tug thug	tree three	true threw

th/*th*	thigh thy	teeth teethe	lath lathe
	sooth soothe	ether either	bath bathe

th/z	lather laser	seethe seize	thee Z
	teethe tease	then Zen	breathe breeze

List 3.12. Phonetic Alphabet and English Spellings

The following lists can be helpful when you look up the pronunciation of a word in a language with which you are not familiar. It is generally used in linguistic study, not ESL instruction.

Consonant Sounds

International Phonetic Symbol	English Orthographic Equivalent (Spelling)	Example
b	b	box
d	d	do
f	f	fast
g	g	gone
h	h	hat
k	k	book
l	l	lit
m	m	me
n	n	now
ŋ	ng	ring
p	p	pit
r	r	red
s	s	sit
ʃ	sh	shed
t	t	tack
θ	th	think
ð	th	they
v	v	vast
w	w	west
y	y	yet
z	z, s	zoo, rise
ʒ	s	treasure
tʃ	ch	cheat
dʒ	dg	fudge

Vowels

International Phonetic Symbol	English Orthographic Equivalent (Spelling)	Example
a	o	hot
æ	a	hat
e	a	ate
ɛ	e	met
i	e	each
ɪ	I	fit
ɔ	aw	saw
o	o	hold

International Phonetic Symbol	English Orthographic Equivalent (Spelling)	Example
u	oo	soon
U	oo	foot
ə	u	but
ə	a, e, i, o, u	about, written, terrible, occur

Diphthongs

International Phonetic Symbol	English Orthographic Equivalent (Spelling)	Example
aɪ	i	tie
aʊ	ow	cow
ɔɪ	oi, oy	boy

List 3.13. Stress and Intonation Patterns in Words

The *rhythm* of a language is the pattern in speech caused by the position of stressed and unstressed syllables and by changes in intonation.

Stress is the relative emphasis, accent, or degree of loudness placed on a syllable or word. In a word, the stress or accent is the result of pronouncing the word part slightly louder or longer than other parts of the word.

Intonation is the relative level of pitch in a spoken sentence. There are four speech pitches: below normal, normal, somewhat above normal, and very much above normal. Stress within a sentence occurs when words are pronounced at pitches above normal.

Stress Patterns in Words

Practice applying these five guidelines will help ESL/ELLs recognize and understand the patterns and use them to pronounce new vocabulary.

1. Stress or accent is usually placed on the part of the word that carries the most meaning, such as the base or root in a polysyllabic word. Example: reWRITten.
2. Prefixes and suffixes usually are not stressed. Examples: unPLUGged, prePARE, TALKed, PORTable.
3. Nouns, verbs, and adjectives of two or more syllables often are stressed on the first syllable, unless the first syllable is a prefix. Examples: CHARacter, CELebrate, BEAUTiful.
4. Stress is usually placed on the syllable before suffixes beginning with the letter i:

ive	iant	ial	ic	ion	io	iate
iar	ify	ily	ish	iary	iable	

5. The first word in a compound word is usually stressed. Example: BANDstand, HEADset.

Practice for Stress Patterns in Words

Words with Prefixes

reWIND	unPAID	preDICT	exCEL
exHAUST	inCLUDE	inFECT	reWRITE
rePAINT	unHAPPY	unABLE	reMIND
deBATE	deFEND	overWHELM	overDUE
aSIDE	enCLOSE	prePARE	proTECT

Words with Suffixes

SLOWly	FASTer	SPEAKing	AWful
FILTHy	SICKly	LOVEly	DRYing
BAKery	KINDness	HELPful	DRINKable
TALKing	TEACHer	ACTor	SERVant
SPEEDily	SMALLest	CAREless	LIFElike

Words with Prefixes and Suffixes

unWORKable	imPOSSible	reFINing	deSCRIPtion
unCERTain	reMAINing	underSTANDing	reMARKable
unTIMEly	inCORRECTly	unREADable	reSPECTable
rePAYment	preSCRIPtion	inSISTant	inSPIRing
preDICTed	obSERVant	preshisTORic	unNATURal

Polysyllabic Words

RAdio	CARpenter	SENator	GASoline
POLitics	OCcupy	TENtative	HISTory
ALgebra	COUNtryman	STEReo	LABoratory
MASCuline	FEMinine	AGriculture	LIbrary
MINister	PRESident	CALendar	FURNiture

Compound Words

BASEball	NOTEbook	SIDEwalk	SNOWflake
DISHwasher	BRIEFcase	HAIRcut	WATERfall
TEXTbook	OUTfit	NEWSpaper	HEADache
TOOTHbrush	AIRport	POPcorn	SKATEboard
CLASSroom	HEADlight	OVERcoat	SKYlight

Words with "i" Suffixes

diRECTive	inCENTive	reMEDial	cusTODial
biONic	oPINion	hisTORical	inCENDiary
ecoNOMics	neCESSity	comPANion	faMILiar
inSATiable	interMEDiary	eNORMity	scenERio
ofFICiate	doMINion	preVENTive	alLUVial

List 3.14. Stress and Intonation Patterns in Sentences

The rhythmic rise and fall of a language is one of its distinctive features. Children often mimic speaking a language other than their own by verbalizing strings of nonsense syllables in the rhythmic pattern they have heard. The *rhythm* of a language is the result of the position of stressed and unstressed syllables and of changes in intonation.

Practice applying these five guidelines will help ESL/ELLs recognize and adopt the patterns of stress and intonation used in American English.

1. Content-bearing words (nouns, verbs, adjectives, and adverbs) are usually stressed and function words (prepositions, conjunctions, articles, and pronouns) usually are not.
2. Words may be stressed for emphasis, as in NO, you may NOT go.
3. The interrogative words—who, what, where, when, why, and how—are usually stressed in questions.
4. When one word in a sentence ends in a consonant sound and the next word begins with a vowel sound, the pause or juncture between the two words is reduced and the beginning vowel sound is weakened.

   For example, the sentence *The fish are swimming* is pronounced

   /The FISHer SWIMming./

   The stresses occur on the content words *fish* and *swim* but not on the article, the weakened verb, or the suffix.

5. When one word in a sentence ends with a vowel sound and the next word begins with a vowel sound, the juncture between the words is filled with a /w/ or /y/ sound. Examples:

See it.	Say it.	Sew it.	Do it.
See/y/it.	Say/y/it.	Sew/w/it.	Do/w/it.

   Phonemic stress changes the meaning of the sentence. Consider the differences in meaning of the following sentence when different elements of the sentence are stressed:

   The GIRL lost the book.
   The girl LOST the book.
   The girl lost the BOOK.

Intonation Patterns

American English sentences generally follow two basic intonation patterns. The first is called *rising and falling*, the second is called *rising*.

Rising and Falling

In this pattern, the speaker's pitch gradually rises throughout the sentence and then falls on the last word. The falling pitch indicates the end of the sentence and is followed by the juncture (silent space) between sentences.

The rising and falling pattern is common for sentences that are simple statements, commands, or questions beginning with an interrogatory word. Examples:

I have a HEADache.
Open the WINdow.
Where are you GOing?

Rising

In this pattern, the speaker's pitch gradually rises throughout the sentence, ending in a higher than normal pitch. This pattern is common for questions requiring a yes or no answer, for tag questions—that is, for questions consisting of a statement with an interrogatory phrase added at the end—or for direct address. In direct address, the rise in pitch occurs on the person's name, not on the title or other descriptive words. Examples:

Is it time to GO?
She didn't leave, DID SHE?
Dr. Snow, are you THERE?

Practice stress and intonation patterns by having students mimic *left-to-right strings* or *right-to-left strings*.

Left-to-Right Strings

Build the sentence from left to right by adding a word or phrase. Students mimic your intonation as in:

I see.
I see a dog.
I see a big dog.
I see a big, black dog.
I see a big, black dog barking.
I see a big, black dog barking at the mailman.

Right-to-Left Strings

Build the sentence from right to left by adding a word or phrase. Students mimic your intonation as in:

park.
to the park.
going to the park.
He was going to the park.

List 3.15. Tongue Twisters

People have used tongue twisters for decades to warm up before speaking and singing performances, to correct poor speech habits and articulation errors, and to reduce native accents. Tongue twisters are great practice for auditory awareness, sound discrimination, and articulation. While fast repetitions may leave students laughing, slow, very careful practice by ESL/ELL students leaves them smiling because their English pronunciation skills have been improved.

Start by having students read a repeater three times quickly. After the laughter subsides, break down the phrase and model the pronunciation of each word, having students echo your sounds. After all words in the phrase are done, repeat. When most students can pronounce the individual words, switch to a backward buildup. That is, begin with the last word in the phrase, then say the last word and the one preceding it, and so on until you are saying the entire phrase. Backwards buildup helps fluency and develops a normal speaking cadence. Beginning with easier tongue twisters will help students gain confidence.

Repeaters

A regal rural ruler

Baboon bamboo

Cheap ship trips

Crisco crisps crusts

Girl gargoyle, guy gargoyle

Greek grapes

Irish wristwatch

Itchy inchworms

Knapsack straps

Lemon liniment

Mrs. Smith's Fish Sauce Shop

Peggy Babcock

Pug puppy

Red leather, yellow leather

Selfish shellfish

Shredded Swiss cheese

Smashed shrimp chips

The myth of Miss Muffett

Three free throws

Tiny orangutan tongues

Toy boat

Tragedy strategy

Truly plural

Urgent detergent

One-Liners

A box of mixed biscuits, a mixed biscuit box.

A noisy noise annoys an oyster.

An icehouse is not a nice house.

Andy ran from the Andes to the Indies in his undies.

Black bugs bleed black blood.

Do drop in at the Dewdrop Inn.

Even Edith eats eggs.

Five minutes to eight, not five minutes to wait.

For fine fish phone Phil.

Fred fed Ted bread, and Ted fed Fred bread.

Friday's Five Fresh Fish Specials.

Give me some ice, not some mice.

How much wood would a woodchuck chuck if a woodchuck could chuck wood?

Is there a pleasant peasant present?

Lesser leather never weathered lesser wetter weather.

Lesser weather never weathered lesser wetter leather.

Lot lost his hot chocolate at the loft.

Mix, Miss Mix!

Please pay promptly.

Seven silly Santas slid on the slick snow.

Seven silly swans swam silently seaward.

She sells sea shells by the seashore, and the shells she sells are sea shells.

Sheep shouldn't sleep in a shack. Sheep should sleep in a shed.

Silly Sally slid down a slippery slide.

Six sharp smart sharks.

Six sick snakes sit by the sea.

Six slippery snails slid slowly seaward.

Six thick thistle sticks.

Strong sharks sink ships.

Ten tiny tin trains toot ten times.

That bloke's back brake-block broke.

The big black-backed bumblebee.

The cat catchers can't catch caught cats.

The sheik's sixth sheep's sick.

The summer school, not a summer's cool.

The sun shines on shop signs.

Thin sticks, thick bricks.

Three free thugs set three thugs free.

Two toads were totally tired.

Which witch wished which wicked wish?

Whistle for the thistle sifter.

Will you, William?

Stories

A big black bug bit a big black bear and the big black bear bled blood.

A big bug bit the little beetle but the little beetle bit the big bug back.

A flea and a fly flew up in a flue. Said the flea, "Let us fly!" Said the fly, "Let us flee!" So they flew through a flaw in the flue.

A tree toad loved a she-toad that lived up in a tree. She was a three-toed tree toad but a two-toed toad was he.

Betty Botter had some butter, "but," she said, "this butter's bitter. If I bake this bitter butter, it would make my batter bitter."

Fuzzy Wuzzy was a bear, Fuzzy Wuzzy had no hair. Fuzzy Wuzzy wasn't fuzzy, was he?

I thought a thought, but the thought I thought wasn't the thought I thought I thought.

On two thousand acres, too tangled for tilling, where thousands of thorn trees grew thrifty and thrilling, Theophilus Twistle, less thrifty than some, thrust three thousand thistles through the thick of his thumb!

Once upon a barren moor there dwelt a bear, also a boar. The bear could not bear the boar. The bear thought the boar a bore. At last that bear could bear no more of that boar that bored him on the moor and so one morn' he bored that boar. That boar will bore the bear no more.

One-One was a racehorse. Two-Two was one too. When One-One won one race, Two-Two won one too.

Our Joe wants to know if your Joe will lend our Joe your Joe's banjo. If your Joe won't lend our Joe your Joe's banjo, our Joe won't lend your Joe our Joe's banjo when our Joe has a banjo!

Suddenly swerving, seven small swans swam silently southward, seeing six swift sailboats sailing sedately seaward.

Two witches bought two wrist watches, but which witch wore which wrist watch?

Unique New York, you need New York, you know you need unique New York.

Whether the weather is hot, whether the weather is cold, whether the weather is either or not, it is whether we like it or not.

Section Four

Vocabulary Builders

List 4.1. Synonyms

English has many synonyms because it has evolved from many languages, each bringing its own word for common ideas. Synonyms have similar literal meanings (denotations) but are used to convey variations in meaning (connotations) for more precise representation of ideas. Some synonyms show the range or power associated with a trait or concept, for example, *mist, drizzle, shower, rain,* and *downpour*. Others have positive or negative associations, for example, *slender, reedy, skinny, thin, boney, willowy,* and *emaciated*. And still others show different user characteristics or style, for example, *cradle, cot, bed, bunk,* and *sack*. Expanding ELLs' vocabulary with synonyms will enable them to be more precise in their speaking and writing, as well as increase their understanding of nuanced language.

ability, power, skill, talent, aptitude
able, adept, adroit, skillful, talented
about, almost, nearly, near, approximately
accident, disaster, mishap, incident, calamity
achievement, feat, accomplishment, attainment, fulfillment
agree, consent, assent, concede, concur
anger, ire, displeasure, animosity, rage
answer, respond, reply, retort, rejoin
ask, beg, request, implore, beseech
baby, toddler, newborn, infant, child
bizarre, odd, weird, exotic, peculiar
blue, navy, powder blue, periwinkle, indigo
boat, ship, sloop, canoe, steamer

bother, annoy, vex, irritate, disturb
boy, chap, guy, fellow, lad
brave, bold, daring, adventurous, courageous
brown, tan, beige, chocolate, coffee
buy, purchase, get, acquire, obtain
chair, stool, bench, rocker, recliner
cheap, low-cost, inexpensive, economical, reasonable
clear, see-through, sheer, transparent, translucent
come, arrive, enter, turn up, appear
correct, true, accurate, exact, faultless
crazy, mad, insane, lunatic, demented
do, act, perform, execute, accomplish
drink, sip, slurp, chug, imbibe
eat, munch, gobble, chomp, consume
empty, vacant, void, unoccupied, unfilled
enemy, adversary, foe, rival, antagonist
excitement, gusto, zest, flavor, pleasure
fair, just, fitting, proper, equitable
fat, obese, fleshy, corpulent, plump
fight, disagree, brawl, feud, quarrel
fix, mend, repair, amend, restore
food, chow, provisions, groceries, victuals
friend, pal, companion, mate, acquaintance
game, sport, recreation, pastime, amusement
girl, lass, miss, young lady, teenybopper
give, provide, present, award, bestow
go, leave, exit, depart, be off
good, virtuous, honorable, pious, upright
green, forest, olive, jade, emerald
happy, cheerful, merry, joyous, ecstatic
hard, difficult, perplexing, arduous, troublesome
hat, cap, bonnet, fedora, lid
hate, detest, abhor, despise, loathe
have, own, possess, hold, control
help, aid, assist, foster, support
hit, beat, strike, pound, thrash
holy, religious, pious, saintly, devout
honest, open, candid, frank, truthful
hurt, injure, abuse, mistreat, damage
hut, shack, cabin, cottage, bungalow
idea, notion, concept, principle, thought
important, significant, relevant, leading, essential
invent, design, devise, construct, create
job, employment, occupation, profession, work
join, connect, attach, unit, append

large, great, huge, immense, gigantic
laugh, giggle, chortle, snicker, guffaw
law, rule, edict, regulation, principle
learn, study, find out, discover, investigate
love, affection, attachment, passion, devotion
morning, daybreak, dawn, sunup, daylight
music, song, notes, tune, melody
near, adjoining, neighboring, adjacent, bordering
night, evening, sunset, dusk, dark
price, cost, value, worth, expense
quick, fleet, nimble, agile, swift
quiet, still, silent, hushed, soundless
red, cherry, ruby, crimson, scarlet
religion, faith, belief, creed, doctrine
report, announce, proclaim, declare, notify
same, uniform, unvarying, homogeneous, equivalent
see, view, perceive, apprehend, notice
shape, form, mold, design, fashion
show, present, display, exhibit, demonstrate
sleep, nap, doze, snooze, slumber
sly, sneaky, cunning, crafty, artful
small, little, wee, slight, diminutive
smile, grin, beam, smirk, leer
spirit, life, vitality, energy, enthusiasm
stay, remain, wait, rest, dwell
story, account, report, narration, description
strange, abnormal, unusual, irregular, atypical
strict, stern, severe, rigid, harsh
strong, powerful, robust, hearty, brawny
stupid, dull, incompetent, senseless, obtuse
sure, certain, assured, confident, positive
surprise, amazement, awe, astonishment, bewilderment
swift, speedy, fast, lively, rapid
take, grab, seize, grasp, snatch
take, steal, pinch, pilfer, lift
teach, educate, instruct, train, develop
track, mind, observe, study, monitor
travel, trip, expedition, voyage, journey
try, attempt, endeavor, strive, undertake
want, desire, crave, long for, yearn for
wash, clean, bathe, cleanse, swab
wide, vast, spacious, boundless, prodigious
wind, breeze, gust, draft, puff
wise, sage, sensible, intelligent, learned
yell, scream, howl, shout, shriek

List 4.2. Antonyms

Learning antonym pairs helps build vocabulary knowledge quickly. Many times one word will already be known, and matching it with its opposite makes it easy to double word knowledge. Some antonyms may be thought of as at different ends of a continuum of a quality; others are truly opposites.

above	below	day	night
absent	present	dead	alive
abundant	scarce	deep	shallow
accept	refuse	depth	height
accurate	inaccurate	despair	hope
add	subtract	dirty	clean
admit	deny	disappear	appear
advance	retreat	distant	close
agree	disagree	distribute	gather
all	none	doubtful	sure
always	never	dull	exciting
answer	question	dwarf	giant
arrive	leave	early	late
ask	answer	east	west
asleep	awake	employee	employer
attack	defend	empty	full
back	front	encourage	discourage
before	after	entrance	exit
begin	end	even	odd
bent	straight	exhale	inhale
better	worse	expensive	cheap
big	little	famous	unknown
bitter	sweet	fast	slow
black	white	fat	thin
blame	praise	find	lose
bless	curse	first	last
boy	girl	floor	ceiling
build	destroy	forward	backward
buy	sell	freeze	thaw
careless	careful	frequent	seldom
casual	formal	friend	enemy
cellar	attic	generous	stingy
child	adult	gentle	rough
come	go	give	get
contract	expand	go	stop
courageous	cowardly	good	bad
dark	light	happy	sad
dawn	dusk	hard	soft

he	she	play	work
healthy	ill	polite	rude
heaven	hell	possible	impossible
heavy	light	poverty	wealth
help	hinder	public	private
here	there	quiet	noisy
high	low	remember	forget
hill	valley	rich	poor
host	guest	right	wrong
import	export	same	different
in	out	sharp	dull
increase	decrease	simple	complex
innocent	guilty	singular	plural
inside	outside	small	large
interior	exterior	sober	drunk
internal	external	something	nothing
join	separate	sow	reap
landlord	tenant	speaker	listener
lead	follow	stale	fresh
left	right	start	stop
lend	borrow	success	failure
light	dark	superior	inferior
long	short	susceptible	immune
lost	found	tall	short
loud	soft	tame	wild
love	hate	temporary	permanent
majority	minority	then	now
many	few	thoughtful	thoughtless
mature	immature	to	from
maximum	minimum	together	apart
more	less	top	bottom
morning	evening	true	false
most	least	ugly	beautiful
narrow	wide	up	down
natural	artificial	vacant	occupied
near	far	vertical	horizontal
neat	messy	victory	defeat
new	old	virtue	vice
noisy	quiet	visible	invisible
north	south	war	peace
old	new	weak	strong
on	off	wet	dry
open	close	wise	foolish
optimist	pessimist	with	without
over	under	yes	no

List 4.3. American Idioms

American English is chock full of idioms—phrases that mean something other than the meaning of their individual words—and their frequent use poses real challenges to ELLs. In the following sentence pairs the first sentence includes one or more idioms and the second sentence presents equivalent information without using idioms. Idioms need to be learned as whole units. Many of the specialized vocabulary lists in this volume contain additional context-specific idioms. An idiom dictionary—paperback or online—is an important resource for intermediate or advanced ELLs.

It's about time you showed up.
You finally arrived.

He's afraid of his own shadow.
He's easily frightened.

We're working against the clock.
We haven't much time.

All systems go.
Everything is ready.

I'm all thumbs.
I'm clumsy.

She went all out with her baking.
She baked all that she could.

I asked for a ballpark figure on the cost of
   the trip.
I asked for an estimated cost for the trip.

We were banking on George's help.
We were relying on George's help.

Elena's a big fan of hip-hop.
Elena likes hip-hop.

We had a blast at the mall.
We had fun at the mall.

It costs an arm and a leg.
It's very expensive.

He's asleep at the switch.
He's not paying attention.

She's at sixes and sevens.
She's not organized.

I'll take a baker's dozen.
I'll take thirteen.

Tom is a real ball of fire.
Tom is good and quick.

Stop beating around the bush.
Stop avoiding the issue.

Carl's just biding his time.
Carl's just waiting for a chance.

Ned is boning up on his German.
Ned is reviewing his German
   lessons.

The bottom line is NO!
The final answer is NO!

The show brought down the house.
The show was a great success.

Don't burn the midnight oil.
Don't stay up too late.

I'm going to catch forty winks.
I'm going to take a nap.

Jill caught his eye.
Jill attracted his attention.

He had his wings clipped.
His activities were restricted.

Tara gave him the cold shoulder.
Tara ignored him.

The prisoner came clean.
The prisoner confessed.

Hal's a company big shot.
Hal's an important person in the company.

He was dead to the world.
He was in a deep sleep.

Bill is down in the dumps.
Bill is depressed.

Drop me a line soon.
Write me a letter soon.

He was the fair-haired boy.
He was the favorite.

Her feet are on the ground.
She is sensible.

No one can fill his shoes.
No one can replace him.

They flew the coop.
They disappeared.

Get off my back.
Stop bothering me.

Gail got the ax.
Gail was fired from her job.

I think I got the feel of it.
I think I have learned to do it.

We just got wind of it.
We just heard about it.

Go fly a kite.
Go away.

John's a good egg.
John is a good person.

Mom's got a green thumb.
Mom is a successful gardener.

The girls are having a ball.
The girls are enjoying themselves.

I think he has a screw loose.
I think he's a little crazy.

Keep your head above water.
Stay out of trouble.

My heart goes out to her.
I feel sorry for her.

I have to hit the books tonight.
I have to study tonight.

I have a little hole-in-the-wall.
I have a small, inexpensive apartment.

Gene is always in a fog.
Gene is always confused.

Joe's in hot water.
Joe's in trouble.

It's still up in the air.
It's still undecided.

Just jump through the hoops.
Just do what you are told to do.

Keep your nose clean.
Stay out of trouble.

Keep the ball rolling.
Continue the activity.

I will leave no stone unturned.
I will try everything.

Let your hair down tonight.
Relax tonight.

He lost his shirt on that bet.
He lost his fortune on that bet.

It happens once in a blue moon.
It happens very seldom.

Our plans are still up in the air.
Our plans are still not decided.

I didn't know he was so well-off.
I didn't know he was wealthy.

Let's zero in on that idea.
Let's focus our attention on that idea.

He's still on the fence.
He's still undecided.

Did he pop the question?
Did he ask you to marry him?

I put two and two together.
I used the facts to make my decision.

By evening she was run ragged.
By evening she was very tired.

I see the light now.
I understand now.

We did it on a shoe string.
We did it with very little money.

Don't spread yourself thin.
Don't do many things at once.

You bet.
Certainly.

He took pains with his work.
He was very careful with his work.

The boys thumbed a ride home.
The boys hitchhiked home.

I'll do it when hell freezes over.
I'll never do it.

Can you lend me a hand?
Can you help me?

Mr. Divens has a heart of gold.
Mr. Divens is kind and generous.

Give me a break, will you?
Stop bothering me, will you?

He zonked out in the chair.
He fell asleep in the chair.

Cut it out, will you?
Stop doing that, will you?

It's raining cats and dogs.
It's raining very hard.

Tony doesn't have a prom date; Jill's in the
    same boat.
Tony doesn't have a prom date; Jill doesn't
    have one either.

Harry put his foot in his mouth again.
Harry said something that made him appear
    foolish again.

This letter belongs in the circular file.
This letter belongs in the trash.

His yellow hat made him stand out in
    the crowd.
He was easy to find in the crowd because
    of his yellow hat.

Please get in touch with me by Friday.
Please telephone or write to me by Friday.

Hang on and I'll ask my sister if she has
    the tickets.
Wait while I ask my sister if she has the
    tickets.

Don't give up now, you've almost got it.
Don't quit now, you've almost got it.

I'd give my right arm to know what
    he said.
I'd pay a large price to know what
    he said.

I never believed he'd turn his back on me like this.
I never believed he would leave me.

Karyn's new job was in the bag.
The arrangements for Karyn's new job were complete.

I was banking on getting that raise.
I believed I was getting that raise.

Carol spilled the beans about Arne's surprise party.
Carol told someone about Arne's surprise party.

I've been beating my brains out trying to find the answer.
I've worked hard to find the answer.

I don't know if he'll beat the rap.
I don't know if the court will find him innocent.

When Tommy was late, Anna was beside herself with fear.
When Tommy was late, Anna was extremely fearful.

Art surprised everyone when he made it big.
Art surprised everyone when he became a success.

I will never have another blind date!
I will never again agree to a date arranged by other people in which I do not know the person.

Cory missed the boat when he turned down the boss's offer.
Cory missed a good opportunity when he turned down the boss's offer.

Tom said he has a bone to pick with Penny.
Tom said he has problem to resolve with Penny.

The president discussed the issue with his brain trust.
The president discussed the issue with his group of experts.

They found a bug in the mayor's phone.
They found a hidden listening device in the mayor's phone.

He turned his room upside down looking for his wallet.
He looked everywhere in his room for his wallet.

Ahmed got cold feet when he reached the diving board.
Ahmed was nervous when he reached the diving board.

I think I'll just bum around the museum for an hour or so.
I think I'll wander around in the museum for an hour or so.

Bundle up or you'll catch a cold.
Dress warmly or you'll become ill.

I bumped into my old boyfriend at the game last night.
I met my former boyfriend at the game last night.

No one bought his excuse for being late again.
No one believed his excuse for being late again.

I'm tired; I think I'll call it a day.
I'm tired; I think I'll stop working now.

It never crossed my mind that it was a fake diamond.
I did not think that it was a fake diamond.

I'm too shy; I don't think I'm cut out to be an actress.
I'm too shy; I don't think I have the right qualities to be an actress.

This car can stop on a dime.
This car can stop very quickly.

His constant singing can drive you
   to drink.
His constant singing can irritate you.

Ella was always on the edge.
Ella was always very nervous.

While she was sick, she fell behind her class
   in math.
While she was sick, she did not continue in
   math at the same pace as her classmates.

Taking drugs is playing with fire.
Taking drugs is very dangerous.

Mom will hit the ceiling when she sees
   this mess.
Mom will be very angry when she sees this mess.

It was hard to hold my tongue while I
   listened to the lies.
While I listened to the lies, I was very
   tempted to speak out against them.

He was put in a hospital because he lost
   his mind.
He was put in a hospital because he became
   insane.

Aspirin is an over-the-counter drug.
Aspirin can be purchased without a doctor's
   prescription.

Kim had taken great pains with the sign and
   it looked great.
Kim had been very careful making the sign
   and it looked great.

Nina passed a remark about Georgio's haircut.
Nina said something unkind about
   Georgio's haircut.

The man's mother passed away in April.
The man's mother died in April.

Ed's car was stolen and he tried to pin it
   on Tony.
Ed's car was stolen and he blamed Tony.

Steve decided he would pop the question on
   Rose's birthday.
Steve decided he would propose marriage
   on Rose's birthday.

If we put our heads together we could think
   of a good present.
If we work together we could think of a
   good present.

She ran into her secretary at the library.
She unexpectedly met her secretary at the
   library.

Bob's father was in his second childhood.
Bob's father was old and returning to
   childish behavior.

It's about time you got here!
Finally you've arrived!

Cindy burst into tears.
Cindy started to cry.

Amos can really carry a tune.
Amos can sing well.

Jaime cleared the table.
Jaime removed the dishes and other things
   from the table.

Hector cleared the fence easily.
Hector jumped over the fence and there was
   space between him and the fence.

Come to think of it, I already have a red
   sweater.
I remember now that I already have a red
   sweater.

We have to cover a lot of ground before this
   works.
We have to do many more things before this
   will work.

I wouldn't hold my breath waiting for a
   lower price.
It is not likely that it will be sold at a lower price.

Did Marianne do the dishes before she left?
Did Marianne wash the dishes before she left?

All the preparation went down the drain
  when the game was cancelled.
All the preparation was wasted when the
  game was cancelled.

Please move, I need some elbow room.
Please move, I need some space for myself.

Every so often I think about my uncle.
Occasionally I think about my uncle.

Caleb and Raoul had a falling out last week.
Caleb and Raoul had a disagreement last week.

It's time to get busy on my project.
It's time to start my project.

Tony gets on my nerves.
Tony annoys me.

Don't forget to give me a call when you arrive.
Don't forget to call me on the phone when
  you arrive.

She gave the woman a piece of her mind.
She told the woman what she thought and felt.

Mom went overboard on the food for
  the party.
Mom prepared too much food for the party.

Olivia has a real sweet tooth.
Olivia likes candy and other sweet-tasting
  things.

I buy all of his hit movies.
I buy all of his movies that are very
  popular.

I'll see if we have it in stock.
I'll see if we have it here at the store.

The juniors and seniors were in the same boat.
The juniors and seniors had the same
  situation.

I'm just about finished with this book.
I am nearly finished with this book.

The baby kept me up all weekend.
The baby prevented me from sleeping all
  weekend.

Could you give me a lift to school tomorrow?
Could you give me a ride to school tomorrow?

Jody lost her temper at the meeting.
Jody became angry at the meeting.

You can make a bundle doing that.
You can earn a lot of money doing that.

The election was neck and neck.
The number of votes for the candidates was
  nearly even.

Do you need a hand?
Do you need help?

I'm using my nest egg for travel.
I'm using the money I have saved for
  travel.

It's neither here nor there.
It is not important.

It's no laughing matter.
It is a serious matter.

Building the box was no picnic.
Building the box was not easy.

No wonder they look alike—they're cousins.
It is not a surprise that they look alike—
  they are cousins.

Now and then we look at the old photos.
Occasionally we look at the old photos.

Lunch will be on the house Thursday.
Lunch will be free on Thursday.

This was a piece of cake.
This was easy.

Richard and Karyn tied the knot in Las Vegas.
Richard and Karyn got married in Las Vegas.

List 4.4. English-Spanish Cognates

Cognates are words in different languages that have the same ancestry and, as a result, similar spellings and meanings. Spanish and English have thousands of words that share the same etymology and thus many pairs look similar, sound alike, and have similar meanings. Students who begin English language instruction after they have developed literacy skills in Spanish benefit from learning the English cognates of familiar words. This knowledge makes it possible for them to gain fluency more rapidly and communicate on a higher level, even while learning basic English grammar.

To help with their spelling, students should know some of the common equivalent suffixes. For example, if the Spanish cognate ends in *-ción*, its English cousin will end in *-tion*.

English	Spanish	English	Spanish
-ary	-ario	-ty	-dad
-ic	-ico	-ical	-ico
-ent	-ente	-ment	-mento
-ly	-mente	-ence	-encia
-ance	-ancia	-ous	-oso
-ant	-ante	-y	-ia or -io

English	Spanish	English	Spanish
abandon	abandonar	active	activo
abdomen	abdomen	actor	actor
abdominal	abdominal	actress	actriz
abhor	aborrecer	adhere	adherir
abort	abortar	adhesion	adhesión
absolute	absoluto	administer	administrar
absorb	absorber	administration	administración
absorbent	absorbente	admirable	admirable
abstract	abstracto	admiration	admiración
absurd	absurdo	admire	admirar
academy	academia	admission	admisión
acceleration	aceleración	adolescent	adolescente
accent	acento	adore	adorar
acceptable	aceptable	adult	adulto
accessory	accesorio	adventure	aventura
accident	accidente	adverb	adverbio
accidental	accidental	adversary	adversario
accompany	accompañar	adverse	adverso
acid	ácido	affable	afable
acre	acre	affirm	afirmar
acrobat	acróbata	affirmative	afirmativo

English	Spanish	English	Spanish
aggravating	agravante	cancel	canceler
agility	agilidad	candle	candela
agony	agonia	canoe	canoa
agriculture	agricultura	capital	capital
airline	aerolínea	captain	capitán
airplane	aeroplano	carpenter	carpintero
alarming	alarmante	category	categoría
alcohol	alcohol	central	central
allergy	alergia	chance	chance
alphabet	alfabeto	character	carácter
alter	alterar	characteristic	característica
ambiguous	ambiguo	chocolate	chocolate
ambition	ambición	circulation	circulación
ample	amplio	circumstance	circunstancia
anatomy	anatomia	clinic	clínica
animal	animal	collaborate	colaborar
annual	anual	colony	colonia
April	abril	combination	combinación
arid	árido	comic	cómico
arrogant	arrogante	commercial	comercial
aspirin	aspirina	complete	completo
assembly	asamblea	complication	complicación
asthma	asma	concert	concierto
attraction	atracción	concise	conciso
austere	austero	confidence	confidencia
authority	autoridad	conflict	conflicto
aviator	aviador	constant	constante
		construction	construcción
balance	balanza	control	control
bank	banco	correspondence	correspondencia
bar	barra	crater	cráter
bicycle	bicicleta	creation	creación
billion	billón	credit	ecrédito
biography	biografia	crystal	cristal
biology	biologia	culture	cultura
block	bloque		
bottle	botella	debate	debate
brutal	brutal	decide	decidir
		defend	defender
cabin	cabina	deliberate	deliberar
calcium	calcio	delicate	delicado
calculate	calcular	democracy	democracia
calendar	calendario	department	departamento
calm	calma	dependent	dependiente

English	Spanish	English	Spanish
describe	describir	friction	fricción
description	descripción	function	función
destruction	destrucción	fundamental	fundamental
determine	determinar		
dictionary	diccionario	gala	gala
direction	dirección	galaxy	galaxia
director	director	gallant	galante
division	división	gallon	galón
divorce	divorcio	gas	gas
dormitory	dormitorio	general	general
dragon	dragón	generous	generoso
drama	drama	geometry	geometría
dual	dual	gradual	gradual
		grammatical	gramático
ecology	ecologia	guard	guardia
economy	economía		
ecosystem	ecosistema	habit	hábito
education	educación	halo	halo
effective	efectivo	handicap	handicap
element	elemento	hardware	hardware
emphatic	enfático	helicopter	helicóptero
energy	energía	hereditary	hereditario
essential	esencial	hero	héroe
esteem	estima	heroine	heroína
evacuation	evacuación	history	historia
evaluation	evaluación	hobby	hobby
evaporate	evaporar	hockey	hockey
evasive	evasivo	honest	honesto
excellence	excelencia	honor	honorar
exhibition	exhibición	honorable	honorable
exotic	exótico	horror	horror
expedition	expedición	hospital	hospital
extreme	extremo	human	humano
		hysterical	histérico
factor	factor	idea	idea
fantastic	fantástico	ideal	ideal
fascinating	fascinante	identification	identificación
fault	falta	idol	ídolo
figure	figura	ignorant	ignorante
float	flotar	illegal	ilegal
fossil	fósil	illusion	ilusión
fragile	frágil	imagine	imaginar
fragment	fragmento	immigrant	inmigrante

English	Spanish	English	Spanish
immune	immune	lavender	lavanda
important	importante	legal	legal
impressive	impresionante	legible	legible
improbable	improbable	lemonade	limonada
inclination	inclinación	liberal	liberal
incorrect	incorrecto	license	licencia
independent	independiente	limitation	limitación
index	indice	liquid	liquido
indigestion	indigestión	liquor	licor
indirect	indirecto	literature	literatura
individual	individuo	lubricant	lubricante
infant	infante		
inform	informar	magic	mágico
inhale	inhalar	magnetic	magnético
innovation	innovación	magnificent	magnifico
insect	insecto	magnitude	magnitud
insult	insulto	majesty	majestad
intense	intenso	manager	mánager
interactive	interactivo	mango	mango
interest	interés	mania	manía
interior	interior	manual	manual
international	internacional	manuscript	manuscrito
Internet	Internet	mark	marca
interpretation	interpretación	massacre	masacre
intolerable	intolerable	mathematics	matemáticas
introduction	introducción	matrix	matriz
invent	inventar	medication	medicación
inventor	inventor	medieval	medieval
invisible	invisible	mediocre	mediocre
involve	envolver	melon	melón
		memorable	memorable
jet	jet	memory	memoria
judicial	judicial	mental	mental
justice	justicia	menu	menú
		Mercury	Mercurio
kerosene	kerosena	merit	mérito
ketchup	ketchup	microphone	micrófono
kiwi	kiwi	microscope	microscópio
		migration	migración
labor	laborar	mineral	mineral
laboratory	laboratorio	minute	minuto
larva	larva	mission	misión
lava	lava	model	modelo

English	Spanish	English	Spanish
molecule	molécula	part	parte
monument	monumento	partial	parcial
moral	moral	participate	participar
morbid	mórbido	participant	participante
mortal	mortal	pass	pasar
mosquito	mosquito	passion	pasión
motel	motel	pasture	pasto
motor	motor	pause	pausa
music	música	perfume	perfume
		permit	permitir
nation	nación	person	persona
national	nacional	petition	petición
natural	natural	pharmacy	farmacia
nautical	náutico	phobia	fobia
nerve	nervio	planet	planeta
nitrogen	nitrógeno	plate	plato
north	norte	platform	plataforma
nuclear	nuclear	pleasant	placentero
number	número	poet	poeta
numerous	numeroso	politics	politica
		practice	práctica
object	objetar	prefer	preferir
observe	observar	preliminary	preliminar
obstruction	obstrucción	premise	premisa
occupant	ocupante	president	presidente
offensive	ofensivo	prevention	prevención
official	oficial	principal	principal
olive	oliva	process	proceso
operation	operación	producer	productor
opinion	opinión	product	producto
opponent	oponente	pronounce	pronunciar
optimism	optimismo	proportion	proporción
oral	oral	protest	protestar
organization	organización	provision	provisión
original	original	prudent	prudente
ornament	ornamento	public	público
oval	ovalado	punctual	puntual
oxygen	oxígeno		
		radio	radio
pajamas	pijama	rational	racional
palace	palacio	reason	razón
papaya	papaya	recommend	recomendar
parade	parada	refine	refinar
park	parque		

English	Spanish	English	Spanish
reform	reforma	stereo	estéreo
remedy	remedio	submarine	submarino
represent	representar	suburb	suburbio
republic	república	supervisor	supervisor
reside	residir	supreme	supremo
resolution	resolución	suspension	suspensión
respond	responder	symbolic	simbólico
responsible	responsable		
restaurant	restaurante	tobacco	tabaco
result	resulta	tardy	tardío
reversible	reversible	taxi	taxi
revoke	revocar	telephone	teléfono
revolutionary	revolucionario	telescope	telescopio
ridiculous	ridículo	television	televisión
robust	robusto	temperamental	temperamental
romantic	romántico	tennis	tenis
rugby	rugby	tension	tensión
rural	rural	terrific	terrorífico
		tolerance	tolerancia
salmon	salmón	tornado	tornado
sandal	sandalia	total	total
satellite	satélite	tradition	tradición
satisfaction	satisfacción	traitor	traidor
sauna	sauna	tranquil	tranquilo
secretary	secretario	trivial	trivial
segment	segmento	tunnel	túnel
segregation	segregación		
sensation	sensación	uniform	uniforme
sentence	sentencia	union	unión
serial	serial	universal	universal
series	serie	urban	urbano
sermon	sermón	usual	usual
shorts	shorts		
simple	simple	vacant	vacante
siren	sirena	vacation	vacación
slogan	eslogan	vampire	vampiro
sociable	sociable	vandalism	vandalismo
solar	solar	vanguard	vanguardia
solid	sólido	variable	variable
solo	solo	verbal	verbal
solution	solución	vertical	vertical
soprano	soprano	viable	viable
special	especial	vibration	vibración

English	Spanish	English	Spanish
villain	villano	Web	web
virile	viril		
visible	visible	yard	yarda
vision	visión	yoyo	yoyó
visit	visita		
visual	visual	zipper	ziper
vocabulary	vocabulario	zombie	zombi
vocal	vocal	zone	zona
vocation	vocación	zoo	zoo
volume	volumen		

List 4.5. English-French Cognates

Cognates—words in different languages that have similar spellings and meanings based on a shared ancestry—can help ESL/ELL students rapidly increase their understanding of English vocabulary. French-speaking students who are learning English must be careful not to assume that all English words that are spelled like French words have the same meaning. "True friends," or *vrais amis,* are English-French pairs that do have similar spellings and meanings, for example, *guitar* and *guitare.* However, there are many, many English-French word pairs that are "false friends," or *faux amis.* For example, in English the word *main* means "key" or "essential, while in French *main* means "hand"; and the word *addition* in English means to "add" but in French *addition* refers to a restaurant bill.

To help with spelling, students should know some of the common equivalent suffixes: For example, a cognate that ends in *-k* in English often ends in *-que* in French.

English	French	English	French
-y	-e	-ly	-ment
-er	-re	-ck	-que
-ary	-aire	-ed	-e
-or	-eur	-ory	-oire
-ist	-iste	-ization	-isation
-ic or –ical	-ique	-ous	-eux or –euse

English	French	English	French
absence	absence	arrive	arriver
absolutely	absolument	artist	artiste
accent	accent	aspirin	aspirine
accept	accepter	attention	attention
activity	activité	authority	autorité
actor	acteur	automatic	automatique
actress	actrice	autumn	automne
admire	admirer	avenue	avenue
adore	adore		
adult	adulte	banana	banane
agency	agence	bank	banque
agreeable	agréable	beauty	beauté
agriculture	agriculture	bicycle	bicyclette
aid	aider	biology	biologie
airport	aéroport	bleu	bleu
alarm	alarme	blizzard	blizzard
album	album	blue	bleu
alligator	alligator	bulletin	bulletin
alphabet	alphabet		
animal	animal	café	café
apartment	appartement	candidate	candidat
applaud	applaudir	canyon	canyon
apricot	abricot	cape	cape
arrange	arranger	center	centre

English	French	English	French
change	change	flatterer	flatteur
check	chèque	fruit	fruits
cheeseburger	cheeseburger		
chocolate	chocolat	globe	globe
client	client	glory	gloire
cola	cola	government	gouvernement
color	couleur	graffiti	graffiti
comfortable	confortable	grand	grand
composition	composition	guitar	guitare
constellation	constellation		
continent	continent	hazard	hasard
continue	continuer	hello	allô
correction	correction	hospital	hôpital
couple	couple	hotel	hôtel
coupon	coupon	humid	humid
cousin	cousin		
		impatient	impatient
dance	danser	insist	insister
December	décembre	invite	inviter
decision	décision		
democracy	démocractie	jacket	jaquette
demonstration	demonstration		
dentist	dentiste	lamp	lampe
dessert	dessert	lesson	leçon
detail	détail	liberty	liberté
dictionary	dictionnaire	license	licence
dinner	diner	linguistic	linquistique
disk	disque	liquid	liquide
edition	édition	machine	machine
elastic	élastique	magnificent	magnifique
electron	électron	management	management
elegant	élégant	manager	manager
elementary	élémentaire	mark	marque
enemy	ennemi	marriage	mariage
equivalent	équivalent	martyr	martyr
error	erreur	maxim	maxime
evaporate	évaporer	May	mai
excellent	excellent	meander	meander
exception	exception	media	media
excuse	excuse	medicine	médicine
exercise	exercice	memorable	memorable
		memory	mémoire
fatigued	fatiqué	mention	mention
finish	finir	menu	menu

English	French	English	French
message	message	participant	participant
metropolitan	métropolitain	passport	passeport
migration	migration	pay	payer
million	million	peach	pêche
miracle	miracle	perfume	parfum
missile	missile	peril	peril
mission	mission	pharmacy	pharmacie
modern	moderne	photocopier	photocopieur
module	module	photography	photographie
molecule	molécule	poet	poète
monster	monster	pork	porc
monument	monument	prepare	preparer
multiple	multiple	pretend	pretendre
multiplication	multiplication	professor	professeur
muscle	muscle	program	programme
music	musique	pronunciation	pronunciation
nation	nation	radio	radio
nationality	nationalité	reserve	reserver
naturally	naturellement	respond	repondre
nectarine	nectarine	restaurant	restaurant
negative	négatif	ridiculous	ridicule
negotiation	négociation		
neutron	neutron	safari	safari
no	non	salad	salade
November	novembre	sandwich	sandwich
number	nombre	sauce	sauce
numeric	numérique	science	science
		scooter	scooter
obey	obeir	script	script
object	objet	segment	segment
objective	objectif	September	septembre
odor	odeur	serpent	serpent
office	office	sign	signer
omelet	omelette	sincerely	sincèrement
onion	oignon	society	societé
operation	opération	soup	soupe
opinion	opinion	statue	statue
orange	orange	success	succés
		surely	surement
page	page	sweater	sweater
painter	peintre		
paper	papier	table	table
parents	parents	tea	thé
park	parc	telephone	téléphone

English	French	English	French
temperature	température	vender	vendeur
terror	terreur	verdict	verdict
tiger	tigre	victim	victime
toast	toast	visible	visible
tomato	tomate	vitamin	vitamine
torment	tourment		
tourist	touriste	waterproof	waterproof
train	traine	web	web
transfer	transferer	webcam	webcam
		weekend	week-end
ulcer	ulcère	western	western
uncle	oncle		
unity	unite	xylophone	xylophone
university	université		
urban	urbain	yoga	yoga
urn	urne		
		zebra	zebra
vacant	vacante	zero	zero
vacation	vacances	zest	zeste
valley	vallée	zigzag	zigzag
vein	veine	zoom	zoom

List 4.6. English-German Cognates

Many words in English, Spanish, French, and German have common roots in Latin. For example, the words *father* in English, *padre* in Spanish, *pater* in French, and *vater* in German are all descendants of the Latin word *pater*. Cognates are pairs of words from different languages that have similar spellings and meanings based on such a shared ancestry. Recognizing cognates can help students rapidly increase their understanding of English vocabulary. Not all word pairs that are spelled alike in two languages have the same or similar meaning. These "false friends," or *falsche Freunde*, can lead the language learner astray. For example, in German *fast* means "almost," *fade* is "boring," *Fabrik* means "factory," a *Catcher* is a "wrestler," a *Chef* is the "department head," and a *billion* is a "trillion."

To help with spelling, students should know some of the common equivalent suffixes and related spelling patterns. For example, a cognate that ends in *-ct* in English often ends in *-kt* in German, as in *architect* and *architekt*.

English	German	English	German
-y	-ie	-ct	-kt
-le	-el	-ive	-iv
-k	-ch	-d	-t
-ic	-isch	-sh	-sch
-y	-g	c- or ch-	k-
-mb	-mm	f-	v-
gh	ch	th	d
f	b	v	b

English	German	English	German
acceptable	akzeptabel	athlete	Athlet
active	aktiv	atlas	Atlas
address	Adresse	August	August
affair	Affäre	auto	Auto
agent	Agent		
alcohol	Alkohol	baby	Baby
algebra	Algebra	bakery	Backerie
all	alle	ball	Ball
allergy	Allergie	balloon	Ballon
alphabet	Alphabet	banana	Banane
analysis	Analyse	band	Band
anatomy	Anatomie	bank	Bank
apple	Apfel	bar	Bar
April	April	barrier	Barriere
aquarium	Aquarium	beer	Bier
archaeology	Archaologie	begin	beginnen
architect	Architekt	best	bester
argument	Argument	biology	Biologie
arm	Arm	blizzard	Blizzard
astronaut	Astronaut	blond	blond

English	German	English	German
book	Buch	energy	Energie
bus	Bus	exact	exakt
butter	Butter	exclusive	exklusiv
		experiment	Experiment
cable	Kabel	explosion	Explosion
café	Café		
calendar	Kalender	fable	Fabel
camera	Kamera	fact	Fakt
canal	kanal	factor	Faktor
candidate	Kandidat	false	falsch
carrot	Karotte	family	Familie
cat	Katze	fan club	Fanklub
centimeter	zentimeter	farmhouse	Farmhaus
chance	Chance	father	Vater
chocolate	Schokolade	figure	Figur
cigarette	Zigarette	finger	Finger
clown	Clown	fish	Fisch
club	Club	fitness	Fitness
computer	Computer	fossil	Fossil
concert	Konzert	friend	Freund
conservative	konservativ	frost	Frost
control	kontrolle		
cost	kosten	gallon	Gallone
creative	kreativ	gang	Gang
curve	Kurve	garage	Garage
		garden	garten
December	Dezember	general	generell
decimal	Dezimal	generation	Generation
design	Design	glass	Glas
diamond	Diamant	God	Gott
director	Direktor	gold	Gold
discipline	Disziplin	gymnastics	Gymnastik
discussion	Diskussion		
dumb	dumm	hamburger	Hamburger
		hand	Hand
effective	effectiv	hello	hallo
elastic	elastisch	here	hier
electron	Elektron	hobby	Hobby
elegance	Eleganz	hotel	Hotel
elegant	elegant	humor	Humor
element	Element	hundred	hundert
elephant	Elefant		
e-mail	E-Mail	idea	Idee
emblem	Emblem	ideal	ideal
end	Ende	idol	Idol

English	German	English	German
illustrate	illustrieren	new	neu
industry	Industrie	November	November
instrument	Instrument		
intelligent	intelligent	object	Objekt
international	international	October	Oktober
		officer	Offizier
January	Januar	often	oft
jazz	Jazz	omelet	Omelett
jeans	Jeans	orchestra	Orchester
journalist	Journalist	organization	Organisation
justice	Justiz		
		panic	Panik
ketchup	Ketchup	paper	Papier
		park	Park
learn	lernen	partner	Partner
legal	legal	passive	passiv
lemonade	Limonade	pause	Pause
license	Lizenz	person	Person
local	lokal	picnic	Picknick
		plan	Plan
magazine	Magazin	planet	Planet
make	machen	popular	popular
manager	Manager	press	Presse
mango	Mango	professor	Professor
market	Markt	program	Programm
maximum	Maximum	puzzle	Puzzle
medicine	Medizin		
meter	Meter	quiz	Quiz
microscope	Mikroskop		
minimum	Minimum	regular	regulär
minus	minus	religion	Religion
minute	Minute	respect	Respekt
mission	Mission	result	Resultat
mobile	mobil	rock concert	Rockkonzert
moment	Moment	rock group	Rockgruppe
monster	Monster		
moral	Moral	sandal	sandale
mother	Mutter	send	senden
motor	Motor	sensation	Sensation
museum	Museum	September	September
music	Musik	shock	Schock
		sit	sitzen
name	Name	situation	Situation
nation	Nation	social	Sozial
nature	Natur	sock	Socke

English	German	English	German
sofa	Sofa	vampire	Vampir
sport	Sport	variable	variable
state	Staat	verb	Verb
		vibration	Vibration
talent	Talent	video camera	Videokamera
taxi	Taxi	vision	Vision
tea	Tee	volleyball	Volleyball
telephone	Telefon		
test	Test	waltz	Walzer
theater	Theater	warm	warm
theory	Theorie	wild	wild
ton	Tonne	winter	Winter
tourist	Tourist	work	Werk
tunnel	Tunnel		
		yacht	Yacht
under	unter	zebra	Zebra
uniform	Uniform	zenith	Zenith
university	Universität	zigzag	zickzack

List 4.7. Collocations

Patterns of word usage develop in all spoken languages. When two or more words occur together with regularity, they are called a *collocation*. Some collocations are longstanding, others are very recent—*ice cream sundae* and *shock and awe*, for example. Over time their usage may become so common that they become a compound word, an idiom, or even a well-worn cliché. Because collocations are customary, learning them helps ESL/ELL students speak more authentic American English. The following list will get you started. Begin a word wall for collocations that students find in different settings. For example, *take notes, take courses, study hard, hit the books, get a grade,* and *get an A* are all school-related collocations. Some groups of words appear not only together but also in a particular order. If a speaker violates the informal rule for their order, the person's speech is jarring and often considered incorrect. *Cream and sugar, bacon and eggs,* and *black and white* are some examples. See List 4.8, on nonreversible pairs, for others.

achieve a goal

act out
act up
alternate route

any news?

April showers

around the corner
ask out
autumn leaves

bank on it
beginning to end
bottom of my heart

break a lease

break a promise

break a record

break a window

break the law

break the rules

breakfast cereal
catch a ball
catch a bus

catch a cold
catch a movie
catch someone's attention

catch someone's eye

coffee and cake
come down with a cold

completely fooled
completely useless
cream and sugar
crystal clear
do a favor

do damage
do harm
do justice
do research
do the job

do the laundry

do your best

down in the dumps
down the drain

easy does it
exotic birds
fast-food restaurant
filthy rich
find a cure

find a seat

find happiness

find the answer

find time

flip a coin
get a grade

get going
get the runaround
go bad

go crazy

go for a ride
go missing

go overboard

go overseas

go to the gym
grab a bite
hard to believe
hardly a reason
have a baby
have a ball

have a chance

have a dream

have a drink

have a headache
have a party

have a problem

have a seat

have an operation
have breakfast
have dinner
have fun
have the time

heavy hitter

heavy load

high and mighty

high note

hit a home run
hit it on the head

hit the books
hit the roof
hit the spot

hold someone's attention

hot, humid, and hazy
in a pinch
in over his head

just around the corner

keep the change

knife and fork
lightening speed
make a call
make a comment
make a date
make a decision
make a discovery
make a list
make a promise
make a suggestion
make a turn

make an effort
make needed changes

make noise
make peace

make preparations
make progress
make trouble

measure up
meet someone
milk and cookies
mind is made up
miss an opportunity

miss by a mile

miss the flight

miss the point

never a dull moment
off ramp
on the chin
once in a while
once upon a time
one at a time
ongoing investigation
out of context

out of the box
out of touch

over and out

over the hill

paper or plastic?

pay a compliment

pay a visit

pay attention

pay the bill

pie a la mode
postage stamp
price you have to pay

priority seating
quick as a whip
reach a goal

rising star
rock and roll

round and round
save a life

save a seat

save energy

save space

save time

see you later
set a date
short and sweet
sincere apology
singsong

sobering thought

soup and salad
soup of the day
spilt milk
spring flowers

starting gate
straight ahead

study hard
sweet spot

tag along
take a bath
take a break
take a left

take a picture
take a ride
take a seat

take a shower
take a taxi

take a temperature

take a test
take courses
take notes
take turns
text message
there's no going back
this and that
turn it down
turn it over
turn it upside down
unavoidably detained
up a creek

up the street
use the ATM
utter nonsense
utterly amazed
wash and dry

wash the dishes

well-worn cliché
what's up?

win over

worn out

List 4.8. Nonreversible Pairs

Nonreversible pairs are collocations that always appear in the same order. Some show temporal sequence, such as *cause and effect;* but for most there are no rules to guide the order—they are simply customary. Fill-ins, sequencing word cards, and oral and aural repetition are useful teaching strategies to help ESL/ELL students master these word pairs.

Adam and Eve	high and dry	rise and fall
back and forth	hit and run	salt and pepper
bacon and eggs	husband and wife	shirt and tie
bed and breakfast	in and out	shock and awe
birds and bees	Jack and Jill	shoes and socks
black and white	knife and fork	short and fat
bought and sold	ladies and gentlemen	slip and slide
bread and butter	law and order	soap and water
bread and water	life or death	sooner or later
bride and groom	live and learn	stars and stripes
business and pleasure	live or die	stem and leaf
cause and effect	lock and key	strawberries and cream
coat and tie	lost and found	suit and tie
coffee and doughnuts	man and wife	supply and demand
cream and sugar	mattress and box spring	sweet and sour
crime and	mean and nasty	table and chairs
punishment	mean and ugly	tall and thin
cup and saucer	name and address	thick and thin
day and age	nice and easy	thunder and lightning
day and time	oil and gas	touch and go
dead or alive	oil and vinegar	travel and entertainment
fish and chips	oil and water	trial and error
food and drink	peaches and cream	up and down
front and center	pen and pencil	up or down
fun and games	pork and beans	war and peace
get up and go	pots and pans	wash and dry
ham and eggs	profit and loss	wash and wear
hammer and nail	rain or shine	wine and cheese
have and have not	read and write	
have and hold	right or wrong	

List 4.9. Phrasal Verbs—Separable

Phrasal verbs are made from a verb plus adverbs and prepositions. Phrasal verbs are frequently encountered in conversation. Many add emphasis or detail (for example, *bring out* or *wake up*), although some are idioms and cannot be understood from their literal meanings (such as *fed up with*).

Phrasal verbs that have direct objects can be separated. For example, in the following sentences the direct objects are underlined and the phrasal verbs are in italics. The meaning is clear both ways:

Jackie will *put off retirement* until she has more savings.
Jackie will *put retirement off* until *she* has more savings.

Note that if the direct object is a pronoun, we always separate the phrasal verb. For example, we could say, *Bring* it *back* tomorrow, but we would never say, *Bring back* it tomorrow.

Add on (add)	Jacob added on the cost of dessert to the bill.
	Jacob added the cost of dessert on to the bill.
	Jacob added it on to the bill.
Add up (add)	We added up the price of tickets and food and were surprised.
	We added the price of tickets and food up and were surprised.
	We added them up and were surprised.
Back up (support)	Lisa backed up her files before she went home.
	Lisa backed her files up before she went home.
	Lisa backed them up before she went home.
Bring back (return)	I have to bring back my library books today.
	I have to bring my library books back today.
	I have to bring them back today.
Bring on (cause)	Shouting will bring on a sore throat quickly.
	Shouting will bring a sore throat on quickly.
	Shouting will bring it on quickly.
Bring out (show)	Mom will bring out the best china for company.
	Mom will bring the best china out for company.
	Mom will bring it out for company.
Bring up (raise)	Joe wants to bring up his children on a farm.
	Joe wants to bring his children up on a farm.
	Joe wants to bring them up on a farm.
Call off (cancel)	Ryan called off the strike at midnight.
	Ryan called the strike off at midnight.
	Ryan called it off at midnight.
Carry out (complete)	The team will carry out the drill on the practice field.
	The team will carry the drill out on the practice field.
	The team will carry it out on the practice field.
Check out (investigate)	Alice checks out errors.
	Alice checks errors out.
	Check it out before agreeing.

Close down (shut)	The police closed down the expressway this morning.
	The police closed the expressway down this morning.
	The police closed it down this morning.
Cross off (draw line through)	Cross off Margaret from the speakers' list.
	Cross Margaret off the speakers' list.
	Cross her off the speakers' list.
Do over (do again)	I don't want to do over the schedule.
	I don't want to do the schedule over.
	I don't want to do it over.
Draw up (prepare)	I have to draw up a new will this year.
	I have to draw a new will up this year.
	I have to draw one up this year.
Figure out (solve)	Jim can figure out any math problem easily.
	Jim can figure any math problem out easily.
	Jim can figure them out easily.
Fill in (complete)	The captain was filling in all the bunks.
	The captain was filling all the bunks in.
	The captain was filling all of them in.
Get across (explain)	Jennifer tried to get across her reasons at the meeting.
	Jennifer tried to get her reasons across at the meeting.
	Jennifer tried to get them across at the meeting.
Give away (distribute)	Eve gave away several old paintings.
	Eve gave several old paintings away.
	Eve gave them away.
Give out (distribute)	Tom will give out copies of his new book at the meeting.
	Tom will give copies of his new book out at the meeting.
	Tom will give it out at the meeting.
Give up (surrender)	Geoff did not give up his plan.
	Geoff did not give his plan up.
	Geoff did not give it up.
Hand in (submit)	We have to hand in our papers on Wednesday.
	We have to hand our papers in on Wednesday.
	We have to hand them in on Wednesday.
Hand out (distribute)	Jenn was handing out apples at the festival.
	Jenn was handing apples out at the festival.
	Jenn was handing them out at the festival.
Hand over (give)	Marianne was happy to hand over her work to her assistant.
	Marianne was happy to hand her work over to her assistant.
	Marianne was happy to hand it over to her assistant.

Hang up (place on hook)	Louise always hangs up her coat in the closet.
	Louise always hangs her coat up in the closet.
	Louise always hangs it up in the closet.
Keep out (prevent entry)	The fence keeps out stray dogs.
	The fence keeps stray dogs out.
	The fence keeps them out.
Knock down (destroy)	The bulldozer will knock down the garage first.
	The bulldozer will knock the garage down first.
	The bulldozer will knock it down first.
Look over (review)	The choir master looked over the sheet music.
	The choir master looked the sheet music over.
	The choir master looked it over.
Look up (locate)	Ms. Polk told the students to look up the answer in the book.
	Ms. Polk told the students to look the answer up in the book.
	Ms. Polk told the students to look it up in the book.
Phase in (start slowly)	We are phasing in the new health plan.
	We are phasing the new health plan in.
	We are phasing it in.
Pick up (collect)	Terry will pick up her son at the airport on Friday.
	Terry will pick her son up at the airport on Friday.
	Terry will pick him up at the airport on Friday.
Pull off (succeed)	The committee pulled off a great party last year.
	The committee pulled a great party off last year.
	The committee pulled a great one off last year.
Put away (store)	Tell the children to put away their toys now.
	Tell the children to put their toys away now.
	Tell the children to put them away now.
Put away (store)	Please put away your notes and books.
	Please put your notes and books away.
	Please put them away.
Put back (restore)	Alex put back the book before he left the room.
	Alex put the book back before he left the room.
	Alex put it back before he left the room.
Put down (lay)	Steven put down the cup on the counter.
	Steven put the cup down on the counter.
	Steven put it down on the counter.
Put off (delay)	Anisa wants to put off the test until Tuesday.
	Anisa wants to put the test off until Tuesday.
	Anisa wants to put it off until Tuesday.
Put up (hang)	Aunt Kathy put up the curtains before the holiday.
	Aunt Kathy put the curtains up before the holiday.
	Aunt Kathy put them up before the holiday.

Rule out (exclude)	Always rule out failure when you plan.
	Always rule failure out when you plan.
	Always rule it out when you plan.
Set up (arrange)	Tom set up my television on Saturday.
	Tom set my television up on Saturday.
	Tom set it up on Saturday.
Sort out (solve)	The class will sort out the book problem next week.
	The class will sort the book problem out next week.
	The class will sort it out next week.
Sum up (tell main points)	Don summed up the main points.
	Don summed the main points up.
	Don summed them up.
Take down (write)	The secretary will take down minutes of the meeting.
	The secretary will take minutes down at the meeting.
	The secretary will take them down at the meeting.
Take on (assume)	Diana agreed to take on more clients when Lee left.
	Diana agreed to take more clients on when Lee left.
	Diana agreed to take them on when Lee left.
Take out (remove)	Bob has to take out the trash early Monday morning.
	Bob has to take the trash out early Monday morning.
	Bob has to take it out early Monday morning.
Take over (control)	Susan will take over the billing next month.
	Susan will take the billing over next month.
	Susan will take it over next month.
Think through (consider)	My advice is to think through the options before deciding.
	My advice is to think the options through before deciding.
	My advice is to think them through before deciding.
Throw out (discard)	Ahmed throws out his old shoes every year.
	Ahmed throws his old shoes out every year.
	Ahmed throws them out every year.
Try on (test)	Gloria likes to try on fancy hats at the mall.
	Gloria likes to try fancy hats on at the mall.
	Gloria likes to try them on at the mall.
Try out (test)	Chris asked the students to try out the new scale in class.
	Chris asked the students to try the new scale out in class.
	Chris asked the students to try it out in class.
Turn down (refuse)	Marie had to turn down Chuck's offer of dinner.
	Marie had to turn Chuck's offer of dinner down.
	Marie had to turn it down.

Turn in (submit)	Juan must turn in his homework before leaving for gym.
	Juan must turn his homework in before leaving for gym.
	Juan must turn it in before leaving for gym.
Turn off (shut off)	Samantha, turn off the light when you leave.
	Samantha, turn the light off when you leave.
	Samantha, turn it off when you leave.
Turn on (start)	Please turn on the television.
	Please turn the television on.
	Please turn it on.
Wake up (awaken)	Jared can wake up his brother with music.
	Jared can wake his brother up with music.
	Jared can wake him up with music.
Work out (solve a problem)	Mike and Nancy will work out vacation arrangements soon.
	Mike and Nancy will work vacation arrangements out soon.
	Mike and Nancy will work them out soon.

List 4.10. Phrasal Verbs—Inseparable

Phrasal verbs that do not have direct objects cannot be separated. For example, the sentence, "We *check up on* everyone before we hire them" cannot be rewritten as "We *check* everyone *up on* before we hire them."

Account for (explain)	Can you account for the missing donuts?
Believe in	The majority of people around the world believe in God.
Break down (stop working)	Dad didn't want the car to break down on the trip.
Brush up (review)	Janet was brushing up on her biology over the weekend.
Catch up with (reach a similar point)	I don't have the time to catch up with every technology.
Check up on (investigate)	We check up on everyone before we hire them.
Come out (make public)	When report cards come out, some children are not happy.
Come up (mention)	Your name came up in the meeting.
Come up with (produce)	That's the best answer anyone has come up with lately.
Cut down on (lessen)	The factory owner agreed to cut down on fuel use.
Deal with (act)	Gabriela had to deal with many new people at work.
Decide on (select)	Scott decided on a trip to the marina.
Get along with (relate well)	Andrew can get along with anyone.
Get back from (return)	When did you get back from your trip?
Get behind in (lag)	Mary did not want to get behind in her school work.
Get in (arrive)	Arun gets in early on Mondays.
Get over (recover)	Jessica is getting over the flu.
Get through (survive)	Philip will get through this crisis too.
Get up (leave bed)	It was hard to get up this morning.
Give in (surrender)	I gave in after she asked me the third time.
Give up (surrender)	Don't give up on your friends.
Go into (be detailed)	We will go into the plans at a later date.
Go over (review)	Darin has to go over the regulations.
Go through (survive)	It's amazing what you can go through smiling.
Go under (fail)	The company almost went under twice last year.
Hit on (think of)	The girls hit on a new idea for a video game.
Keep on (continue)	Jaime will keep on working until it's done.
Look after (take care of)	Jennifer had to look after her friend.
Look for (search)	Priam is looking for her sweater.
Look forward to (anticipate)	We are looking forward to finishing the book.
Look into (investigate)	John will look into the cost of the trip.

Look out for (watch for)	Look out for falling rocks on that road.
Make up (resolve issues)	The two friends made up after a long time.
Pass out (faint)	The man passed out when he heard he'd won the lottery.
Pull out (discontinue)	We pulled out of the contract just in time.
Pull through (survive)	He pulled through the difficult operation.
Put up with (endure)	There's no reason to put up with this nonsense.
Put up with (tolerate)	Don't put up with lame excuses.
Run into (meet by chance)	Charlotte ran into her teacher at the grocery store.
Run out of (have no more)	Angela ran out of spinach.
Rush into (hurry)	You shouldn't rush into business deals.
Set off (leave)	Bill set off at 6:00 A.M. for the airport.
Show up (appear)	Look who showed up early!
Sink in (be understood)	I wonder if it will ever sink in that honesty is the best policy.
Speak up (speak louder)	Can you speak up?
Stand for (represent)	This candidate stands for fairness and honesty.
Stand in (replace)	Abel has to stand in for Roger tonight because Roger is sick.
Take charge of (be responsible for)	Nick took charge of the golf clubs.
Talk about	What do you want to talk about now?
Took off (left)	The jumbo jet took off on time.
Turn down (reject)	Meg couldn't turn down David's offer.
Turn out (arrive)	At camp, we turned out by the flag at 8:00 A.M.
Wait for (be patient)	I can't wait for the news.
Wear out (become worn)	His running shoes wear out every few months.

List 4.11. Words with Multiple Meanings

Words with multiple meanings can be challenging. Use context clues to determine which meaning applies. These words are *homographs,* that is, they are spelled the same but have different meanings.

arms	He placed the child in her mother's *arms.*
	The rebels needed to buy *arms* to fight the war.
bail	We had to *bail* to keep the boat from sinking.
	She was released from jail when she paid $500 *bail.*
ball	The *ball* rolled under the table.
	The women wore their prettiest dresses to the *ball.*
bank	You can cash your check at the *bank.*
	We had a picnic on the *bank* of the river.
	You can *bank* on it if Vikas promises you something.
bark	Did you hear the dog *bark?*
	The *bark* on the old tree is dry and brittle.
bat	A *bat* flew from the barn and frightened me.
	The children played with the *bat* and ball.
bend	Copper wire is easy to *bend.*
	The boat sailed around the *bend* in the river.
	Mom will *bend* the no-snack rule sometimes.
bit	Jenn checked the *bit* in the horse's mouth.
	I *bit* into the apple.
	It will take just a *bit* longer.
	Ritesh changed the drill *bit* and then made a hole for the screw.
block	Don't *block* the driveway with your bike.
	Eileen straightened the *block* of wood on the bench.
	We walked three *blocks* before we saw the store.
blow	The wind began to *blow* and the leaves fell.
	The *blow* to his head knocked the fighter out.
board	It's almost time to *board* the plane.
	Andrew bounced on the diving *board.*
	Jackie made a presentation to the school *board.*
boil	Amaruta showed the doctor the *boil* on her finger.
	Boil some water for tea, please.
bowl	Chuck likes to *bowl* on Thursdays.
	Mike had a *bowl* of soup.
bridge	We crossed the *bridge* over the Raritan River.
	Bridge is a card game for four people.
	The ball hit him on the *bridge* of his nose.
brush	The dog hid the bone in the *brush* behind the house.
	We found the paint *brush* in the cellar.
	The girls had to *brush* up on their history before taking the test.
	Brush your teeth at least twice a day.
can	I bought a *can* of soda.
	Can I come with you?

case	She put her eyeglasses in their *case*.
	The lawyer won her first *case*.
	Sri ordered a *case* of soda for the party.
check	Camille wrote the *check*.
	Samantha likes to *check* my math.
	Jim put a *check* next to each CD he planned to buy.
compound	The soldiers surrounded the enemy *compound*.
	A *compound* sentence is made of two clauses.
count	The duke, *count*, and earl received awards.
	The child is learning to *count* from one to ten.
court	The lawyer tried the case in *court*.
	Adam and Chris work out at on the basketball *court* on Wednesdays.
cover	Put the *cover* on the pot.
	I pulled a *cover* over my legs because I was cold.
	I listened to a new *cover* of one of my favorite songs.
	His *cover* was blown when his neighbor recognized him and said hello.
crown	The princess wore a small *crown*.
	The doctor put six stitches near the *crown* of the boy's head.
cue	The actor missed his *cue* and did not say his line.
	He held the *cue* steady and aimed at the eight-ball.
date	Bill asked Martina for a *date*.
	Today's *date* is March 28.
digest	Gloria liked reading the *digest* because it had good short stories.
	It takes time to *digest* a big meal.
	There's too much information to *digest* at one time.
fair	The weather was *fair* on the day of the race.
	The judge's decision was *fair*.
	We went on the rides at the *fair*.
fan	Taimur is a baseball *fan*; he never misses a game.
	It's very warm; please, turn on the *fan*.
file	Put your papers in the *file*.
	The children marched in single *file*.
	The prisoner used a *file* to cut the metal bar.
firm	When he finished college, Abdul joined a law *firm*.
	Apples should be *firm*, not soft.
fold	*Fold* your paper in half.
	Viktor took care of the sheep in the *fold*.
game	It sounded exciting, so I was *game* to try it.
	Poker is his favorite card *game*.
grave	The coffin was lowered into the *grave*.
	There was no laughter on the *grave* occasion.
hide	The belts were made from the *hide* of a cow.
	I usually *hide* the gifts for the children's birthdays.
hold	David put the supplies in the ship's *hold*.
	Hold the camera still or the photo will not be good.

jam	I tried to *jam* one more coat into the full closet.
	We put strawberry *jam* on our toast.
	We were stuck in a traffic *jam* for an hour.
jar	The loud noise *jarred* the old man.
	Put the *jar* of mustard on the table.
kind	What *kind* of ice cream do you like?
	Bijal was always *kind* and gentle.
last	I hope this will *last* until Tuesday.
	The *last* time I saw her she was very thin.
lean	He *leaned* against the building while he waited.
	The runner was tan and *lean* after the summer's races.
light	Gloria baked muffins that were *light* and tasty.
	Phil turned on the *light* so we could see.
	It was Christopher's turn to *light* the fire.
like	A carton is *like* a box.
	I *like* fudge cookies.
line	We stood in *line* to get tickets.
	Write your name on the *line*.
	I had to learn my *lines* for the play.
list	Make a *list* of things we need from the grocery store.
	If you don't balance the weight on a boat it will *list* to one side.
long	I *long* to go to a quiet beach.
	How *long* is the story?
mean	What did you *mean* when you said that?
	He was *mean* and unkind.
	We calculated the *mean* score for the two teams.
mine	The silver ore is brought out of the *mine* in carts.
	Put your chair next to *mine*.
miss	*Miss* Polk is the new chemistry teacher.
	I will *miss* you when you move to the city.
	That was a *miss,* not a hit.
net	The fish were caught in a *net,* not on hooks.
	After we paid the taxes, our *net* pay was $300.
palm	The gypsy looked at the lines on my *palm*.
	Gerry took many pictures of the *palm* trees in Florida.
paper	Hand me a piece of *paper*.
	We have to do a *paper* on history.
	I read about the election in the daily *paper*.
	Mom hired a man to *paper* the living room.
pen	The pigs live in a *pen*.
	Sign your name with this *pen*.
play	Marianne, Kathryn, and Fred went to see a *play* at the theater.
	Jaime, Jessica, and David can *play* the piano.
	Nick likes to *play* with the kids on Saturdays.
present	John was absent on Friday, not *present*.
	For her birthday Jill received five *presents*.

press	The editor and other members of the *press* took notes.
	Ask the tailor to *press* this skirt.
	Press the button to start the machine.
punch	The *punch* was made from fruit juice and soda.
	Josh *punched* the bag as hard as he could.
quarters	The soldiers marched to their *quarters*.
	I cut the apple into *quarters*.
	I needed four *quarters* for the vending machine.
rare	I like my steak *rare,* not well done.
	Only three people have ever owned this *rare* coin.
rest	Anna will do the *rest* of the shopping.
	After the long walk up the hill, I wanted to *rest*.
roast	I took the *roast* out of the oven.
	Tom was the guest of honor at the annual *roast*.
	Should we *roast* the chicken or fry it?
roll	Jake and his cousin like to *roll* down the grassy hill.
	I had a *roll* with butter for breakfast.
	Ryan was on a *roll*—he just kept winning.
	The teacher calls *roll* every morning.
seal	Don't use the medicine if the safety *seal* is broken.
	We saw the *seals* at the zoo.
second	There are sixty *seconds* in a minute.
	I was *second* today, but tomorrow I might be first.
shape	We exercise to stay in *shape*.
	A triangle is a common *shape*.
	The artist will *shape* the clay with his hands.
show	Jim and Gloria watched their favorite TV *show*.
	Show me how to do it, please.
sign	Please *sign* your name on this line.
	Alex learned to *sign* from a friend.
	Jared pointed to the *sign* for the cafeteria.
snap	The *snap* on my jacket is loose.
	I'll be there in a *snap*.
	Kathy said she heard the branch *snap* just before it fell.
soil	We added fertilizer to the *soil* so the plant would grow stronger.
	The men tried not to *soil* the new carpet.
sole	I ordered the *sole* for lunch because I like fish.
	He was the *sole* survivor of the crash.
	There was a hole in the *sole* of his shoe.
spell	The child learned to *spell* his name.
	The witch put a magic *spell* on the frog.
stable	Put the horses in the *stable*.
	He may leave the hospital if his breathing is *stable*.
steep	The mountain was *steep* and the climb difficult.
	You should *steep* a tea bag for three minutes.
stick	The glue was dried and the stamp would not *stick*.
	We collected *sticks* and leaves for the fire.

stop	The two girls got off at the Nutley *stop*.
	I'll put a *stop* to that nonsense soon.
	A period at the end of a sentence is also called a full *stop*.
	When will you *stop* working?
store	Meg and Alicia met at the *store*.
	Jenn and Benji *store* their camping equipment in the garage.
story	This is a five-*story* building.
	Tell the children a bedtime *story*.
string	Gabriella tied the packages with silver *string*.
	There was a *string* of robberies in the city.
	The children *string* beads to make necklaces.
	He played second *string* when he was a sophomore.
temple	He took two aspirin for the pain in his *temple*.
	The men walked to the *temple* to pray.
tick	*Ticks* are insects that spread Lyme disease.
	Can you hear the clock *tick*?
tire	I never *tire* of hearing my favorite music.
	I had a flat *tire* on my new car.
trade	I'll *trade* you a red one for a green one.
	When he grows up he'll work in his father's *trade*.
trip	Cynda and Jason planned a *trip* for the holidays.
	Jake was careful and did not *trip* over the wires on the floor.
vault	The athlete could *vault* a six-foot barrier with ease.
	The actress put her diamond jewelry in the *vault*.
wake	Be quiet or you will *wake* Maggie up.
	The waves in the *wake* of the speed boat were very high.
	We attended our aunt's *wake* after she died.
watch	Hanna wanted to *watch* Emily draw.
	I have to buy a new battery for my *watch*.
	Darin was keeping *watch* at the pool.
well	I feel very *well* today.
	The boy put the bucket into the *well* to get water.
will	The lawyer wrote a *will* for the old man before he died.
	I *will* see the man tomorrow, not today.
yard	A *yard* is equal to thirty-six inches.
	We had a picnic in the *yard*.

List 4.12. Homophones

Homophones are words that sound the same but have different meanings and usually different spellings. Recognizing homophones is particularly important because computer spell-check programs do not recognize them as spelling errors.

This list contains only homophones that have different spellings. If a pair has the same spelling (for example, *bat* meaning a flying animal and *bat* meaning a club), they are included in the homograph list (4.11). The term *homonym* can include both homophones (same sound) and homographs (same spelling).

Easy Homophones

add	ad		might	mite	
air	heir		missed	mist	
already	all ready		morn	mourn	
ant	aunt		need	knead	
ate	eight		new	knew	gnu
ball	bawl		night	knight	
bare	bear		no	know	
be	bee		oh	owe	
beat	beet		one	won	
been	bin		or	oar	ore
blue	blew		our	hour	
brake	break		pair	pare	pear
by	bye	buy	peace	piece	
close	clothes	cloze	plane	plain	
creek	creak		principal	principle	
dear	deer		rain	reign	rein
die	dye		read	reed	
fair	fare		real	reel	
feet	feat		red	read	
find	fined		right	write	
flower	flour		road	rode	rowed
for	four	fore	sale	sail	
great	grate		see	sea	
heard	herd		seem	seam	
here	hear		sell	cell	
hi	high		sent	cent	scent
hole	whole		shoe	shoo	
horse	hoarse		side	sighed	
I	eye	aye	so	sew	sow
in	inn		some	sum	
its	it's		son	sun	
led	lead		steal	steel	
loan	lone		tail	tale	
made	maid		their	there	they're
meet	meat		through	threw	

to	two	too	weather	whether	
toe	tow		week	weak	
told	tolled		where	wear	ware
way	weigh		your	you're	
we	wee		wood	would	

More Homophones

acts (deeds)   ax (tool)

ad (advertisement)   add (addition)

ads (advertisements)   adz (axlike tool)

aid (assistance)   aide (helper)

ail (be sick)   ale (beverage)

air (oxygen)   heir (successor)

aisle (path)   I'll (I will)   isle (island)

all (everything)   awl (tool)

all together (in a group)   altogether (completely)

already (previous)   all ready (all are ready)

allowed (permitted)   aloud (audible)

altar (in a church)   alter (change)

ant (insect)   aunt (relative)

ante (before)   anti (against)

arc (part of a circle)   ark (boat)

ascent (climb)   assent (agree)

assistance (help)   assistants (those who help)

ate (did eat)   eight (number)

attendance (presence)   attendants (escorts)

aural (by ear)   oral (by mouth)

away (gone)   aweigh (clear anchor)

band (plays music)   banned (forbidden)

bare (nude)   bear (animal)

based (at a base)   baste (cover with liquid)

bazaar (market)   bizarre (odd)

be (exist)   bee (insect)

beach (shore)   beech (tree)

beat (whip)   beet (vegetable)

beau (boyfriend)   bow (decorative knot)

been (past participle of be)   bin (box)

berry (fruit)   bury (put in ground)

berth (bunk)   birth (born)

better (more good)   bettor (one who bets)

billed (did bill)   build (construct)

blew (did blow)   blue (color)

bough (of a tree)   bow (of a ship)

boy (male child)   buoy (floating object) brake (stop)

break (smash)

bread (food)

bred (cultivated)

brewed (steeped)

brood (flock)

brews (steeps)

bruise (bump)

bridal (relating to bride)

bridle (headgear for horse)

but (except)

butt (end)

buy (purchase)

by (near)

bye (farewell)

capital (money, city)

Capitol (building of U.S. Congress)

carat (weight of precious stones)

carrot (vegetable)

carol (song)

carrel (study space in library)

cast (throw, actors in a play)

caste (social class)

ceiling (top of room)

sealing (closing)

cell (prison room)

sell (exchange for money)

cellar (basement)

seller (one who sells)

censor (ban)

sensor (detection device)

cent (penny)

scent (odor)

sent (did send)

cereal (relating to grain)

serial (of a series)

chance (luck)

chants (songs)

chews (bites)

choose (select)

chilly (cold)

chili (hot pepper)

choral (music)

coral (reef)

chorale (chorus)

corral (pen for livestock)

chord (musical notes)

cord (string)

chute (slide)

shoot (discharge gun)

cite (summon to court)

sight (see)

site (location)

claws (nails on animal's feet)

clause (part of a sentence)

click (small sound)

clique (group of friends)

climb (ascend)

clime (climate)

close (shut)

clothes (clothing)

cloze (test)

coal (fuel)

cole (cabbage)

coarse (rough path)

course (school subject)

colonel (military rank)

kernel (grain of corn)

complement (complete set)

compliment (praise)

coop (chicken pen)

coupe (car)

core (center)

corps (army group)

correspondence (letters)

correspondents (writers)

council (legislative body)

counsel (advise)

creak (grating noise)

creek (stream)

crews (groups of workers)

cruise (sail)

cruel (hurting)

crewel (stitching)

currant (small raisin)

current (stream, recent, fast part of)

curser (one who curses)

cursor (moving pointer)

cymbal (percussion instrument)

symbol (sign)

deer (animal) — dear (greeting, loved one)

desert (abandon) — dessert (follows main course of meal)

die (expire) — dye (color)

dine (eat) — dyne (unit of force)

disburse (pay out) — disperse (scatter)

discreet (unobtrusive) — discrete (noncontinuous)

doe (female deer) — dough (bread mixture) — do (musical note)

do (shall) — dew (moisture) — due (owed)

dual (two) — duel (formal combat)

duct (tube) — ducked (did duck)

earn (work for) — urn (container)

ewe (female sheep) — yew (shrub)

eyelet (small hole) — islet (small island)

fair (honest, bazaar) — fare (cost of transportation)

faze (upset) — phase (stage)

feat (accomplishment) — feet (plural of foot)

find (discover) — fined (given penalty of money)

fir (tree) — fur (animal covering)

flair (talent) — flare (flaming signal)

flea (insect) — flee (run away)

flew (did fly) — flu (influenza)

flour (milled grain) — flower (bloom)

for (in favor of) — fore (front part) — four (number 4)

foreword (preface) — forward (front part)

forth (forward) — fourth (after third)

foul (bad) — fowl (bird)

friar (brother in religious order) — fryer (frying chicken)

gate (fence opening) — gait (foot movement)

gilt (golden) — guilt (opposite of innocence)

gnu (antelope) — knew (did know) — new (opposite of old)

gorilla (animal) — guerrilla (irregular soldier)

grate (grind) — great (large)

groan (moan) — grown (cultivated)

guessed (surmised) — guest (company)

hail (ice; salute) — hale (healthy)

hair (on head) — hare (rabbit)

hall (passage) — haul (carry)

hangar (storage building) — hanger (to hang things on)

halve (cut in half) — have (possess)

hart (deer) — heart (body organ)

hay (dried grass) — hey (expression to get attention)

heal (make well) — heel (bottom of foot) — he'll (he will)

hear (listen) — here (this place)

heard (listened) — herd (group of animals)

heed (pay attention) — he'd (he would)

hertz (unit of wave frequency)

hurts (pain)

hi (hello)

high (opposite of low)

higher (above)

hire (employ)

him (pronoun)

hymn (religious song)

hoarse (husky voice)

horse (animal)

hole (opening)

whole (complete)

holy (sacred)

wholly (all)

horde (crowd)

hoard (hidden supply)

hostel (lodging for youth)

hostile (unfriendly)

hour (sixty minutes)

our (possessive pronoun)

hurdle (jump over)

hurtle (throw)

idle (lazy)

idol (god)

in (opposite of out)

inn (hotel)

insight (self-knowledge)

incite (cause)

instance (example)

instants (short periods of time)

insure (protect against loss)

ensure (make sure)

intense (extreme)

intents (aims)

its (possessive pronoun)

it's (it is)

lain (past participle of lie)

lane (narrow way)

lead (metal)

led (guided)

leak (crack)

leek (vegetable)

lean (slender, incline)

lien (claim)

leased (rented)

least (smallest)

lessen (make less)

lesson (instruction)

levee (embankment)

levy (impose by legal authority)

liar (untruthful)

lyre (musical instrument)

lichen (fungus)

liken (compare)

lie (falsehood)

lye (alkaline solution)

lieu (instead of)

Lou (name)

lightening (becoming light)

lightning (occurs with thunder)

load (burden)

lode (vein or ore)

loan (something borrowed)

lone (single)

locks (plural of lock)

lox (smoked salmon)

loot (steal)

lute (musical instrument)

made (manufactured)

maid (servant)

mail (send by post)

male (masculine)

main (most important)

Maine (state)

mane (hair)

maize (Indian corn)

maze (confusing network of passages)

mall (courtyard)

maul (attack)

manner (style)

manor (estate)

mantel (over fireplace)

mantle (cloak)

marshal (escort)

martial (militant)

massed (grouped)

mast (support)

maybe (perhaps, adj.)

may be (is possible, v.)

meat (beef)	meet (greet)	mete (measure)
medal (award)	meddle (interfere)	
might (may, strength)	mite (small insect)	
miner (coal digger)	minor (juvenile)	
missed (failed to attain)	mist (fog)	
moan (groan)	mown (cut down)	
mode (fashion)	mowed (cut down)	
morn (early day)	mourn (grieve)	
muscle (flesh)	mussel (shellfish)	
naval (nautical)	navel (depression on abdomen, type of orange)	
need (require)	knead (mix with hands)	
new (not old)	knew (remembered)	gnu (animal)
night (evening)	knight (feudal warrior)	
no (negative)	know (familiar with)	
none (not any)	nun (religious sister)	
not (in no manner)	knot (tangle)	
oar (of a boat)	or (conjunction)	ore (mineral deposit)
ode (poem)	owed (did owe)	
oh (exclamation)	owe (be indebted)	
one (number)	won (triumphed)	
overdo (go to extremes)	overdue (past due)	
overseas (abroad)	oversees (supervises)	
pail (bucket)	pale (white)	
pain (discomfort)	pane (window glass)	
pair (two of a kind)	pare (peel)	pear (fruit)
palate (roof of mouth)	palette (board for paint)	pallet (tool, straw bed)
passed (went by)	past (former)	
patience (composure)	patients (sick persons)	
pause (brief stop)	paws (feet of animals)	
peace (tranquility)	piece (part)	
peak (mountaintop)	peek (look)	pique (offense)
pearl (jewel)	purl (knitting stitch)	
pedal (ride a bike)	peddle (sell)	
peer (equal)	pier (dock)	
per (for each)	purr (cat sound)	
pi (Greek letter)	pie (kind of pastry)	
plain (simple)	plane (flat surface)	
pleas (plural of plea)	please (to be agreeable)	
plum (fruit)	plumb (lead weight)	
pole (stick)	poll (vote)	
pore (ponder, skin gland)	pour (flow freely)	
pray (worship)	prey (victim)	
presents (gifts)	presence (appearance)	
principal (chief)	principle (rule)	
profit (benefit)	prophet (seer)	
rain (precipitation)	reign (royal authority)	rein (harness)

raise (put up)	raze (tear down)	rays (of sun)
rap (hit, talk)	wrap (cover)	
read (peruse)	reed (plant)	
read (perused)	red (color)	
real (genuine)	reel (spool)	
reek (give off strong odor)	wreak (inflict)	
rest (relax)	wrest (inflict)	
review (look back)	revue (musical)	
right (correct)	rite (ceremony)	write (inscribe)
rime (ice, rhyme)	rhyme (same end sound)	
ring (circular band)	wring (squeeze)	
road (street)	rode (transported)	rowed (used oars)
roe (fish eggs)	row (line, use oars)	
role (character)	roll (turn over, bread)	
root (part of a plant)	route (highway)	
rose (flower)	rows (lines)	
rote (by memory)	wrote (did write)	
rung (step on a ladder, past of ring)	wrung (squeezed)	
sail (travel by boat)	sale (bargain)	
scene (setting)	seen (viewed)	
scull (boat, row)	skull (head)	
sea (ocean)	see (visualize)	
seam (joining mark)	seem (appear to be)	
serf (feudal servant)	surf (waves)	
sew (mend)	so (in order that)	sow (plant)
shear (cut)	sheer (transparent)	
shoe (foot covering)	shoo (drive away)	
shoot (use gun)	chute (trough)	
shone (beamed)	shown (exhibited)	
side (flank)	sighed (audible breath)	
slay (kill)	sleigh (sled)	
sleight (dexterity)	slight (slender)	
soar (fly)	sore (painful)	
sole (only)	soul (spirit)	
some (portion)	sum (total)	
son (male offspring)	sun (star)	
stair (step)	stare (look intently)	
stake (post)	steak (meat)	
stationary (fixed)	stationery (paper)	
steal (rob)	steel (metal)	
straight (not crooked)	strait (channel of water)	
suite (connected rooms)	sweet (sugary)	
tacks (plural of tack)	tax (assess; burden)	
tail (animal's appendage)	tale (story)	
taught (did teach)	taut (tight)	
tea (drink)	tee (holder for golf ball)	

teas (plural of tea)   tease (mock)

team (crew)   teem (be full)

tear (cry)   tier (level)

their (possessive pronoun)   there (at that place)   they're (they are)

theirs (possessive pronoun)   there's (there is)

threw (tossed)   through (finished)

throne (king's seat)   thrown (tossed)

thyme (herb)   time (duration)

tic (twitch)   tick (insect, sound of clock)

tide (ebb and flow)   tied (bound)

to (toward)   too (also)   two (number)

toad (frog)   towed (pulled)

toe (digit on foot)   tow (pull)

told (informed)   tolled (rang)

trussed (tied)   trust (confidence)

vain (conceited)   vane (wind indicator)   vein (blood vessel)

vale (valley)   veil (face cover)

vice (bad habit)   vise (clamp)

vile (disgusting)   vial (small bottle)

wade (walk in water)   weighed (measured
                               heaviness)

wail (cry)   whale (sea mammal)

waist (middle of body)   waste (trash)

wait (linger)   weight (heaviness)

waive (forgive)   wave (swell, motion with hand)

ware (pottery)   wear (have on)   where (what place)

way (road)   weigh (measure heaviness)

ways (plural of way, shipyard) weighs (is this heavy)

we (pronoun)   wee (small)

weak (not strong)   week (seven days)

we'll (we will)   wheel (circular frame)

weather (climate   whether (if)
characteristic)

weave (interlace)   we've (we have)

we'd (we would)   weed (plant)

which (what one)   witch (sorceress)

while (during)   wile (trick)

whine (complaining sound)   wine (drink)

who's (who is)   whose (possessive of who)

wood (of a tree)   would (is willing to)

worst (most bad)   wurst (sausage)

yoke (harness)   yolk (egg center)

you (pronoun)   ewe (female sheep)   yew (evergreen tree)

you'll (you will)   yule (Christmas)

your (possessive pronoun)   you're (you are)

See also List 4.13: Homographs and Heteronyms.

List 4.13. Homographs and Heteronyms

Homographs are words that are spelled the same but have different meanings and different origins. Many other words have multiple meanings, but according to dictionary authorities, what makes these words homographs is that they have different origins as well. Some homographs are also heteronyms, meaning they have a different pronunciation, often caused by changing syllable stress (for example, cón-sole versus con-sóle) or vowel shift. These can also be called homonyms. They are marked with an asterisk (*).

august* (majestic)	August (eighth month of the year)	
axes* (plural of ax)	axes (plural of axis)	
band (group of musicians)	band (thin strip for binding)	
bass* (low male voice)	bass (kind of fish)	
baste (pour liquid on while roasting)	baste (sew with long stitches)	
batter (liquid mixture used for cakes)	batter (baseball player)	
bay (part of a sea)	bay (aromatic herb)	
bear (large animal)	bear (support, carry)	
bill (statement of money owed)	bill (beak)	
bow* (weapon for shooting arrows)	bow (forward part of a ship)	bow (bend in greeting or respect)
box (four-sided container)	box (kind of evergreen shrub)	box (strike with the hand)
buck (male deer)	buck (slang for dollar)	
capital (money)	capital (punishable by death)	
carp (complain)	carp (kind of fish)	
chap (crack or become rough)	chap (boy or man)	
chop (cut with something sharp)		
chop (cut of meat)		
chuck (throw or toss)	chuck (cut of beef)	
clip (cut)	clip (fasten)	
close* (shut)	close (near)	
cobbler (one who mends shoes)	cobbler (fruit pie with one crust)	
colon (mark of punctuation)	colon (lower part of the large intestine)	
compact* (firmly packed together)	compact (agreement)	
con (swindle)	con (against)	
console* (cabinet)	console (ease grief)	

contract* (written agreement)   contract (withdraw)

content* (all things inside)   content (satisfied)

converse* (talk)   converse (opposite)

corporal (of the body)   corporal (low-ranking officer)

count (name numbers in order)   count (nobleman)

counter (long table in a store or restaurant)   counter (one who counts)   counter (opposite)

crow (loud cry of a rooster)   crow (large black bird)   Crow (tribe of Native American Indians)

cue (signal)   cue (long stick used in a game of pool)

curry (rub and clean a horse)   curry (spicy seasoning)

date (day, month, and year)   date (sweet dark fruit)

defer (put off)   defer (yield to another)

demean (lower in dignity)   demean (humble oneself)

desert* (dry barren region)   desert (go away from)

die (stop living)   die (tool)

do* (act; perform)   do (first tone on the musical scale)

dock (wharf)   dock (cut some off)

does* (plural of doe)   does (present tense of to do)

dove* (pigeon)   dove (did dive)

down (from a higher to a lower place)   down (soft feathers)   down (grassy land)

dredge (dig up)   dredge (sprinkle with flour or sugar)

dresser (one who dresses)   dresser (bureau)

drove (did drive)   drove (flock, herd, crowd)

dub (give a title)   dub (add voice or music to a film)

duck (large wild bird)   duck (lower suddenly)   duck (type of cotton cloth)

ear (organ of hearing)   ear (part of certain plants)

egg (oval or round body laid by a bird)   egg (encourage)

elder (older)   elder (small tree)

entrance* (going in)   entrance (delight, charm)

excise* (tax)   excise (remove)

fair (beautiful, lovely)   fair (just, honest)   fair (showing of farm goods)

fair (bazaar)

fan (devise to stir up the air)   fan (admirer)

fast (speedy)

fast (go without food)

fawn (young deer)

fawn (try to get favor by slavish acts)

fell (did fall)

fell (cut down a tree)

fell (deadly)

felt (did feel)

felt (type of cloth)

file (drawer; folder)

file (steel tool to smooth material)

file (material)

fine (high quality)

fine (money paid as punishment)

firm (solid, hard)

firm (business, company)

fit (suitable)

fit (sudden attack)

flag (banner)

flag (get tired)

flat (smooth)

flat (apartment)

fleet (group of ships)

fleet (rapid)

flight (act of flying)

flight (act of fleeing)

flounder (struggle)

flounder (kind of fish)

fluke (lucky stroke in games)

fluke (kind of fish)

fly (insect)

fly (move through the air with wings)

foil (prevent carrying out of plans)

foil (metal sheet)

foil (long narrow sword)

fold (bend over on itself)

fold (pen for sheep)

forearm (part of the body)

forearm (prepare for trouble ahead)

forge (blacksmith shop)

forge (move ahead)

forte* (strong point)

forte (loud)

found (did find)

found (set up, establish)

founder (sink)

founder (one who establishes)

frank (hotdog)

frank (bold talk)

Frank (man's name)

fray (become ragged)

fray (fight)

fresh (newly made, not stale)

fresh (impudent, bold)

fret (worry)

fret (ridge on a guitar's neck)

fry (cook in shallow pan)

fry (young fish)

fuse (slow-burning wick)

fuse (melt together)

gall (bile)

gall (annoy)

game (pastime)

game (lame)

gauntlet (challenge)

gauntlet (protective glove)

gin (alcoholic beverage)

gin (apparatus for separating seeds from cotton)

gin (card came)

gore (blood)

gore (wound from a horn)

gore (three-sided insert of cloth)

grate (framework for burning fuel in a fireplace)

grate (have an annoying effect)

grave (place of burial)   grave (important, serious)   grave (carve)

graze (feed on grass)   graze (touch lightly in passing)

ground (soil)   ground (did grind)

grouse (game bird)   grouse (grumble, complain)

gull (sea bird)   gull (cheat, deceive)

gum (sticky substance from certain trees)   gum (tissue around teeth)

guy (rope, chain)   guy (fellow)

hack (cut roughly)   hack (carrier or car for hire)

hail (pieces of ice that fall like rain)   hail (shouts of welcome)

hamper (hold back)   hamper (large container or bucket)

hatch (bring forth young from an egg)   hatch (opening in a ship's deck)

hawk (bird of prey)   hawk (peddle goods)

haze (mist, smoke)   haze (bully)

heel (back of the foot)   heel (tip over to one side)

hide (conceal, keep out of sight)   hide (animal skin)

hinder (stop)   hinder (rear)

hold (grasp and keep)   hold (part of ship or place for cargo)

husky (big and strong)   husky (sled dog)

impress (have a strong effect on)   impress (take by force)

incense* (substance with a sweet smell when burned)   incense (make very angry)

intern* (force to stay)   intern (doctor in training at a hospital)

intimate* (very familiar)   intimate (suggest)

invalid* (disabled person)   invalid (not valid)

jam (fruit preserve)   jam (press or squeeze)

jerky (with sudden starts and stops)   jerky (strips of dried meat)

jet (stream of water, steam, or air)   jet (hard black soil)   jet (type of airplane)

jig (dance)   jig (fishing lure)

job* (work)   Job (biblical man of patience)

jumper (person or thing that jumps)   jumper (type of dress)

junk (trash)   junk (Chinese sailing ship)

key (instrument for locking and unlocking)   key (low island) kind (friendly, helpful)   kind (same class)

lap (body part formed   lap (drink)   lap (one course traveled)
when sitting)

lark (small songbird)   lark (good fun)

lash (cord part of a whip)   lash (tie or fasten)

last (at the end)   last (continue, endure)

launch (start out)   launch (type of boat)

lead* (show the way)   lead (metallic element)

league (measure of   league (group of persons or
distance)   nations)

lean (stand slanting)   lean (not fat)

leave (go away)   leave (permission)

left (direction)   left (did leave)

lie (falsehood)   lie (place oneself in a flat
position, rest)

light (not heavy)   light (not dark)   light (land on)

like (similar to)   like (be pleased with)

lime (citrus fruit)   lime (chemical substance)

limp (lame walk)   limp (not stiff)

line (piece of cord)   line (place paper or fabric
inside)

list (series of words)   list (tilt to one side)

live* (exist)   live (having life)

loaf (be idle)   loaf (shaped as bread)

lock (fasten door)   lock (curl of hair)

long (great measure)   long (wish for)

loom (frame for weaving)   loom (threaten)

low (not high)   low (cattle sound)

lumber (timber)   lumber (move along
heavily)

mace (club, weapon)   mace (spice)

mail (letters)   mail (flexible metal
armor)

maroon (brownish red   maroon (leave helpless)
color)

mat (woven floor covering)   mat (border for picture)

match (stick used to light   match (equal)
fires)

meal (food served at a   meal (ground grain)
certain time)

mean (signify, intend)   mean (unkind)   mean (average)

meter (unit of length)   meter (poetic rhythm)   meter (device that
measures flow)

might (past of may)   might (power)

mine (belonging to me)   mine (hole in the earth
to get ores)

minute* (sixty seconds)   minute (very small)

miss (fail to hit)

miss (unmarried woman or girl)

mold (form, shape)

mold (fungus)

mole (brown spot on the skin)

mole (small underground animal)

mortar (cement mixture)

mortar (short cannon)

mount (high hill)

mount (go up)

mule (cross between donkey and horse)

mule (type of slipper)

mum (silent)

mum (chrysanthemum)

nag (scold)

nag (old horse)

nap (short sleep)

nap (rug fuzz)

net (open-weave fabric)

net (remaining after deductions)

nip (small drink)

nip (pinch)

number (numeral)

number (past tense of numb)

object* (a thing)

object (to protest)

pad (cushion)

pad (walk softly)

page (one side of a sheet of paper)

page (youth who runs errands)

palm (inside of hand)

palm (kind of tree)

patent (right or privilege)

patent (type of leather)

patter (rapid taps)

patter (light, easy walk)

pawn (leave as security for loan)

pawn (chess piece)

peaked* (having a point)

peaked (looking ill)

peck (dry measure)

peck (strike at)

pen (instrument for writing)

pen (enclosed yard)

pile (heap or stack)

pile (nap on fabrics)

pine (type of evergreen)

pine (yearn or long for)

pitch (throw)

pitch (tar)

pitcher (container for pouring liquid)

pitcher (baseball player)

poach (trespass)

poach (cook an egg)

poker (card game)

poker (rod for stirring a fire)

pole (long piece of wood)

pole (either end of the earth's axis)

policy (plan of action)

policy (written agreement)

Polish* (from Poland)

polish (shine)

pool (tank with water)

pool (game played with balls on a table)

pop (short, quick sound) | pop (dad) | pop (popular)

post (support) | post (job or position) | post (system for mail delivery)

pound (unit of weight)	pound (hit hard again and again)	pound (pen)
present* (not absent)	present (gift)	present (to introduce formally)
press (squeeze)	press (force into service)	
primer* (first book)	primer (something used to prepare another)	
produce* (vegetables)	produce (make something)	
prune (fruit)	prune (cut, trim)	
pry (look with curiosity)	pry (lift with force)	
pump (type of shoe)	pump (machine that forces liquid out)	
punch (hit)	punch (beverage)	
pupil (student)	pupil (part of the eye)	
quack (sound of a duck)	quack (phony doctor)	
racket (noise)	racket (paddle used in tennis)	
rail (bar of wood or metal)	rail (complain bitterly)	
rank (row or line)	rank (having a bad odor)	
rare (unusual)	rare (not cooked much)	
rash (hasty)	rash (small red spots on the skin)	
ream (500 sheets of paper)	ream (clean a hole)	
rear (back part)	rear (bring up)	
record* (music disk)	record (write down)	
recount (count again)	recount (tell in detail)	
reel (spool for winding)	reel (sway under a blow)	reel (lively dance)
refrain (hold back)	refrain (part repeated)	
refuse* (say no)	refuse (waste, trash)	
rest (sleep)	rest (what is left)	
rifle (gun with a long barrel)	rifle (ransack, search through)	
ring (circle)	ring (bell sound)	
root (underground part of a plant)	root (cheer for someone)	
row* (line)	row (use oars to move a boat)	row (noisy fight)
sage (wise person)	sage (herb)	
sap (liquid in a plant)	sap (weaken)	
sash (cloth worn around the waist)	sash (frame of a window)	
saw (did see)	saw (tool for cutting)	saw (wise saying)
scale (balance)	scale (outer layer of fish and snakes)	scale (series of steps)
school (place for learning)	school (group of fish)	
scour (clean)	scour (move quickly over)	
scrap (small bits)	scrap (quarrel)	

seal (mark of ownership)   seal (sea mammal)

sewer* (one who sews)   sewer (underground pipe
                                        for wastes)

shark (large meat-eating   shark (dishonest person)
    fish)

shed (small shelter)   shed (get rid of)

shingles (roofing materials)   shingles (viral disease)

shock (sudden violent   shock (thick bushy mass)
disturbance)

shot (fired a gun)   shot (worn out)

slug (small slow-moving   slug (hit hard)
    animal)

sock (covering for foot)   sock (hit hard)

soil (ground, dirt)   soil (make dirty)

sole (type of fish)   sole (only)

sow* (scatter seeds)   sow (female pig)

spar (mast of a ship)   spar (argue)   spar (mineral)

squash (press flat)   squash (vegetable)

stake (stick or post)   stake (risk or prize)

stalk (main stem of a plant)   stalk (follow secretly)

stall (place in a stable for   stall (delay)
    one animal)

staple (metal fastener for   staple (principal element)
    paper)

steer (guide)   steer (young male cattle)

stem (part of a plant)   stem (stop, dam up)

stern (rear part of a ship)   stern (harsh, strict)

still (not moving)   still (apparatus for making
                                        alcohol)

stoop (bend down)   stoop (porch)

strain (pull tight)   strain (group with an
                                   inherited quality)

strand (leave helpless)   strand (thread or string)

strip (narrow piece of   strip (remove)
    cloth)

stroke (hit)   stroke (pet, soothe)   stroke (an illness)

stunt (stop growth)   stunt (bold action)

sty (pen for pigs)   sty (swelling on eyelid)

subject* (topic)   subject (put under)

swallow (take in)   swallow (small bird)

tap (strike lightly)   tap (faucet)

tarry* (delay)   tarry (covered with tar)

tart (sour but agreeable)   tart (small fruit-filled pie)

tear* (drop of liquid from   tear (pull apart)
    the eye)

temple (building for   temple (side of forehead)
    worship)

tend (incline to)   tend (take care of)

tender (not tough)   tender (offer)

till (until)   till (plow the land)

tip (end point)   tip (slant)   tip (present of money for services)

toast (browned bread slices)   toast (wish for good luck)

toll (sound of a bell)   toll (fee paid for a privilege)

top (highest point)   top (toy that spins)

troll (ugly dwarf)   troll (method of fishing)

unaffected (not influenced)   unaffected (innocent)

will (statement of desire for distribution of property after one's death)   will (is going to)   will (deliberate intention or wish)

wind* (air in motion)   wind (turn)

wound* (hurt)   wound (wrapped around)

yak (long-haired ox)   yak (talk endlessly)

yard (enclosed space around a house)   yard (thirty-six inches)

yen (strong desire)   yen (unit of money in Japan)

See also List 4.12: Homophones.

Section Five

Grammar

List 5.1. Basic Sentence Patterns

Students find it helpful to have models for basic sentence patterns. It helps them learn English word order and reminds them of how articles and other parts of speech are used. Compound patterns may be taught at the same time as simple patterns if students understand the use of compounds in spoken English.

Simple Patterns

N/V
noun/verb

The boys/ran.
Four women/sewed.
The faucet/dripped.
A balloon/burst.
Children/laughed.

N/V/AD
noun/verb/adverb

The glass/broke/suddenly.
I/drove/home.
We/left/early in the morning.
Darin/trained/all season.
Adam/fished/often.

N/V/N
noun/verb/noun

Christopher/planned/the trip.
The artist/painted/a picture.
The choir/sings/hymns.
An elephant/eats/peanuts.
The cat/caught/a mouse.

N/V/N/N
noun/verb/noun/noun

Jenn/made/Benji/a sandwich.
Tom/bought/Chris/flowers.
Mom/bought/them/tickets.
The representatives/elected/David/chairman.
Philip/called/Alex/his cousin.

N/V/N/ADJ   **noun/verb/noun/adjective**

Jared/found/the door/open.
You/are driving/me/crazy.
Meg/made/the house/cozy.
Alicia and Samantha/painted/the room/green.
The frosting/made/the cake/fattening.

N/LV/N   **noun/linking verb/noun**

Mike/is/a banker.
The party/will be/a surprise.
The owner/was/a musician.
The desk/could have been/an antique.
The drivers/were/professionals.

N/LV/ADJ   **noun/linking verb/adjective**

Love/is/grand.
Gloria/seems/pleased.
The apples/were/tart.
Jim/feels/energetic.
The potatoes/tasted/salty.

Compound Patterns

N/V   **noun/verb**

Lisa and Steven/studied.
The roses and begonias/bloomed.
The old lady/complained and complained.
The tigers/roared and attacked.
The mother and child/watched and smiled.
David and Andrew/sailed and swam.

N/V/AD   **noun/verb/adverb**

The books and papers/were scattered/on the desk.
Your letter and package/arrived/yesterday.
She/typed and filed/expertly.
They/designed and painted/carefully.
The thief/entered/slowly and noiselessly.
The guests/gathered/on the deck and in the house.

N/V/N   **noun/verb/noun**

The principal and teachers/greeted/the students.
Hydrogen and oxygen/form/water.
Jason/sorted and stacked/his bills.
Cynda/picked and arranged/the flowers.
Gabriela/purchased/some coffee and biscuits.
Ryan/wore/a jacket and tie.

N/V/N/N   **noun/verb/noun/noun**

Jackie and Nancy/gave/Gerry/hugs.
Chuck/planned and built/Marie/a bookcase.

Kathy/gave/Emily and Maggie/kisses.
Nick/cooked/Camille/shrimp and scallops.

N/V/N/ADJ   **noun/verb/noun/adjective**

The heat and humidity/made/Jake/tired.
The judge/thought and called/the winner/exceptional.
The surprise/made/Jaime and Jessica/happy.
Phil/found/Gloria/interesting and beautiful.

N/LV/N   **noun/linking verb/noun**

Emily and Hanna/are/sisters.
You/can and will be/a winner.
Michael/is/a reader and a writer.

N/LV/ADJ   **noun/linking verb/adjective**

The coffee and tea/were/hot.
Reading/is and will be/necessary.
The model/is/tall and slender.

List 5.2. Question and Answer Sentence Patterns

English provides many options for asking and answering questions. Be sure to introduce students to alternate question and response patterns, and discuss the level of formality that each type conveys. Students who have gained some knowledge of English through instruction that focused on reading and writing may find the flexibility more challenging than those who have learned English through a model that focused on listening and speaking.

There are six major sentence patterns for asking questions, and several answer forms:

1. Question words
2. Inverted word order
3. Emphatic or request words
4. Tag questions
5. Closed questions
6. Open questions

Question Words

Who called the taxi?	Victor.
	Victor called.
	Victor called it.
	Victor called the taxi.
Who is waiting?	Bijal.
Who's waiting?	Bijal is.
	Bijal is waiting.
What is in the box?	A vase.
What's in the box?	A vase is.
	A vase is in the box.
Where are you going?	The store.
Where're you going?	To the store.
	I'm going to the store.
When are you leaving?	In an hour.
	I'm leaving in an hour.
Why did he call?	To get the answer.
Why'd he call?	He called to get the answer.
How much does it cost?	Three dollars.
	It costs three dollars.

Inverted Word Order

Are you tired?	Yes, I am.	No, I'm not.
Aren't you tired?	Yes, I am.	No, I'm not.
Is he hungry?	Yes, he is.	No, he's not.
Isn't he hungry?	Yes, he is.	No, he isn't.

Is it time to go?	Yes, it is.	No, it's not.
Isn't it time to go?	Yes, it is.	No, it isn't.
Will you be going?	Yes, I will.	No, I won't.
Won't you be going?	Yes, I will.	No, I won't.
Have you had a cold?	Yes, I have.	No, I haven't.
Haven't you had a cold?	Yes, I have.	No, I haven't.

Emphatic or Request Words

Did it fall?	Yes, it did.	No, it didn't.
Do you like it?	Yes, I do.	No, I don't.
Does he have one?	Yes, he does.	No, he doesn't.
May I have some?	Yes, you may.	No, you may not.
Can we leave?	Yes, we can.	No, we can't.
Should I speak?	Yes, you should.	No, you shouldn't.
Have they gone?	Yes, they have.	No, they haven't.
Has she finished?	Yes, she has.	No, she hasn't.
Would you take this?	Yes, I would.	No, I wouldn't.

Question Tags

I'm on next, aren't I?	I'm not on next, am I?
You're tall, aren't you?	You're not tall, are you?
She's busy, isn't she?	She's not busy, is she?
It's over, isn't it?	It's not over, is it?
We're young, aren't we?	We're not young, are we?
They're smiling, aren't they?	They're not smiling, are they?
I was hungry, wasn't I?	I wasn't hungry, was I?
You're ill, weren't you?	You weren't ill, were you?
He was broke, wasn't he?	He wasn't broke, was he?
We were silly, weren't we?	We weren't silly, were we?
They were new, weren't they?	They weren't new, were they?
You'll go, won't you?	You won't go, will you?
They'll go, won't they?	They won't go, will they?
She can go, can't she?	She can't go, can she?
We can go, can't we?	We can't go, can we?
They do know, don't they?	They don't know, do they?
She did write, didn't she?	She didn't write, did she?
It looks good, doesn't it?	It doesn't look good, does it?
The jet has landed, hasn't it?	The jet hasn't landed, has it?
He had won, hadn't he?	He hadn't won, had he?
I have missed, haven't I?	I haven't missed, have I?
I could do it, couldn't I?	I couldn't do it, could I?
They would do it, wouldn't they?	They wouldn't do it, would they?
We should do it, shouldn't we?	We shouldn't do it, should we?

Closed Questions—Yes or No Answers

Does Marina like ice cream?

Doesn't Marina like ice cream?

Marina likes ice cream, doesn't she?

Open Questions—Various Answers Possible

What does Ritesh like?

What doesn't Ritesh like?

List 5.3. Negative Sentence Patterns

There are three common ways to express negation in English: negate the verb in the sentence, negate a noun in the sentence, or use a special negative word.

Negating the Verb

To negate the verb in a sentence, add *not* between the auxiliary and the main verb. If the verb does not have an auxiliary, use its emphatic transformation and the auxiliary *do* or *does*. Contractions are frequently used in negative sentences. Examples:

Positive	Transformation	Negative
I see it.	I do see it.	I do not see it.
		I don't see it.
I have it.	I do have it.	I do not have it.
		I don't have it.
He carries them.	He does carry them.	He does not carry them.
		He doesn't carry them.
I saw it.	I did see it.	I did not see it.
		I didn't see it.
He could fix the tire.		He could not fix the tire.
		He couldn't fix the tire.
I will go to the store.		I will not go to the store.
		I won't go to the store.
We were going swimming.		We were not going swimming.
		We weren't going swimming.
It is time to go.		It is not time to go.
		It isn't time to go.

Negating a Noun

To negate a noun, add *no* before the noun. Examples:

We have time to spare.	We have no time to spare.
I found money in the park.	I found no money in the park.
Photographs were taken on Friday.	No photographs were taken on Friday.

Using a Special Negative Word

These words are also used to express negation: *nobody, nothing, nowhere, none, no one,* and *neither.* Examples:

Nobody found Marianne's wallet.	There was nothing left in the jar.
Nowhere is more beautiful than this valley.	None of the babies cried.
No one knew how to turn off the generator.	Neither Kathryn nor Fred saw it.

List 5.4. Active/Passive Sentence Patterns

The verb in a sentence is in the active voice when the subject is the doer or agent of the action. The verb is in the passive voice when the subject is the receiver of the action. The doer or agent of the action is not always stated in a passive sentence.

Active	**Passive**
Anthony broke the window.	The window was broken by Anthony.
	The window was broken.
A neighbor is watching her.	She is being watched by a neighbor.
I am not considering the costs.	The costs are not being considered.
He is stirring the soup.	The soup is being stirred by him.
The music excites me.	I am excited by the music.
Librarians order books.	Books are ordered by librarians.
We make decisions daily.	Decisions are made daily.
Farmers grow grain.	Grain is grown by farmers.
They do not trade jobs often.	Jobs were not traded often by them.
She usually makes the tea.	The tea is usually made by her.
Someone stole the car.	The car was stolen.
They voted Dawn treasurer.	Dawn was voted treasurer.
Sissy gave Jake a watch.	Jake was given a watch by Sissy.
Jose did not paint the house.	The house was not painted by Jose.
Ellen slammed the door shut.	The door was slammed shut.
The boys didn't rake the leaves.	The leaves weren't raked by the boys.
The teacher graded the tests.	The tests were graded.
Congress raised the taxes.	The taxes were raised by Congress.
Phil drank the soda.	The soda was drunk by Phil.
Jill will not call Rosa.	Rosa will not be called by Jill.
Harry will fix the VCR.	The VCR will be fixed.
They will break the record.	The record will be broken by them.
We will bring the boxes.	The boxes will be brought by us.
Andy will tease Annette.	Annette will be teased by Andy.
I will operate the machine.	The machine will be operated by me.
Ed will appoint the captain.	The captain will be appointed by Ed.
I will not do it.	It will not be done by me.
Someone will take us.	We will be taken by someone.

List 5.5. The Parts of Speech

The English language classifies words into eight categories, or parts of speech:

noun	verb	adjective	adverb
pronoun	conjunction	preposition	interjection

The parts of speech are the building blocks of the language. The categories explain how a word is *used* in written and spoken language. In English, the same word can be used in more than one way. For example, in the sentence,

I *talk* to my friend everyday.

the word *talk* is used as the *verb* or action of the sentence. But in this sentence,

Her *talk* about hats was boring.

the word *talk* is used as a *noun* or the subject of the sentence.

The *syntax* of a language is the set of rules for using the different parts of speech to form sentences grammatically. In addition to helping us speak and write clearly, our knowledge of these rules or patterns (syntax clues) helps us to understand the meaning of unfamiliar words. For example, in the sentence

The *glicker* explained why he was late.

we can tell that a *glicker* is a *person* because the word is used as a *noun*, and that the *glicker* is *male* because of the *pronoun he* referring back to *glicker*. Understanding the parts of speech and their use in sentences will also help students improve their listening and reading comprehension.

Noun

A *noun* names or points out a person, place, thing, or idea. It can act or be acted upon. Examples: *teacher, home, bike, democracy.*

A *proper noun* names a specific person, place, or thing. Always capitalize a proper noun. Examples: *Jennifer, New Jersey, North Sea, Eiffel Tower, Central Park.*

A *common noun* names one of a class or group of persons, places, or things. Common nouns are not capitalized. Examples: *boy, president, state, sea, building.*

In sentences, nouns are used as subjects, direct objects, indirect objects, or objects of prepositions:

Subject	The dog barked.
Direct object	John broke the lock.
Indirect object	I gave Christine the book.
Object of preposition	We went to the park.

Pronoun

A *pronoun* is used in place of a noun. Different pronoun forms are used to show:

- person (first, second, or third)
- number (singular or plural)
- gender (masculine, feminine, or neuter)
- case (nominative, possessive, or objective).

In addition, there are different types of pronouns for special purposes.

Personal pronouns refer to one or more individuals or things (*we, it*).

Interrogative pronouns are used to ask questions (*who, what*).

Relative pronouns relate groups of words to nouns or other pronouns (*that, which*).

Indefinite pronouns make a general reference; they do not point to a specific person or thing (*each, someone*).

Demonstrative pronouns are used to point out or identify a noun (*this, those*).

Reflexive pronouns emphasize and refer back to the noun (*itself, ourselves*).

See List 5.14, on pronouns, and List 5.15, on possessive forms, for additional information and examples.

Adjective

An *adjective* describes a noun or a pronoun and tells what kind, how many, or which one.

Examples: *lazy, beautiful, three, that*.

See List 5.16, on adjectives, for additional information and examples.

Verb

A *verb* shows a physical or mental action, or the state of being of a subject.

Examples: *build, wish, climb, feel, seem, understand*.

There are three types of verbs: transitive, intransitive, and linking.

- A *transitive verb* relates an action that has an object.

    Example: Janet *made* the cards.
- An *intransitive verb* does not have an object.

    Example: Cody and Sophia *smiled*.
- A *linking verb* connects the subject and a word that describes or relates to the subject.

    Example: Brad *looks* proud.

Verbs take different forms to show person, voice, tense, and mood.

See List 5.6, on verbs, for more information and examples.

Adverb

An *adverb* describes a verb, an adjective, or another adverb by providing information about where, when, how, how much or to what extent. Many adverbs are formed by adding the suffix *-ly* to an adjective or noun.

Examples: *outside, later, seriously, few*.

See List 5.17, on adverbs and adverbial phrases, for more information and examples.

Conjunction

A *conjunction* is used to join words, phrases, or clauses.

Examples: *and, because, however, but*.

See List 5.19, on conjunctions, for more information and examples.

Preposition

A *preposition* shows the relationship of a noun or pronoun to another word. A prepositional phrase is made up of a preposition and a noun with its modifiers. Prepositional phrases may indicate an indirect object, or act as adverbs of time or place.

Examples: *to* the girl (indirect object), *on* the bed (adverb), *across* the street (adverb), *before* noon (adverb).

See List 5.20, on prepositions, for additional information and a list of common prepositions.

Interjection

An *interjection* is a word that is used alone to express strong emotion.

Examples: *Wow! Congratulations! Damn! Bravo!*

List 5.6. Verbs

Verbs show physical or mental action or the state of being of a subject. For example, *sit, think, swim, breathe, appear* and *know* are all verbs. Verbs take different forms to show person, voice, tense, and mood.

Person

Person refers to the subject of the verb.

It can be first, second, or third person, singular or plural.

Verbs use different endings and forms to show person.

	Singular	**Plural**
1st person	I	We
2nd person	You	You
3rd person	He, she, it	They

Voice

Verbs have an active and a passive voice.

A verb is in the active voice when the subject is the agent or doer of the action.

A verb is in the passive voice when the subject is the receiver of the action.

Examples:

Active	Marie baked the pie.
Passive	The pie was baked by Marie.

Tense

Verb tense shows the time of the action.

The *simple* tenses are the present, the past, and the future.

The *perfect* tenses are the present perfect, past perfect, and future perfect.

The *progressive* tenses are the present progressive, present perfect progressive, past perfect progressive, and future perfect progressive.

See List 5.19, on verb conjugation, for additional information and examples.

Mood

Verb moods help show the intention of the speaker or writer.

The three moods are indicative, imperative, and subjunctive.

- The *indicative mood* is used to make statements or ask questions.

    Examples: I baked an apple pie. Where did you get that hat?

- The *imperative mood* is used for commands or requests.

    Examples: Wash your hands. Please go to the store.

- The *subjunctive mood* is used to express a wish, a condition contrary to fact, or a request.

    Examples: I wish I were taller. If I begin this project, will you finish it for me? If I had dealt you another card, would you have won?

Verbs can also be transitive, intransitive, or linking.

- A *transitive verb* conveys an action that has an object.
    Example: Camille *baked* the bread.
- An *intransitive verb* does not have an object.
    Example: The baby *cried.*
- A *linking verb* connects the subject and a word that describes or relates to the subject.
    Example: The old man *seems* tired.

Verbs have five *principle parts:* infinitive, present, present participle, past, and past participle.
Regular verbs form their past and past participle by adding the suffix *-d* or *-ed* to the verb base.
Examples: *look, looked, looked; thank, thanked, thanked.*
Irregular verbs do not follow this pattern and their past and past participle forms must be learned.
Examples: *go, went, gone; see, saw, seen; bit, bit, bitten.*

	Regular Verb	**Irregular Verb**
Infinitive	to mend	to go
Present	mend	go
Present participle	mending	going
Past	mended	went
Past participle	mended	gone

The verb *to be* is a special case. It has irregular present forms:

Infinitive	to be
Present	am, are, is
Present participle	being
Past	was
Past participle	been

See List 5.11, on irregular verb forms, for a complete list.
Auxiliary verbs, also called *helping verbs,* are used with the main verb to show tense and mood. They include the forms of *be, have,* and *do.*
Examples: *will* go, *has been* crying, *had* gone, *did* say.
Modal auxiliary verbs are also helping verbs and are used to indicate possibilities, obligations, abilities, desires, permissions, needs, willingness, requests, and viewpoints.
Examples: You *may* stay out late. I *ought* to call home. He *must* leave now.
Modals include:

be able	could	have to	must	should
be supposed to	had better	may	ought to	will
can	have got to	might	shall	would

A verb is in the *active voice* when the subject is the doer or agent of the action.
Example: *Marie baked* the pie.

List 5.7. Verb Conjugation

To conjugate a verb is to write or say its forms for each person, number, tense, and mood. The following example is a conjugation of the regular verb *to cover*. The principle parts of the verb are:

| to cover | cover | covering | covered | covered |

Active Voice, Indicative Mood

Tense	Singular	Plural
Present	I cover	We cover
	You cover	You cover
	He covers	They cover
	She covers	
	It covers	
Present progressive	I am covering	We are covering
	You are covering	You are covering
	He is covering	They are covering
	She is covering	
	It is covering	
Past	I covered	We covered
	You covered	You covered
	He covered	They covered
	She covered	
	It covered	
Past progressive	I was covering	We were covering
	You were covering	You were covering
	He was covering	They were covering
	She was covering	
	It was covering	
Future	I will cover	We will cover
	You will cover	You will cover
	He will cover	They will cover
	She will cover	
	It will cover	
Future progressive	I will be covering	We will be covering
	You will be covering	You will be covering
	He will be covering	They will be covering
	She will be covering	
	It will be covering	
Present perfect	I have covered	We have covered
	You have covered	You have covered
	He has covered	They have covered
	She has covered	
	It has covered	

Tense	Singular	Plural
Present perfect progressive	I have been covering You have been covering He has been covering She has been covering It has been covering	We have been covering You have been covering They have been covering
Past perfect	I had covered You had covered He had covered She had covered It had covered	We had covered You had covered They had covered
Past perfect progressive	I had been covered You had been covered He had been covered She had been covered It had been covered	We had been covered You had been covered They had been covered
Future perfect	I will have covered You will have covered He will have covered She will have covered It will have covered	We will have covered You will have covered They will have covered
Future perfect progressive	I will have been covered You will have been covered He will have been covered She will have been covered It will have been covered	We will have been covered You will have been covered They will have been covered
Conditional	I would cover You would cover He would cover She would cover It would cover	We would cover You would cover They would cover
Conditional progressive	I would be covered You would be covered He would be covered She would be covered It would be covered	We would be covered You would be covered They would be covered
Conditional perfect	I would have covered You would have covered He would have covered She would have covered It would have covered	We would have covered You would have covered They would have covered
Conditional perfect progressive	I would have been covered You would have been covered He would have been covered She would have been covered It would have been covered	We would have been covered You would have been covered They would have been covered

Active Voice, Imperative Mood

Singular	Plural
cover	cover

Active Voice, Subjunctive Mood

Tense	Singular	Plural
Present	if I cover	if we cover
	if you cover	if you cover
	if he covers	if they cover
	if she covers	
	if it covers	
Past	if I covered	if we covered
	if you covered	if you covered
	if he covered	if they covered
	if she covered	
	if it covered	
Future	if I should cover	if we should cover
	if you should cover	if you should cover
	if he should cover	if they should cover
	if she should cover	
	if it should cover	

Passive Voice, Indicative Mood

Tense	Singular	Plural
Present	I am covered	We are covered
	You are covered	You are covered
	He is covered	They are covered
	She is covered	
	It is covered	
Present progressive	I am being covered	We are being covered
	You are being covered	You are being covered
	He is being covered	They are being covered
	She is being covered	
	It is being covered	
Past	I was covered	We were covered
	You were covered	You were covered
	He was covered	They were covered
	She was covered	
	It was covered	
Past progressive	I was being covered	We were being covered
	You were being covered	You were being covered
	He was being covered	They were being covered
	She was being covered	
	It was being covered	

Tense	Singular	Plural
Future	I will be covered You will be covered He will be covered She will be covered It will be covered	We will be covered You will be covered They will be covered
Present perfect	I have been covered You have been covered He has been covered She has been covered It has been covered	We have been covered You have been covered They have been covered
Past perfect	I had been covered You had been covered He had been covered She had been covered It had been covered	We had been covered You had been covered They had been covered
Future perfect	I will have been covered You will have been covered He will have been covered She will have been covered It will have been covered	We will have been covered You will have been covered They will have been covered

Passive Voice, Imperative Mood

Singular	Plural
be covered	be covered

Passive Voice, Subjunctive Mood

Tense	Singular	Plural
Present	if I am covered if you are covered if he is covered if she is covered if it is covered	if we are covered if you are covered if they are covered
Past	if I were covered if you were covered if he was covered if she was covered if it was covered	if we were covered if you were covered if they were covered
Future	if I should be covered if you should be covered if he should be covered if she should be covered if it should be covered	if we should be covered if you should be covered if they should be covered

List 5.8. Sentence Patterns Using *To Be*

Following is a helpful list of the affirmative and negative forms of the verb *to be* in the common tenses. Repetitions using temporal words or phrases will help learners recognize the appropriate forms and develop fluency. For example: Now, I am hungry. Yesterday, I was hungry. Tomorrow I will be hungry.

Present Tense

I am hungry.	I am not hungry.
I'm hungry.	I'm not hungry.
You are hungry.	You are not hungry.
You're hungry.	You aren't hungry.
He is hungry.	He is not hungry.
He's hungry.	He isn't hungry.
She is hungry.	She is not hungry.
She's hungry.	She isn't hungry.
It is hungry.	It is not hungry.
It's hungry.	It isn't hungry.
We are hungry.	We are not hungry.
We're hungry.	We aren't hungry.
You are hungry.	You are not hungry.
You're hungry.	You aren't hungry.
They are hungry.	They are not hungry.
They're hungry.	They aren't hungry.
It is time to go.	It isn't time to go.
It's time to go.	It's not time to go.
There is time to spare.	There isn't time to spare.
There's time to spare.	There's no time to spare.
This is the car.	This isn't the car.
These are the cars.	These aren't the cars.

Past Tense

I was hungry.	I was not hungry.
	I wasn't hungry.
You were hungry.	You were not hungry.
	You weren't hungry.
He was hungry.	He was not hungry.
	He wasn't hungry.
She was hungry.	She was not hungry.
	She wasn't hungry.
It was hungry.	It was not hungry.
	It wasn't hungry.

We were hungry.

You were hungry.

They were hungry.

It was time to go.
There was time to spare.

This was the car.
These were the cars.

We were not hungry.
We weren't hungry.
You were not hungry.
You weren't hungry.
They were not hungry.
They weren't hungry.

It wasn't time to go.
There wasn't time to spare.
There was no time to spare.
This wasn't the car.
These weren't the cars.

Future Tense

I will be. . . .
I'll be. . . .
You will be. . . .
You'll be. . . .
He will be. . . .
He'll be. . . .
She will be. . . .
She'll be. . . .
It will be. . . .
It'll be. . . .

We will be. . . .
We'll be. . . .
You will be. . . .
You'll be. . . .
They will be. . . .
They'll be. . . .

This will be. . . .
This'll be. . . .
These will be. . . .
These'll be. . . .
There will be. . . .
There'll be. . . .

I will not be. . . .
I won't be. . . .
You will not be. . . .
You won't be. . . .
He will not be. . . .
He won't be. . . .
She will not be. . . .
She won't be. . . .
It will not be. . . .
It won't be. . . .

We will not be. . . .
We won't be. . . .
You will not be. . . .
You won't be. . . .
They will not be. . . .
They won't be. . . .

This will not be. . . .
This won't be. . . .
These will not be. . . .
These won't be. . . .
There will not be. . . .
There won't be. . . .

Present Perfect Tense

I have been. . . .
I've been. . . .
You have been. . . .
You've been. . . .
He has been. . . .

I have not been. . . .
I haven't been. . . .
You have not been. . . .
You haven't been. . . .
He has not been. . . .

He's been. . . .
She has been. . . .
She's been. . . .
It has been. . . .

It's been. . . .
We have been. . . .
We've been. . . .
You have been. . . .
You've been. . . .
They have been. . . .
They've been. . . .

This has been. . . .
This's been. . . .
These have been. . . .
These've been. . . .
There has been. . . .
There's been. . . .

He hasn't been. . . .
She has not been. . . .
She hasn't been. . . .
It has not been. . . .

It hasn't been. . . .
We have not been. . . .
We haven't been. . . .
You have not been. . . .
You haven't been. . . .
They have not been. . . .
They haven't been. . . .

This has not been. . . .
This hasn't been. . . .
These have not been. . . .
These haven't been. . . .
There has not been. . . .
There hasn't been. . . .

Past Perfect Tense

I had been. . . .
I'd been. . . .
You had been. . . .
You'd been. . . .
He had been. . . .
He'd been. . . .
She had been. . . .
She'd been. . . .
It had been. . . .
It'd been. . . .

We had been. . . .
We'd been. . . .
You had been. . . .
You'd been. . . .
They had been. . . .
They'd been. . . .
This had been. . . .
This'd been. . . .
These had been. . . .
These'd been. . . .
There had been. . . .
There'd been. . . .

I had not been. . . .
I hadn't been. . . .
You had not been. . . .
You hadn't been. . . .
He had not been. . . .
He hadn't been. . . .
She had not been. . . .
She hadn't been. . . .
It had not been. . . .
It hadn't been. . . .

We had not been. . . .
We hadn't been. . . .
You had not been. . . .
You hadn't been. . . .
They had not been. . . .
They hadn't been. . . .
This had not been. . . .
This hadn't been. . . .
These had not been. . . .
These hadn't been. . . .
There had not been. . . .
There hadn't been. . . .

Future Perfect Tense

I shall have been. . . .
I'll have been. . . .
You will have been. . . .
You'll have been. . . .
He will have been. . . .
He'll have been. . . .
She will have been. . . .
She'll have been. . . .
It will have been. . . .
It'll have been. . . .

We shall have been. . . .
We'll have been. . . .
You will have been. . . .
You'll have been. . . .
They will have been. . . .
They'll have been. . . .

This will have been. . . .
This'll have been. . . .
These will have been. . . .
These'll have been. . . .
There will have been. . . .
There'll have been. . . .

I shall not have been. . . .
I shan't have been. . . .
You will not have been. . . .
You won't have been. . . .
He will not have been. . . .
He won't have been. . . .
She will not have been. . . .
She won't have been. . . .
It will not have been. . . .
It won't have been. . . .

We shall not have been. . . .
We shall not have been. . . .
You will not have been. . . .
You won't have been. . . .
They will not have been. . . .
They won't have been. . . .

This will not have been. . . .
This won't have been. . . .
These will not have been. . . .
These won't have been. . . .
There will not have been. . . .
There won't have been. . . .

List 5.9. Subject-Verb Agreement

English grammar uses multiple signals to indicate number. A statement about a *singular subject* will use the *singular verb form,* and a statement about a *plural subject* requires the use of a *plural verb form.* Examples:

Singular	**Plural**
The *box is* on the table.	The *boxes are* on the table.
I was packing my suitcase when he called.	*We were* packing our suitcases when he called.
That *artist paints* well.	Those *artists paint* well.

Compound subjects refer to more than one doer or agent of the action in the sentence, and therefore need plural verbs. Examples:

The *driver checks* the truck every night.	The *driver and mechanic check* the truck every night.
Amruta is asleep in the family room.	*Amruta and Taimur are* asleep in the family room.
Thunder frightens many people.	*Thunder and lightening frighten* many people.

The following *indefinite pronouns* are *singular* and take singular verbs: *anybody, anyone, each, either, everybody, everyone, neither, nobody, no one, one, somebody, someone.* Examples:

Is *anybody* home?
Anyone may apply for the scholarship.
Of the five models, *each* has a special feature.
Either Rose or Sharon has the list.
Everybody needs a dream.
Nobody answers the phone after six o'clock.
Somebody has to fix the flat tire.
Someone is peering in the window.

The following *indefinite pronouns* are *plural* and take plural verbs: *several, both, many, few.* Examples:

Several of the applicants are waiting in the hall.
Both seem interested in taking economics courses.
Many are not in favor of the new parking regulations.
Few of the students returned to the dorm before noon.

The following *indefinite pronouns* can be either *singular* or *plural* depending on the meaning of the sentence: *some, none, all, most, any.* Use a singular verb form if the pronoun refers to a single quantity; use a plural verb form if the pronoun refers to more than one unit of something. Examples:

Some of the *work is* very difficult.
Some of the *cookies are* burned.
All of the *coffee has been* drunk.
All of the *tickets have been* turned in.
Most of the *food is* in the refrigerator.
Most of the choir *members are* on the bus.

There is a useful test for determining whether to use the singular or plural verb form. Substitute *he, it,* and *they* for the subject in the sentence. If *he* or *it* makes sense, the subject is singular and takes a singular verb; if *they* makes sense, the subject is plural and takes a plural verb.

Sometimes the subject and verb are separated by adjectives, adverbs, phrases, and even clauses. Don't be confused by the intervening words. Isolate the subject and verb and apply the rules of agreement. Examples:

Each of the bridges and tunnels in the counties of Cambria and Tuxedo *is* painted grey.

The girl's *parents,* as well as the high school principal, *were* anxious to hear what happened at the tournament.

List 5.10. Time Agreement

Time agreement refers to the consistent use of a tense in a spoken or written sentence, paragraph, or other unit of communication. Providing exercises in which ESL/ELL students mark the verbs and discuss their tense and spelling helps develop their recognition of agreement patterns. Begin with prose that includes only regularly formed tenses—for example, past tense using *-ed* or *-d*—to allow students to develop some experience with the rule of agreement. Next, review irregular verb forms and provide correct examples in prose using both regular and irregular forms. After students become adept at recognizing the forms, they will be more successful with time agreement in their speaking and writing. Here are some examples to get you started:

Correct	Yesterday Ahmed washed the car, polished the trim, and cleaned the windows.	All verbs are in the past tense and are regularly formed.
	During the show Roger slept, Tim whispered to Joshua, Bijal made notes, and Alice took photographs.	All verbs are in the past tense but several have irregular forms.
	Next week the band will record a new song, their agent will set up interviews, and the writer will begin a biography of the band leader.	All verbs are in the future tense.
Incorrect	Last semester we studied hard, read lots of books, and wonder who got an A on each test.	Two verbs are in the past tense and one is in the present tense.
Corrected	Last semester we studied hard, read lots of books, and wondered who got an A on each test.	All three verbs are now in the past tense.
Incorrect	We will visit the museum on Friday. Once there we have to keep to our tight schedule or miss the train home.	One verb is in the future tense, the other two verbs are in the present tense.
Corrected	We will visit the museum on Friday. Once there we will have to keep to our tight schedule or we will miss the train home.	All verbs are in the future tense.

Permitted Tense Shifts

Sometimes a sentence tells about an event that happened before or that will happen after the time of the main action in the sentence. To show this change in time, different tenses are used. Examples:

Same time	The man told us that the boat was destroyed.	Both events, the telling and the destroying, happened in the past.
	On Friday we will know what John will do.	Both events, the knowing and the doing, will happen in the future.

Before	The man told us that the boat had been destroyed ten years ago.	The destruction of the boat happened before the man told about it.
	We know what John did.	John's action happened before the knowing.
After	The man told us that the boat will be destroyed next summer.	The destruction is expected to occur after the telling about the boat.
	We know what John will do.	John's action is expected to occur after the knowing.

List 5.11. Irregular Verb Forms

Many high-frequency verbs have irregular forms and need to be studied. Focus on a few at a time. Introduce them in the context of a conversation or story. Students need practice changing the action from present to future to past and back again, both orally and in written assignments.

Present	Past	Past Participle
arise	arose	arisen
awake	awoke	awakened
be	was, were	been
bear	bore	borne
beat	beat	beaten
become	became	became
begin	began	begun
bet	bet	bet
bid	bid	bid
bind	bound	bound
bite	bit	bitten
bleed	bled	bled
blow	blew	blown
break	broke	broken
breed	bred	bred
bring	brought	brought
broadcast	broadcast	broadcast
build	built	built
burn	burned, burnt	burned, burnt
burst	burst	burst
buy	bought	bought
cast	cast	cast
catch	caught	caught
choose	chose	chosen
cling	clung	clung
come	came	come
creep	crept	crept
cut	cut	cut
deal	dealt	dealt
dig	dug	dug
do	did	done
draw	drew	drew
dream	dreamed, dreamt	dreamed, dreamt
drink	drank	drunk
drive	drove	driven
eat	ate	eaten
fall	fell	fallen
feed	fed	fed
feel	felt	felt

Present	Past	Past Participle
fight	fought	fought
find	found	found
flee	fled	fled
fling	flung	flung
fly	flew	flown
forbid	forbade	forbidden
forecast	forecast	forecast
foretell	foretold	foretold
forget	forgot	forgotten
forgive	forgave	forgiven
forsake	forsook	forsaken
freeze	froze	frozen
get	got	got
give	gave	given
go	went	gone
grind	ground	ground
grow	grew	grown
hang	hung	hung
have	had	had
hear	heard	heard
hide	hid	hidden
hit	hit	hit
hold	held	held
hurt	hurt	hurt
keep	kept	kept
kneel	knelt	knelt
knit	knit, knitted	knit, knitted
know	knew	known
lay	laid	laid
lead	led	led
leap	leaped	leapt
leave	left	left
lend	lent	lent
let	let	let
lie	lay	lain
lose	lost	lost
make	made	made
mean	meant	meant
meet	met	met
mistake	mistook	mistaken
overtake	overtook	overtaken
pay	paid	paid
prove	proved	proven
put	put	put
quit	quit	quit
read	read	read

Present	Past	Past Participle
rid	rid	rid
ride	rode	ridden
ring	rang	rung
rise	rose	risen
run	ran	run
saw	sawed	sawed, sawn
say	said	said
see	saw	seen
seek	sought	sought
sell	sold	sold
send	sent	sent
set	set	set
sew	sewed	sewn, sewed
shake	shook	shaken
shave	shaved	shaven
shear	sheared	shorn
shine	shone	shone
shoot	shot	shot
show	showed	shown
shut	shut	shut
sing	sang	sung
sink	sank	sunk
sit	sat	sat
slay	slew	slain
sleep	slept	slept
slide	slid	slid
slit	slit	slit
smell	smelled, smelt	smelled, smelt
speak	spoke	spoken
speed	sped	sped
spell	spelled	spelt
spend	spent	spent
spill	spilled	spilt
spin	spun	spun
spit	spat	spat
split	split	split
spread	spread	spread
spring	sprang	sprung
stand	stood	stood
steal	stole	stolen
stick	stuck	stuck
sting	stung	stung
stink	stank	stunk
strew	strewed	strewn
strike	struck	struck, stricken
string	strung	strung

Present	Past	Past Participle
strive	strove	striven
swear	swore	sworn
sweep	swept	swept
swell	swelled	swollen
swim	swam	swum
swing	swung	swung
take	took	taken
teach	taught	taught
tear	tore	torn
tell	told	told
think	thought	thought
throw	threw	thrown
thrust	thrust	thrust
undertake	undertook	undertaken
undergo	underwent	undergone
understand	understood	understood
upset	upset	upset
wake	woke	woken
wear	wore	worn
weave	wove	woven
weep	wept	wept
wet	wet	wet
win	won	won
wind	wound	wound
withdraw	withdrew	withdrawn
wring	wrung	wrung
write	wrote	written

List 5.12. Contractions

Contractions are shortened forms of words in which two words are squeezed together, eliminating sounds and letters. An apostrophe is used to show where letters have been eliminated. For example, *does not* becomes *doesn't*. Contractions are necessary elements of fluent speech. They are also a marker of casual conversation. Some spellings are irregular. For example, *will not* becomes *won't*. Many students confuse the pronoun *its* with the contraction *it's*. To check which word and spelling is needed, try replacing the word with *it is*. If the sentence makes sense, use the contraction.

I am	I'm	I have	I've
you are	you're	you have	you've
he is	he's	he has	he's
she is	she's	she has	she's
it is	it's	it has	it's
we are	we're	we have	we've
you are	you're	you have	you've
they are	they're	they have	they've
what is	what's	what have	what've
that is	that's	that have	that've
who is	who's	who has	who's
who are	who're	who have	who've
here is	here's	would have	would've
there is	there's	could have	could've
should have	should've	might have	might've
let us	let's	there have	there've
I would	I'd	I had	I'd
you would	you'd	you had	you'd
she would	she'd	she had	she'd
he would	he'd	he had	he'd
it would	it'd	it had	it'd
we would	we'd	we had	we'd
they would	they'd	they had	they'd
there would	there'd	there had	there'd
who would	who'd	who had	who'd
I will	I'll	can not	can't
you will	you'll	do not	don't
she will	she'll	will not	won't
he will	he'll	is not	isn't
it will	it'll	should not	shouldn't
we will	we'll	could not	couldn't
you will	you'll	would not	wouldn't
they will	they'll	are not	aren't
that will	that'll	does not	doesn't
these will	these'll	was not	wasn't
those will	those'll	were not	weren't
there will	there'll	has not	hasn't
this will	this'll	had not	hadn't
what will	what'll	have not	haven't
who will	who'll	must not	mustn't
did not	didn't	might not	mightn't
need not	needn't		

List 5.13. Plurals

Plurals, the noun forms that refer to more than one, are usually formed by adding *-s* to the singular form. If the singular noun ends in *-s, -sh, -ch, -x,* or *-z,* the plural is formed by adding *-es.* Examples:

cat	cats	dish	dishes
floor	floors	fox	foxes
cabinet	cabinets	waltz	waltzes
smile	smiles	floss	flosses
disk	disks	bench	benches

The plurals of words ending with a consonant followed by *-y* are formed by changing the *-y* to *-i* and adding *-es.* The plurals of words ending with a vowel followed by *-y* are formed by adding *-s.*

city	cities	valley	valleys
baby	babies	trolley	trolleys
rally	rallies	turkey	turkeys
lady	ladies	alley	alleys
country	countries	key	keys

The plurals of most nouns ending with *-f* or *-fe* are formed by adding *-s;* for some, the plurals are formed by changing the *-f* to -v and adding *-es.*

gulf	gulfs	knife	knives
chief	chiefs	half	halves
belief	beliefs	leaf	leaves
safe	safes	self	selves

The plurals of most nouns ending with *-o* preceded by a consonant are formed by adding *-es.* The plurals of most nouns ending in *-o* preceded by a vowel are formed by adding *-s.*

hero	heroes	radio	radios
potato	potatoes	studio	studios
tomato	tomatoes	video	videos

The plurals of compound words are formed by making either the base noun or the second noun plural.

brother-in-law	brothers-in-law
passer-by	passers-by
raincoat	raincoats
sandbox	sandboxes

The following nouns are some that have *irregular plural forms:*

alumna	alumnae	basis	bases
alumnus	alumni	bison	bison
analysis	analyses	cactus	cacti
axis	axes	child	children

corps	corps	mouse	mice
crisis	crises	oasis	oases
criterion	criteria	ovum	ova
curriculum	curricula	ox	oxen
datum	data	person	people
deer	deer	piano	pianos
diagnosis	diagnoses	radius	radii
die	dice	salmon	salmon
Eskimo	Eskimos	scissors	scissors
fish	fish, fishes	series	series
foot	feet	sheep	sheep
fungus	fungi	species	species
goose	geese	stimulus	stimuli
hypothesis	hypotheses	syllabus	syllabi
louse	lice	synthesis	syntheses
man	men	that	those
means	means	this	these
medium	media	tooth	teeth
millennium	millennia	trout	trout
moose	moose	woman	women

List 5.14. Pronouns

Pronouns take the place of nouns. Different forms are used to show person, number, gender, and case. There are personal, interrogative, relative, indefinite, demonstrative, and reflexive pronouns.

- *Personal pronouns* refer to one or more individuals or things. They may be in the nominative, objective, or possessive case and they show gender and number.

		Nominative	**Objective**	**Possessive**
Singular	1st person	I	me	my, mine
	2nd person	you	you	your
	3rd person			
	Masculine	he	him	his
	Feminine	she	her	her
	Neuter	it	it	its
Plural	1st person	we	us	our, ours
	2nd person	you	you	your, yours
	3rd person	they	them	their, theirs

I took my sister to *her* doctor.
They check *their* mailbox more than *I* check *mine.*
His family has *its* favorite holidays; does *yours*?
She gave *us* a new table for *our* kitchen.

- *Interrogative pronouns* are used to ask questions. Examples:

Who unlocked the car door?
What fell out of the tree?
To *whom* did you give the message?
Whose book is on the steps?
Which is the most expensive perfume?

- *Relative pronouns* relate groups of words to nouns or other pronouns. Examples:

Grandpa was the one *who* built the picnic table.
The video *that* is now playing is my favorite.
Their house, *which* has a garden in bloom, is very inviting.
There are people in the town *whom* I have not met.
I spoke to the child *whose* kitten had climbed the tree.

- *Indefinite pronouns* refer to general rather than specific persons or things. Be sure to use the singular verb form with singular indefinite pronouns.

Singular indefinite pronouns include *one, each, either, neither, everyone, no one, anybody, somebody, nobody, everybody, anyone,* and *someone.*

Neither of the boys wants to have lunch now.
No one has a good idea for the bulletin board.
Everyone goes to the movies at least once a year.
Each of the games takes twelve minutes to play.

Plural indefinite pronouns include *several, both, many,* and *few.*

Several boys want to follow George to the gate.
Few were returned because they didn't fit.
Both had long brown hair and brown eyes.
Many come to the resort to escape the city's noise.

The indefinite pronouns—*some, none, all, most,* and *any*—can be either singular or plural depending on the meaning of the sentence.

Some of the marks come off easily.
Some of the work is done.
All of the flowers are dead.
All of the paint has been scraped off.

- Demonstrative pronouns—*that, this, these, those,* and *such*—identify or point out nouns.

  This is more fragile than *that.*
  These are my favorites, not *those.*
  I had not seen a jewel *such* as *that* before.

- *Reflexive pronouns* are used when the object of a verb or preposition refers back to the subject. They are also used to add emphasis to the subject. They are formed with the suffixes *-self* and *-selves.*

	Singular	**Plural**
1st person	myself	ourselves
2nd person	yourself	yourselves
3rd person	himself	themselves
	herself	
	itself	

The boys helped *themselves* to the cookies.
Mary made the lamp by *herself.*
We tried to occupy *ourselves* during the long storm.
The sculptor *himself* showed us the statue.

List 5.15. Possessive Forms

There are four usual ways to show possession or ownership:

1. *Using possessive pronouns. Hers* was hanging on the hook.
2. *Using possessive adjectives. Her* hat was hanging on the hook.
3. *Adding -'s.* Corina*'s* hat was hanging on the hook.
4. *Using the words* of *or* belonging to. The hat *belonging to* Corina was hanging on the hook.

- *Possessive pronouns* take the place of nouns and are indicators of ownership.

	Singular	**Plural**
1st person	mine	ours
2nd person	yours	yours
3rd person		
Masculine	his	theirs
Feminine	hers	theirs
Neuter	its	theirs

> *Mine* ran out of ink; may I borrow *yours*?
> *Theirs* is parked in the garage; *hers* is at the curb.
> *Yours* is still warm; *mine* got cold already.

- *Possessive adjectives* are used with nouns and indicate ownership. Examples: *my* hat, *our* tickets.

	Singular	**Plural**
1st person	my	our
2nd person	your	your
3rd person		
Masculine	his	their
Feminine	her	their
Neuter	its	their

> *My* skates are very old; *their* skates are brand-new.
> *Its* fur was covered with a dusting of snow.
> *Our* long-time relationship was based on trust.

- *Adding -'s* is another way to show possession. For most singular nouns and irregularly formed plurals, add -'s; however, if the noun is plural and ends in s, just add the apostrophe. Exceptions are guided by pronunciation.

Diane's book	the picture's frame	the class's teacher
Louise's desk	the boss's phone	the classes' teacher
the queens' crowns	the bosses' phones	the roses' color
children's toys	mice's tails	for goodness' sake

- Using the words *of* or *belonging to* also shows possession. Examples:

the mayor *of* the town
the laughter *of* children
the scent *of* a rose
the temperature *of* the water
the cat *belonging to* Susan
the car *belonging to* Eileen
a book *belonging to* Valerie

List 5.16. Adjectives

An adjective describes a noun or pronoun, tells what kind or how many, or points out which one. Adjectives can be single words, phrases, or clauses. Adjective phrases are also called *adjectival phrases*. Examples:

What Kind	How Many	Which One
lazy	several	this
of great value	three	that was painted red
powerful	few	those
green	some	these

A *descriptive* adjective tells about a quality of the noun. Examples: *pretty* girl, *soft* pillow, *yellow* ribbon.

A *limiting* adjective puts boundaries on a noun or limits it. The three types of limiting adjectives are possessive adjectives, demonstrative adjectives, and interrogative adjectives. Examples: *his* sweater, *this* chair, *whose* sandwich.

A *proper* adjective is derived from a proper noun. Examples: *Italian* bread, *Irish* coffee.

Comparisons Using Adjectives

Adjectives can show the *degree* to which a quality is associated with a noun or pronoun by using either the comparative or the superlative form of the adjective.

The *comparative* form adds *-er* to the adjective or adds the word *more* before the adjective. Most one-syllable and some two-syllable adjectives use *-er*, and longer adjectives use *more*.

pretty	prettier	irritating	more irritating
dark	darker	spongy	more spongy

The superlative form adds *-est* to the adjective or adds the word *most* before the adjective. Most one-syllable and some two-syllable adjectives use *-est*, and longer adjectives use *most*.

tall	tallest	stubborn	most stubborn
dark	darkest	complex	most complex

The *comparative* form is used for comparisons with *one* other while the *superlative* form is used for comparisons of *two or more*. Examples:

Positive	Comparative	Superlative
Dennis is a lazy boy.	Dennis is lazier than Elise.	Dennis is the laziest of the three children.
The famous skater won the gold medal.	The more famous skater of the two won.	The most famous skater on the team won.

Adjectives can also show a *negative* comparison. Use *less* for a negative comparison and *least* for a negative superlative adjective. Examples:

eager	less eager	least eager
strong	less strong	least strong
drastic	less drastic	least drastic
interesting	less interesting	least interesting
expensive	less expensive	least expensive

Some adjectives have *irregular* comparative and superlative forms:

good	better	best
bad	worse	worst
little	less	least
much	more	most
many	more	most

The following adjectives have only one form:

dead	pregnant	perfect
infinite	perpetual	alive

List 5.17. Adverbs and Adverbial Phrases

Adverbs describe verbs, adjectives, or other adverbs by providing information about where, when, or how much. Sometimes they are called adverbs of *manner, place,* or *frequency.* Adverbs can be single words, phrases, or clauses. The regular form is called the *positive* form.

Many adverbs are formed by adding the suffix *-ly* to adjectives.

adjective	+	-ly	=	adverb
correct	+	-ly	=	correctly
dainty	+	-ly	=	daintily
stern	+	-ly	=	sternly
serious	+	-ly	=	seriously
speedy	+	-ly	=	speedily

Comparisons Using Adverbs

Adverbs can show the degree to which a quality is associated with a verb, adjective, or other adverb using either the comparative or superlative form of the adverb.

The *comparative* form adds *-er* to the adverb or adds the word *more* before the adverb. Most one-syllable adverbs use *-er,* and adverbs of more than one syllable use *more.*

soon	sooner	powerfully	more powerfully
late	later	quickly	more quickly

The *superlative* form adds *-est* to the adverb or adds the word *most* before the adverb. Most one-syllable adverbs use *-est,* and adverbs of more than one syllable use *most.*

soon	soonest	powerfully	most powerfully
late	latest	quickly	most quickly

The comparative form is used for comparisons with *one* other while the *superlative* form is used for comparisons of *two or more.* Examples:

Positive	Comparative	Superlative
I expect Kelly to arrive soon.	I expect Kelly to arrive sooner than Elise.	I expect Kelly to arrive the soonest of the three.
Roger spoke sternly to the driver.	Roger spoke more sternly than Hal.	Roger spoke most sternly of all the riders.

Adverbs can also show a *negative* comparison. Use *less* for a negative comparative and *least* for a negative superlative adverb. Examples:

often	less often	least often
frequently	less frequently	least frequently
quickly	less quickly	least quickly

Some adverbs have *irregular* comparative and superlative forms:

well	better	best
badly	worse	worst
much	more	most
far	farther or further	farthest or furthest
little	less	least

The following adverbs have only one form:

afterward	inside	outside
nearby	away	here
there	downstairs	uptown
never	seldom	sometimes
indefinitely	habitually	always
constantly	perpetually	everywhere

Adverbial phrases (also known as *prepositional phrases*) or clauses frequently begin with the following prepositions:

above	He put the sign above the doorbell.
across	The plane flew across the desert.
after	After we finished the game, we drove to the beach.
along	We ran along the shore each morning.
at	I asked him to meet me at the gym.
before	Jenn has to leave before we do.
behind	David put his backpack behind the desk.
beneath	The steward put my suitcase beneath the seat.
beside	I parked my car beside the trailer.
between	John is standing between Mary and Phil.
during	Not a sound was heard during her speech.
in	The lion paced in the cage.
in front	He asked the shortest person to stand in front.
near	The dog slept peacefully near the boy's bed.
on	He placed his trophy on the shelf.
over	We tossed the rope over the fence.
since	The house has been empty since Robert left.
to	The bubbles rose to the top of the liquid.
with	He announced the winners with pleasure.
within	The card was tucked within the folds of paper.

List 5.18. Articles

Articles (also called *determiners* and *noun markers*) are adjectives that precede and identify nouns. A *definite article* designates a particular thing, an *indefinite article* designates one of a class of things, and *partitive articles* designate part of a class.

Definite Articles

Singular	the	Give me the ticket.
Plural	the	Give me the tickets.

Indefinite Articles

Singular	a	I see a box.	Use before nouns beginning with a consonant, except those beginning with *h*.
	an	I see an elephant.	Use before nouns beginning with a vowel or *h*.
Plural	Some	I see some boxes. I see some elephants.	

Partitive Articles

The following partitive articles are used with nouns that can be counted:

few	Jason ate a few raisins.
some	Some toys were left in the playground.
a lot of	I could use a lot of tickets for my friends.
many	Ellen tried many recipes for chocolate cake.

The following partitive articles are used with nouns that cannot be counted:

little	I got a little sleep between meetings.
some	Bring me some hot tea, please.
a lot of	The cancellation caused a lot of trouble.
much	There isn't much rice left in the pantry.

List 5.19. Conjunctions

Conjunctions join words, phrases, and clauses. They coordinate equal sentence parts within a sentence, or they subordinate a dependent clause to an independent clause.

and	Chris is reading a book and Jenn is writing a letter.
but	Nancy wanted to go but Marie did not.
for	The students were tired, for they had waited for the bus for more than two hours.
nor	Neither Jessica nor Jaime were tired after the party.
or	He will finish his report on time or he will not get a good grade.
so	We were in a hurry to leave, so everyone helped pack the car.
still	The sun is shining now; still, it could rain later.
yet	They were happy to graduate, yet they knew they would miss this school.
consequently	Only six team members showed up; consequently, we had to forfeit the game.
furthermore	This class will be cancelled; furthermore, math class will start at 10 A.M.
however	No one earned a B on the last test; however, three students earned A's.
moreover	Sports foster school spirit; moreover, they develop students' self-esteem.
nevertheless	The train was delayed; nevertheless, Mr. Meyers got to his office on time.
therefore	Samantha finished first; therefore, she may choose the next puzzle.
after	After they read the reviews, the cast went to the party.
although	Although I'd heard the song three times a day, I had not tired of it.
as if	He walked into the room as if nothing had happened.
because	Mary Lee smiled broadly because her puppy won Best in Show.
if	If it rains on Saturday, Bob will play golf on Sunday instead.
since	Since he went on a diet, he has lost twelve pounds.
so that	Take the chairs off the stage so that we will have enough room for the piano.
that	We thought that Alicia had baked the cookies.
till	Till we had the accident, the car had not had engine problems.
until	Until we fix the leak we must check the pipes frequently.
when	When it snows my mother likes to bake bread.
where	Meet me at the corner where Main Street intersects with Columbus Avenue.
while	While I waited for the light to change, I looked at the directions and map.

List 5.20. Prepositions

A *preposition* shows the relationship of a noun or pronoun to another word. A *prepositional phrase* is made up of a preposition and a noun with its modifiers. Prepositional phrases may indicate an indirect object or act as adverbs of time or place.

Prepositions Indicating an Indirect Object

An *indirect object* is the receiver of the action of a verb. A prepositional phrase is often used to show who or what is the indirect object. In the following examples the prepositional phrases are in italics.

> Alaine gave the book *to Benjamin.*
> Tom took the heavy package *from Elise.*

Prepositions Indicating Time and Place

Adverbs are used to show the time and place that an action occurred. A prepositional phrase is often used as an adverb to show where or when something happened. In the following examples the prepositional phrases (also called *adverbial phrases*) are in italics.

The mailbox was *near the door.*	(where)
I found my shoes *under the bed.*	(where)
Alex tossed the ball *over the fence.*	(where)
During the day, children played *on the swings.*	(when)
After lunch, Jared took Jake home.	(when)
We will leave the house at *about six o'clock.*	(when)

Common Prepositions

about	between	past
above	beyond	since
across	by	through
after	down	throughout
against	during	to
along	except	toward
amid	for	under
among	from	underneath
around	in	until
at	into	up
before	near	upon
behind	of	with
below	off	within
beneath	on	without
beside	over	

List 5.21. Capitalization

In English, *uppercase* letters are called *capital letters*. Capital letters are used to point something out, show importance, or show respect. They begin sentences and make names and other information stand out among other text. Use a capital letter for the following:

- The first word of every sentence

  Margaret Atwood is one of my favorite authors.
  The car keys are on the table.

- The word I

  "It's not mine," I said.
  Joe and I didn't think it was over already.

- All proper nouns

  The view from the top of the Empire State Building is magnificent.
  I'd like to go to Chicago or San Francisco for vacation.
  Jenn traveled to Wales and El Salvador.

- The names of days, months, and holidays

  Friday
  February
  Fourth of July

- All proper adjectives

  Members of the British and French governments participated in the flag ceremony.
  The figs ripened in the bright California sun.

- The names of religions, their followers, and important (sacred) religious items

  Roman Catholic
  Christians
  the Bible
  the Koran

- The names of departments of government

  Department of the Treasury
  Department of State

- The names of ethnic, social, or other groups

  The Lenni-Lenape tribe lived in New Jersey.
  Both Democrats and Republicans voted for the tax.
  Mr. Philips is a member of the Rotary Club.

- Titles of respect or position

  Reverend Patrick McCarthy
  Senator Jon Ryan
  Superintendent Cox

- The first word in a quotation

  The nurse asked, "How long have you had a fever?"

- The first word in lines of most poetry

  Roses are red,
  Violets are blue.

- Trade or brand names

  Kleenex tissues
  Xerox copier

- The titles of books, newspapers, articles, stories, and magazines

  The Sun Also Rises
  "Forever Is Composed of Nows"
  The New York Times
  "Economists Predict End of Recession"
  Time Out San Francisco

List 5.22. Punctuation

English uses twelve *punctuation marks:* apostrophe, colon, comma, dash, ellipsis points, exclamation point, hyphen, parentheses, period, question mark, quotation marks, and semicolon.

- Use an apostrophe ('):

  To show ownership
  > Malik's radio
  > the Ross's house

  To show the omission of letters in contractions, numbers, and dialect
  > can't
  > class of '11
  > ma'am

  To form the plurals of letters, numbers, and symbols
  > Cross your *t*'s.
  > Jorge got three 100's on his quizzes.
  > There are + *'s* and − *'s* in every situation.

- Use a colon (:):

  Before a list or series
  > Hasan ordered his usual: two cheeseburgers, a large fries, and a large soda.

  After the greeting in a business letter
  > Dear Sir:

  Between the numerals showing the hour and minutes in time
  > 3:45 P.M.

  Before a summary or explanatory statement in a complex sentence
  > In short, these were the alternatives: go to the party alone, wait for Anton to pick me up, or go with Hui-Yin.

- Use a comma (,):

  Between words, phrases, or clauses in a series
  > We need garlic, salt, parsley, pepper, and rosemary.
  > I like to play the piano, to crochet, and to read.

  Between a name and a title
  > Mary Steward, President
  > Shiang-Kwei Chin, Treasurer

  Between the names of the city and state in an address
  > New York, New York
  > Athens, Georgia

  After a noun of direct address
  > Adam, where is your brother?
  > David, do you have my keys?

  After *yes* or *no* at the beginning of a sentence
  > No, I don't want a sandwich.
  > Yes, I'd like to have lunch now.

After an introductory phrase
> In summary, the new product has been proven effective.
> In the meantime, the scouts set up camp near the river.

Between the day and year in dates
> May 27, 1969
> March 28, 1972

Before and after words in apposition
> Jose Marino, the director, spoke to the new employees.
> Elisa Cortine, the soloist, autographed my program.

Before and after direct quotations
> He said, "I'm late," as he rushed passed me.
> "That's not the way I see it," said the young man.

After the greeting in a friendly letter
> Dear Susan,
> Dear Mrs. Monaghan,

After the closing in all letters
> Very truly yours,
> Sincerely,

Before the conjunction in a compound sentence unless the two clauses are short and closely related.
> Karen thought she was afraid of heights, but she changed her mind after looking down from the attic window.
> The day was warm and sunny and there were no clouds in the sky.

Between dependent and independent clauses
> While we waited for the tow truck, we saw the other van loaded down with our gear drive by.
> Since the band left, the hotel lobby has been nearly empty.

Before and after interruptive or explanatory elements in a sentence
> The bell, for example, is solid brass.

Before and after contrasting phrases
> It was Nick, not Chuck, who drove the white car.
> The child was found by the cabdriver, not the fireman.

- Use a dash (—):

Before and after an interruptive element in a sentence
> I took two—two, mind you, not three—tablets.

To mark an abrupt change in tone or thought
> I think I'd like to be—did you see that?

To mark an incomplete thought or unfinished dialogue
> I was wondering whether—

- Use ellipsis points (. . .):

To show there are words missing in a direct quotation
> "The goal of the program . . . was the development of a new political system."

- Use an exclamation point (!):

  To mark the end of an exclamatory sentence
  > Happy birthday!

  After an interjection
  > Aha!

  To mark the end of some commands.
  > Drop that!

- Use a hyphen (-):

  Between spelled-out numbers and fractions
  > For nearly twenty-five years the old men met at the diner for breakfast.
  > Three-fourths of the class knew the answer.

  At the end of a line to divide the last word
  > The room was decorated for the cele-
  > bration.

  Between words in a compound adjective
  > The school bought state-of-the-art computers.

- Use parentheses ( ):

  Before and after material that is explanatory or extra
  > The living room was large (12' $\times$ 26') for an apartment.

  Before and after letters or numbers used in lists included in text.
  > The directions were simple: (1) trace the design on the wood, (2) cut the wood with a coping saw, and (3) sand the edges smooth.

- Use a period (.):

  To mark the end of a statement, command, or request
  > The snowplow cleared the road.
  > Turn to the first page of the test.
  > Put the groceries in the pantry, please.

  After initials or abbreviations
  > C. S. Lewis
  > Sept.

  In currency and decimal numbers
  > $10.00
  > 98.6

  After letters and numbers in outlines
  > A.
  >> 1.
  >> 2.

- Use a question mark (?):

  To mark the end of a question
  > How many books did you read this year?

To indicate doubt
You read two hundred books?

- Use quotation marks (" "):

Before and after a direct quote
Harlan said, "Time is on our side."

Before and after dialogue
"What time would you like to leave?"
"Oh, at about five o'clock, I think."

Before and after titles of songs, short stories, articles, and poems
"Bridge Over Troubled Water"
"The Open Window"

Before and after words used in a new or uncertain way
"Texting" is a recent phenomenon.

- Use a semicolon (;):

Between independent clauses in a compound sentence
George had eaten two sandwiches already; he was beginning to feel full.

Before a conjunction in a complex sentence
The president has made his decision; moreover, the senate committee has agreed.

Between items in a list if they are long or if the items contain commas
Nancy took everything she needed: her well-worn, comfortable shoes; her shopping bag; and of course her wallet.

List 5.23. Common Grammatical Errors

Very often the words *mistake* and *error* are used interchangeably to label something that differs from the accepted standard. In language instruction, mistakes and errors should be differentiated.

Use the word *mistake* when the student produces a spoken or written form that differs from a standard the student knows. For example, the misspelling of a word that the student has previously learned is a mistake. Its correction is a matter for proofreading.

Use the word *error* when the student consistently produces spoken or written forms that differ from the standard when these nonstandard forms are likely the result of the student not knowing the rule or standard or applying a false rule or standard. For example, the misspellings *fone, oxes, elefant,* and *childs* are errors. They show that the student does not yet know the *ph* spelling of /f/ and the plural forms of common irregular nouns. The correction of an error is a matter for instruction.

Common Errors	Examples
Adds articles	After the work, Jorge went home.
	We got a good news about our jobs.
	We need eggs and a sugar.
Adds *-s*	Ana must writes a letter.
	Does he watches TV everyday?
Adds *-ing*	He does working on the car.
	He should mowing the lawn.
Adds *(to) do*	Does he can fix the wheel?
	He does can fix the wheel.
Omits articles	I gave [the] box to [the] nurse.
	She is [the] aunt of [the] girl.
	He was [a] brave soldier.
Substitutes articles	We have a prettiest house in the neighborhood.
	Do you have the question?
Shifts tenses	Tomorrow we will go to the shopping center and have to buy sneakers for gym class.
Includes nonparallel items	William was a good president and smart.
	Picking the berries, making the jam, and the savings are fun.
Uses wrong verb form for singular or plural subjects	The flowers grows in the garden.
	The doctor and nurse speaks to the patient.
	Everybody have a name.
	The baseball player and the coach has taken his place on the stage.
Shifts person	Becky and Zim took the bus to the pier on the island and then we walked to the cottage.
Leaves out necessary sentence elements	Children [are] playing in the park
	Commuters [were] running to catch their trains.
Uses wrong word order	I gave to him the tickets.
	On the shelf the book was found.
Uses wrong pronoun	Jesse and me did the homework.
	Jesse and I did their homework.
	The pilots check his baggage.
Uses wrong word	There are less people in the audience today than yesterday.
	The little girl is very handsome.
	He was not conscience when he arrived at the hospital.

List 5.24. Spelling Rules

English *orthography,* the sound-and-letter relationships better known as spelling, is a challenge to both native and nonnative speakers of the language. Part of its difficulty comes from the fact that many of the words in English are derived from other languages—as many as one hundred other languages. As a result, English spelling is more complex than that of a language with a more limited ancestry. The following guidelines address the most common patterns of sound-and-letter relationships.

1. Before you try to spell a word, say it aloud slowly, one syllable at a time. Listen for the sounds that make up each syllable, and then spell the word syllable by syllable.

2. Every syllable must have one vowel sound. The vowel sound may be spelled with more than one letter. For example, *meeting* has two syllables and two vowel sounds: *the long e* (ē) and an *unaccented short i* (ĭ) or *schwa* (ə). The vowel sounds are spelled *ee* and *i.*

3. Most consonant sounds have regular, consistent spellings.

Sound	Spelling	Example
b	b	baby
d	d	dad
f	f	fat
g	g	get
h	h	hat
l	l	let
m	m	mom
n	n	net
p	p	pin
r	r	rim
s	s	sip
t	t	tap
v	v	vast
w	w	web
y	y	yes
ch	ch	church
wh	wh	when
th	th	thin, that
ng	ng	ring

4. Some consonant sounds have more than one spelling.

k Usually spelled *c* if followed by the vowel *a, o,* or *u.* Examples: *cat, cot, cut.* If the sound is at the end of a word, it is often spelled *-ck.* Examples: *back, tack, stick.*

f Usually spelled *f.* Sometimes spelled *ph* as in *phone, elephant,* and *graph.*

j Usually spelled *j.* If the sound is at the end of the word, it is often spelled *-dge* as in *fudge, judge,* and *edge.* If the sound is followed by the vowel *e, i,* or *y,* it is spelled with a *g.* Examples: *gem, giant, gym.*

s   Usually spelled *s*. If the sound is followed by the vowel *e, i,* or *y*, it may be spelled with a *c*. Examples: *cent, city, cycle.*

z   Usually spelled *z*. Examples: *zoo, ozone, Oz*. Spelled *s* when it is a voiced plural or inflected ending, and sometimes after the letter *o*. Examples: *tables, sits, rose.*

sh   Usually spelled *sh*. Examples: *shine, fashion, flash*. Sometimes spelled *-ti-, -si-,* or *-ci-* as part of suffixes. Examples: *attention, tension, special.*

5. The short vowel sounds have regular spellings.

Sound	Spelling	Example
ă	a	cat
ĕ	e	let
ĭ	i	sit
ŏ	o	cot
ŭ	u	cut

6. The long vowel sounds have several spellings. The spelling used depends on the word's meaning units. Meaning units are prefixes, suffixes, and base words. For example, *long e* may be spelled *e, ea, ee,* or *-y*. In the word *return* it is spelled *e* because it keeps the spelling of the prefix *re*.

Sound	Spelling	Example
ā	a	acorn
	ai	rain
	ay	day
	a__e	tame
ē	e	pretense
	ee	feet
	ea	seat
	-y	lucky
	-ie	Jackie
ī	i	bicycle
	i__e	ice
ō	o	noble
	oa	toast
	o__e	stone
	ow	glow
ū	u	universe
	u__e	tune

7. The vowels in unaccented syllables are pronounced with less emphasis. This reduced sound is called a *schwa* (ə). It sounds similar to a *short u* (ŭ), but its spelling relates to its meaning unit. For example, the word *portable* is made of the base word *port*, meaning "to carry," and the suffix *able*, meaning "able to be." The *a* in *portable* is a vowel in an unaccented syllable and is pronounced ə or ŭ. It keeps its spelling because it is part of the suffix *–able*.

8. *ie* is more common than *ei*. The following well-known rhyme is a good guide:

Use *i* before *e*,
Except after *c*,
Or when sounded like *a*,
As in *neighbor* and *weigh*.

Exceptions you need to learn:

agencies	ancient	conscience	counterfeit
either	efficient	deity	Fahrenheit
fancier	financier	foreign	forfeit
height	kaleidoscope	leisure	neither
protein	proficient	science	seismograph
seize	sheik	society	sovereign
species	weird		

9. When adding a suffix that begins with a vowel to a base word that ends in *e*, drop the *e* before adding the suffix. If the suffix begins with a consonant, keep the final *e* on the base word. Examples:

love + ing   =   loving
love + ly   =   lovely

10. If a base word ends with a vowel followed by a consonant (*-vc*), double the consonant before adding a suffix that begins with a vowel (*-vccv-*). Don't double the consonant before a suffix that begins with a consonant (*-vcc-*). Examples:

tan	+	-ed	=	tanned	vccv-
dim	+	-er	=	dimmer	vccv-
dim	+	-ly	=	dimly	vcc-
commit	+	-ed	=	committed	vccv-
commit	+	-ment	=	commitment	vccv-

11. Common prefixes you should learn to spell:

Prefix	Meaning	Example
anti-	against	antiwar
auto-	self	autobiography
bi-	two	bicycle
cent-	hundred	century
inter-	between	interstate
mid-	middle	midstream
poly-	many	polyglot
pre-	before	predict
re-	again	rerun
sub-	under	submarine
ultra-	beyond	ultraconservative
un-	not	unclear
under-	below	underground

12. Common suffixes you should learn to spell:

Suffix	Meaning	Example
-ist	one who	artist
-or	one who	actor
-hood	state of	childhood
-ation	process of	computation
-ology	study of	biology
-less	without	careless
-ful	full of	fearful
-en	made of	wooden
-ical	relating to	hysterical
-ate	to make	activate
-able	able to be	washable

Section Six

Content Area Words

List 6.1. Mathematics Vocabulary—Basic

For many ESL/ELL students who began their education in other countries, it is in mathematics that they can most readily apply and build on their prior academic knowledge and skills. The international use of common symbols for numbers, operations ($+$, $-$, $\times$, and $\div$), fractions, graphs, and more allow students to "do math" in English. However, math instruction does not stop with practicing already learned computation skills. Basic mathematics vocabulary is presented here in groups progressing from pre-K through grade 3 content. Each group of words contains math content and math instruction vocabulary. The vocabulary words were selected from widely used math texts for the primary grades. See List 2.4: Number Words; List 2.7: Time Words; and List 2.10: Money Words for additional mathematics vocabulary.

Primary grade ESL/ELL students who do not already have math knowledge and skills will also need direct instruction in math to learn concepts such as equals, add, one-to-one correspondence, place, computation rules, and so on. Counting, games, manipulatives, and other active learning strategies work well. For older ESL/ELL students, surveys, graphs, and word problems that deal with personally important information are helpful. Use the words in the following list for word recognition practice, to teach or review math concepts, and to practice word problem skills.

Group I

$+$ addition sign	add	all
$+$ plus sign	addition	all together
$-$ subtraction sign	addition fact	almost
$-$ takeaway sign	addition sentence	amount
$=$ equals sign	addition sign	answer
$\neq$ not equal sign	alike	Arabic numeral

arrange
as long as
baker's dozen
bar graph
before
below
between
big
bigger
biggest
billion
both
center
circle
closed shape
color
column
combine
compare
connect
corner
count
count back
count backward
count on
counting numbers
cup (c)
curve
diagonal
difference
divide
dozen
draw
edge
endpoint
equal
= equal to
estimate
fact family
false
fewer
fewer than
graph
greater
> greater than
greatest
group
grouping

guess
half
heavier
higher
horizontal
how many
hundreds chart
hundreds place
impossible
increase
inside
irregular shape
join
large
larger
largest
last
least
length
less
< less than
lighter
list
long
longer
longest
lower
many
match
measure
measurement
mile (mi)
minus
minus sign
missing
more
more than
most
next
next to
number
number fact
number line
number sentence
numeral
ones place
one-to-one
open shape

order
organize
organized list
over
part
pattern
picture graph
placeholder
place value
predict
prediction
problem
problem solving
question
recognize patterns
rectangle
regroup
related facts
row
ruler
same
scale
score
set
shaded
shape
share
shorter
shorter than
shortest
show
side
similar
size
skip counting
small
smaller
smallest
some
sort
square
story problem
subtract
subtraction
subtraction fact
subtraction sentence
subtraction sign
sum

survey
symbol
table
take away
tall
taller
tallest
tally (tallies)
tally chart
tally mark
temperature
ten
tens place
tenth

thermometer
third
thirteen
thirtieth
thirty
thirty-second
thousand
three
timeline
times
together
total
triangle
true

two-digit number
under
unequal
unit
unknown
use manipulatives
weight (wt)
whole
width (w)
word problem
yard
yardstick
zero

Group II

* multiplication sign
* times sign
× multiplication sign
× times sign
÷ division sign
/ division sign
two-dimensional shape
three-dimensional shape
acre (A)
act out
actual
addend
amount
angle
apply
area
argument
array
associative property
attribute
average
capacity
caret
change
circumference
collection
combine
common factor
common multiple
commutative property

compare
conclusion
cone
congruent
congruent figures
connect
construct
contain
contrast
counting numbers
cube
cubic unit
cup (c)
curve
customary system
customary units
cylinder
data
decimal
decimal number
decrease
decreasing sequences
degree
degrees Celsius
degrees Fahrenheit
denominator
design
diagonal
diagram
diameter

digit
distance
distributive property
divide
dividend
division
divisor
double
doubles
doubles minus one
doubles plus one
doubling
elapsed time
element
equal parts
equally likely
equals
equation
equilateral triangle
equivalent
equivalent fractions
estimation
even
even number
examine
expanded form
explain
explore
face
factor

feet (ft)
fewer
figure
flip (reflection)
foot (ft)
frequency table
gallon (gal)
geometric figure
geometric pattern
geometry
graduated scale
graph
half-gallon
hexagon
horizontal
identify
identity element
identity property
inch (in)
inches (in)
include
increase
increasing sequences
inequality
intersect
intersecting lines
inverse operations
investigate
irrelevant information
key
label
least
less
less likely
likely
line
line graph
line of symmetry
line segment
liter (l)
mass
mean
measure
median
member
mental math
metric
metric system

metric units
mile (mi)
miles (mi)
minute
mixed
mixed number
mode
more likely
multiple
multiple representations
multiplication
multiplication sentence
multiply
name
negative
net
numerator
numeric expression
numeric pattern
octagon
odd
odd number
one-digit number
one-eighth
one-half
one-quarter
operation
opposite
order
ordered pair
ounce (oz)
overestimate
pair
parallel
parallel lines
parallelogram
parentheses
pattern unit
pentagon
per
percent
perimeter
period
perpendicular
physical models
pictograph
pint (pt)
place value

plane
plane figure
point
polygon
positive
possible outcomes
prime number
prism
problem
process of elimination
product
property
protractor
pyramid
quart (qt)
quotient
radius
range
ratio
ray
real-world situation
reasonable estimate
reciprocal
regular shapes
relevant information
remainder
rename
repeated addition
repeated subtraction
represent
rhombus
right angle
right triangle
Roman numerals
rotation
round (rounding)
rounded number
sequence
set of objects
side
sign
similar
simple
simplest form
single
slide (translation)
solid
solution

solve

space

sphere

standard measure

standard units

straight

strategy

sum

symmetrical figure

symmetry

trapezoid

trial and error

triangle

turn (rotation)

underestimate

unequal parts

unit

unit fractions

unit price

unknown

unlikely

value

variable

Venn diagram

vertical

whole number

word form

written representations

yard (yd)

yards (yd)

zero property

List 6.2. Mathematics Vocabulary—Intermediate

This list builds on the mathematics concepts and instructional vocabulary presented in the basic mathematics vocabulary list. It reflects the mathematics curriculum taught and tested in grades 4 through 6. These words are also part of the vocabulary needed for algebra, geometry, and other math courses in high school. Teach math-related affixes and roots to develop students' ability to use structural analysis to read and understand math language.

30-60-90 triangle	commutative property	empty set
45-45-90 triangle	compass	equality
abscissa	complementary	equation
absolute	compound	equiangular triangle
accurate	compound interest	equilateral
act out	computation	equivalent
acute angle	concave	estimate
acute triangle	concentric	evaluate
adjacent	congruent triangles	event
algebra	consecutive	exact
algebraic expression	constant	examine
alternate	construct	example
altitude	convex	experiment
analyze	coordinate	explain
angle ($\angle$)	correlation	explore
answer	corresponding	exponent
apply	cylinder	express
approach	data	extend
approximately	decimal	exterior
arc	decrease	factor (verb)
area	denominator	favorable outcomes
associative property	dependent events	finite
at random	depth	flow chart
average	derive	formula
axis (axes)	describe	frequency
bar graph	determine	geometry
base (of percent)	develop formulas	graph
benchmark	deviation	grid
bisect	diameter	gross
box plot	differentiate	histogram
calculate	digit	hypotenuse
capacity	dimension	identify
cast out	discount	identity
circle graph	discuss	identity property
circumference	disprove	impossible outcomes
coefficient	distributive property	improper
common denominator	dot graph	increase
common factor	drawings	independent event
common multiple	element	infinite

input values
integer
interest
interior
interpret
intersect
intersection of sets
interval
inverse
inverse operation
investigate
irrelevant information
isosceles triangle
justify
label
like denominators
line graph
linear
mean
median
midpoint
midway
minimum
mixed number
mode
model
monitor
multiple
negative
notation
null set
numerator
numeric pattern
numerically
objects
obtuse
odd
open sentence
opposite
order of operations
organize
organized chart
organized list

outcome
outlier
partial
pattern
percent
percentage
percentile
perpendicular lines
perspective drawing
pi (π)
plot
point
poll
predict
prime
principle
probability
probable
proportion
prove
Pythagorean theorem
quadrant
quadrilateral
quantity
radius, radii
range
ranking
rate
rationale
reasonable estimates
recognize
record data
reduce
reflect
reflection
relevant information
rename
repeating decimal
reverse
rule
sale price
sales tax
sampling

satisfies
scale
scientific
sector
segment
set
short division
sign
significant digits
similarities
simple interest
simplest
simplify
single
solution
spatial relationships
square
squared
statistics
stem-and-leaf plot
strategies
string
subset
substitute
substitution
surface area
survey
symbols
translate
tree diagram
trial
trial and error
triangle
union
unlike
unlimited
unmatched
upper limit
variable
verbal expression
vertical
whole
whole number

List 6.3. Social Studies Vocabulary—Basic

Social studies encompasses history, geography, civics, economics, and sociology. Social studies instruction builds a foundation in the early grades around the interdependence of people and the relationship between people and their environment. Social studies also plays a major role in transmitting the American culture and value system, drawing attention to themes of freedom, democracy, courage, frontier blazing, capitalism, and community. The following basic vocabulary of social studies comes from current textbooks for grades 1 to 3 and begins to build this foundation.

abolish	charter	election
Abraham Lincoln	Cherokee	Election Day
administration	Christopher Columbus	Ellis Island
adobe	chronological order	Europe
Africa	citizen	executive branch
ally	citizenship	expedition
amendment	city	explore
American Revolution	city hall	federal
ancestor	civil	firefighter
ancient	civil rights	fleet
anthem	Civil War	founded
area	civilization	freedom
artifact	coal	frontier
Asia	colonists	geography
assembly line	colony	George Washington
Atlantic Ocean	Comanche	government
authority	commerce	governor
balance	communication	harbor
barter	community	history
beliefs	compromise	hogan
Benjamin Franklin	confederate	holiday
bill	Congress	homestead
Bill of Rights	consent	Hopi
biography	Constitution	House of Representatives
black gold	consumer	illegal
branch	continent	immigrant
British	council	indentured servant
budget	country	independence
cabinet	courage	Industrial Revolution
calendar	culture	invention
candidate	customs	Iroquois
capital	Declaration of	Jamestown, Virginia
capitalism	Independence	judicial
cause	demand	justice
cause and effect	democracy	law
celebrations	democrat	leader
century	earn	lean-tos

legal
legislative
letter carrier
Leif Erikson
Lincoln Highway
machine
Magna Carta
mail delivery
majority
map
Mayflower Compact
mayor
Mexico
minority
monarchy
mountain
national
native
Native Americans
Navajo
North America
ocean
opportunity
oral history
Oregon Trail
Pacific Ocean
Parliament
patriot
pilgrim
pioneer
Pledge of Allegiance
Plymouth Rock
police officer
policy
political
Pony Express

possession
Post Road
postal service
Powhatan
prejudice
president
primary
primary sources
prohibit
pueblos
Puritan
railroads
religion
represent
representative democracy
representative government
republic
republican
responsibility
river
sea
Seminole
Senate
sequence
settle
settlers
Shawnee
shelter
Sioux
slavery
slaves
society
South America
Spanish
spending
St. Augustine, Florida

Star Spangled Banner
state
state capital
state government
Statue of Liberty
supply
system
tax
taxation
technology
tepees
Thanksgiving
Thomas Jefferson
timeline
town hall
trade
tradition
transcontinental
  railroad
treaty
tribes
union
unite
United Kingdom
United States
veto
volunteer
vote
voyage
wagon train
Washington, D.C.
westward movement
wigwams
wilderness
worship
Yankee

List 6.4. Social Studies Vocabulary—Intermediate

Social studies in the middle grades places greater emphasis on the relationships among nations and the struggle between political and ideological views. This list builds on basic social studies vocabulary and is based on words in social studies texts and tests for grades 4 through 6. Documentaries are excellent ways to teach social studies vocabulary. Be sure to teach related words and spellings, for example, ally, allies, allied, and alliance.

alien	delegates	Great Depression
alliance	depression	Great Famine
Allied Powers	desegregation	Holocaust
ally	diplomat	Homestead Act
amnesty	disarmament	hostage
apartheid	discrimination	human resources
Articles of Confederation	dissent	humanitarian
assassination	distribution map	immigration
Assembly	divine right	import
atomic bomb	dynasty	inauguration
automation	economy	inflation
Axis powers	electoral vote	initiative
balance of power	emancipation	integration
blockade	Emancipation	interdependent
Boston Tea Party	Proclamation	interstate highway
boundary	embargo	invasion
boycott	emigration	investment
bureaucracy	emperor	Iron Curtain
cabinet	empire	isolationism
capitalism	endangered species	judicial branch
cash crop	equality	laissez-faire
census	Era of Good Feelings	Latin America
Central powers	erosion	legislative branch
checks and balances	ethnic group	legislature
civil rights	evaluate	liberal
cold war	executive branch	literacy
collective bargaining	exile	loyalists
communism	export	majority
compromise	extinct	mandate
concentration camps	fascism	Manifest Destiny
Confederacy	federal	manufacturing
conserve	Federal Reserve	martial law
convention	First Continental Congress	mass production
convert	foreign	meridian
cooperation	free enterprise system	metropolitan area
crisis	free state	middle class
Cuban missile crisis	Free World	Middle East
currency	Gettysburg Address	migrant
customs	globalization	militias

minority
missionary
moderates
monopoly
nationalism
navigation
Nazism
negotiate
neutral
nominate
nonviolence
nuclear weapons
null and void
occupied
opinion
oppression
pacifists
Parliament
passport
patriotism
per capita
persecution
Persian Gulf War
petition
plantation
policy
political party
politics
poll tax
pollution
population density map
postwar
prairie
preamble
precipitation
prejudice
primary
primary source
prime minister
private property
process

proclamation
profit
progressive
prohibit
prohibition
propaganda
protectorate
public opinion
public works
radicals
ratify
rebellion
recall
recession
Reconstruction
recycle
referendum
reform
Reformation
refugee
regulation
Renaissance
repeal
representative
republic
republican
reservation
reserves
resign
resolution
resources
retreat
revenue
revolution
riots
sabotage
saga
savanna
scale
scandal
secession

segregation
senator
Seneca Falls Convention
separation of powers
settlement house
siege
slave state
smuggling
Social Security
socialism
society
sociology
sovereignty
spoils system
standard of living
stock market
strategy
strike
suffrage
supply
Supreme Court
surplus
surrender
survive
sweatshops
terrorism
tolerance
totalitarian
traitor
treason
tyrant
unanimous
underground railroad
union
United Nations
unskilled worker
veto
Vietnam War
war hawks
War of 1812
Watergate scandal

List 6.5. Geography Vocabulary—Basic

Some ESL/ELL students have extensive knowledge of other people, places, cultures, and environments because they have lived in and traveled to many countries. Others have had very limited exposure beyond their family's village and have not encountered information about other communities, land and water forms, map skills, and political geography. Drawing on the knowledge that all students bring about their countries of origin helps set the context for learning about world geography. The words in this list are found in geography units for grades 1 to 3.

adapt	conserve	fertile
address	continent	flag
Africa	contour	forest
alike	country	fossil
arid	county	freedom
Asia	crop	fuel
Atlantic Ocean	crossroads	geography
atlas	crust	glacier
atmosphere	cultivation	globe
Australia	culture	goods
axis	custom	grain
bar graph	data	grasslands
barren	desert	Greece
bay	diagram	grid
border	different	group
boundary	directions	gulf
Canada	discover	Gulf of Mexico
canyons	diversity	habitat
capital	drought	harbor
cardinal directions	earth	harvest
Caribbean Sea	east	hemisphere
cartographer	eastern	highlands
census	eastern hemisphere	hill
central	ecology	history
Central America	economy	holiday
chart	ecosystem	horizon
citizen	endangered	human resources
city	England	ice cap
classify	environment	iceberg
climate	equator	import
coast	ethnic group	income
colony	Europe	industry
communicate	evaporation	interdependence
community	export	invention
compass	factory	inventor
compass rose	farm	island
conservation	farming	job

jungle
lake
landform
landmark
latitude
lava
law
leader
legend
line graphs
livestock
location
locator map
longitude
map
map key
map scale
market
mass
meridian
mesa
Mexico
migration
miner
mineral
moderate
money
monument
motto
mountain
nation
native
natural resource
needleleaf forest climate
needs
neighborhood
nomad
nonrenewable resource
north
North America
North Pole

northern
northern hemisphere
oasis
ocean
oil
Pacific Ocean
peak
peninsula
Phoenicians
physical environment
pie chart
plain
planet
plateau
population
port
prairie
precipitation
president
prime meridian
producer
products
profit
rainfall
rainforest climate
range
recreation
recycle
reduce
region
religion
renewable resource
reuse
river
Rome
route
rule
rural
saving
scale of miles
scarcity

school
sea
season
services
soil
south
South America
South Pole
southern
southern hemisphere
sphere
state
suburb
swamp
symbol
table
temperate climate
temperature
tide
timeline
tools
town
trade
transportation
tropical
tundra climate
urban
valley
vast
vegetation
volcano
volunteer
wants
weather
west
western
western hemisphere
wilderness
world
zone

List 6.6. Geography Vocabulary—Intermediate

This list includes key vocabulary from middle grade geography texts. It builds on concepts presented in the primary grade list.

agriculture	equal area map	metropolitan area
alluvial	erosion	monsoon
altitude	European Union	multiculturalism
Antarctic Circle	evergreen	navigation
anthropology	fault	ocean current
arable	flash flood	oceanography
archipelago	flood plain	parallel
Arctic Circle	foliage	pasture
arid	free trade zone	petroleum
artisan	geologist	physical map
basin	globalization	polar
belt	grasslands	pollution
canal	greenhouse effect	population density
cape	gross national product	rain forest
cash crop	growing season	raw materials
cliff	Gulf Stream	refinery
climate	heritage	relief map
coast	highlands	religion
commercial	homogeneous	resources
competition	humidity	rotation
coniferous	hurricane	sediment
continental divide	hydroelectric	seismograph
crater	inland	silt
crop rotation	international date line	single product economy
cultural region	irrigation	standard of living
current	jet stream	steppe
dam	labor force	strait
death rate	landlocked	subsistence farming
deciduous	latitude	subtropical
deforestation	levee	supply
degree	life expectancy	surplus
delta	longitude	survey
density	lowlands	temperate
desert	mainland	timberline
diversity	manufacture	topography
domestic	map projection	topsoil
drought	marine climate	tourism
ecology	marsh	tributary
economic indicators	meadow	typhoon
economy	megalopolis	vital statistics
elevation	Mercator map	water power

List 6.7. Science Vocabulary—Basic

Primary grade science introduces students to the life cycle, the earth, the solar system, simple machines, weather, and natural systems. Science at this level is learned best through discovery using observation, measurement, classification, data collection, and hypothesis testing. This vocabulary list is drawn from texts for grades 1 through 3. Science words pose significant challenges to ESL/ELL students. Science often uses a common word such as *crust* or *pole* to refer to concepts that are difficult to imagine or understand. Science concepts introduced in the early grades often have vocabulary that is beyond students' decoding skills and instructional reading levels. Science words are often challenging to pronounce and spell. Be sure to teach related terms (such as chemistry, chemist, chemical) and highlight roots and affixes when teaching science words.

absorb	chlorine	dinosaur	food chain
accurate	chlorophyll	direction	food web
adaptation	circuit	disease	force
air	circulation	dissolve	forest
air current	classify	distance	form
air pressure	climate	earth	forward
algae	cloud	earthquake	fossil
amoeba	community	eclipse	freeze
amphibian	compare	ecosystem	fresh water
ancestor	compass	effect	friction
anemometer	competition	electric current	frost
apply	compound	electricity	fruit
arctic	concave	element	fuel
astronaut	conclusion	endangered	fulcrum
astronomer	condense	energy	full moon
atmosphere	conductor	environment	fungus (fungi)
atom	conserve	equator	gas
attract	constant	erosion	germinate
axis	constellation	evaporate	gills
backbone	consumer	evidence	glacier
backward	contain	examine	gram
bacteria	contract	expand	grassland
balance	control	experiment	gravity
barometer	convex	extinct	groundwater
battery	core	Fahrenheit	habitat
behavior	crater	fall	hail
biology	crust	fern	heat
boil	current	fertile	hemisphere
breathe	data	filament	herbivore
carbon dioxide	decay	first quarter	heredity
carnivore	decompose	fish	hibernate
cell	degree	float	host
Celsius	density	flood	human
centimeter	desert	flow	hurricane
chemical change	development	flowers	hypothesis
chemical symbol	dew	focus	iceberg
chemistry	digestion	fog	igneous rock

image	mixture	property	sink
imaginary	model	protein	skeleton
imprint	moisture	prove	skin
incisor	mold	pull	soil
inclined plane	molecule	pulley	solar system
infection	moon	pupil	solid
infer	motion	pure	solution
inherited trait	mountain	push	sound
insect	natural resource	radiant	South Pole
instinct	nectar	rain forest	space
interpret	new moon	rain gauge	speed
investigate	nonliving thing	rainfall	sphere
joint	nonrenewable	ramp	spring
key	resource	range	star
kilogram	North Pole	rate	stem
landform	northern	reaction	stimulus
landslide	nucleus	recycle	stream
leaf (leaves)	observation	reduce	summer
learned trait	observe	reflection	sun
length	omnivore	refraction	surface
lens	opaque	relocate	survive
lever	optical	renewable	switch
life cycle	orbit	resources	system
light	order	repel	taste
liquid	organism	reproduction	temperature
liter	outlet	reptile	texture
living thing	oxygen	reservoir	thermometer
load	parasite	respiration	thunder
lungs	periodic	response	tides
machine	phase	retina	tissue
magnet	physical	reuse	tornado
magnetic field	physical change	revolve	transparent
magnetism	pitch	ridge	treatment
mammal	plain	river	variables
mantle	plane	rock	vibrate
map	planet	root	volcano
marine life	poles	rotate	volume
mass	pollen	ruler	waste
matter	pollution	scale	water cycle
measure	population	screw	water vapor
measuring cup	position	sea water	wave
melt	power	season	weather
melting point	precipitation	sediment	weather vane
mercury	predator	sedimentary rock	weathering
metal	predict	seed	wedge
metamorphic rock	prescribe	seedling	weight
metamorphosis	preserve	senses	wheel and axle
meteor	prey	separate	wind
microscope	prism	series	winter
migrate	produce	shelter	work
mineral	producer	simple machine	

List 6.8. Science Vocabulary—Intermediate

The following list was drawn from vocabulary in science texts for grades 4 through 6 and builds on the basic science vocabulary list. This list helps students work with concepts of biology, ecology, chemistry, and physics. Students need practice in order to recognize multi-word science idioms such as *chain reaction* or *circuit breaker*.

absolute zero	cell cycle	depletion
acceleration	centripetal force	deposition
acid	chain reaction	diffraction
acoustics	charge	diffusion
action	chemical bonding	digestive system
alkaline	chemical equation	dilute solution
alloy	chemical formula	direct current
alternating	chemical reaction	discharge
alternative energy	chlorine	dispersion
aluminum	chromosome	dissect
amino acid	circuit breaker	distillation
ammonia	circulatory system	divergence
amplify	cirrus cloud	diversity
analysis	classification	DNA
anatomy	climate zone	dominant
aneroid barometer	clone	dormant
antibiotic	coefficient	dry cell
Archimedes	cohesion	echo
assimilation	cold front	ecology
astronomy	cold-blooded	efficiency
atomic mass	collision theory	effort
atomic number	color blindness	electrode
autonomic nervous system	combustion	electrolyte
base	compression	electromagnetic
benchmark	concave lens	electron
big bang	concentrate	element
biodiversity	conductor	elevation
biome	convection	embryo
biotechnology	convergence	endangered species
black hole	convex lens	endocrine system
boiling point	corrosion	endoskeleton
bonding	cross-pollination	endothermic
Boyle's Law	crystal	entropy
buoyancy	cumulus cloud	enzyme
calorie	cycle	epicenter
carbohydrate	deceleration	equilibrium
carbon	decibel (dB)	era
carbon cycle	decomposition	erratic
carrier	dehydration	evolution
catalyst	dependence	exoskeleton

exothermic
fault
fiber optics
filter
fission
fluid
fluorescent
focus
formula
frame of reference
freeze
freezing point
frequency
friction
front
fulcrum
fusion
galaxy
gears
gene
generation
generator
genetic engineering
genetics
genus
geology
geothermal energy
germination
gestation
grounded
hazardous waste
heat transfer
heterogeneous
homeostasis
homologous
hormone
horsepower
host
humidity
hybrid
hydrocarbon
hydrochloric acid
hydroelectric
hydrogen
immune
imprint
inborn

incandescent
induction
inert
inertia
infectious
inflammation
infrared ray
inhale
inherited behavior
inner core
inorganic
insoluble
insulate
intensity
interference
international date line
intrusive
inverse
invertebrate
invisible spectrum
ion
irrigation
joule
kinetic energy
kingdom
larva
laser
learned behavior
life span
light year
lightning
litmus
magma
magnetic
magnetic field
malleable
mammal
mechanical advantage
meiosis
membrane
meniscus
metabolism
microorganism
Milky Way
mineral
mitosis
modulation

momentum
muscular system
mutation
nerves
nervous system
neuron
neutral
neutron
niche
nitrogen
noble gas
nomenclature
nonmetal
nuclear energy
nuclear fission
nuclear fusion
nuclear waste
nucleic acid
nutrient
organ
organic
organic rock
osmosis
outer core
output
ovary
oxidation
oxygen
ozone
parallel circuit
pasteurization
periodic
periodic table
peripheral
peristalsis
permanent magnet
permeable
petri dish
petrified
petroleum
pH
photoelectric effect
photon
photosynthesis
physics
pitch
plate tectonics

plateau
polarity
potassium
potential energy
pressure
prey
primary color
probability
projectile
protoplasm
psychological
puberty
pulley
radar
radiation
radioactivity
ratio
raw material
reaction
receptor
recessive
relative humidity
replication
reproduction
resistance
resistor
resonance
respiratory system
retina
reverberation
runoff
saturation
scientific method
scientific name
scientific notation
series circuit
sex-linked trait

sexual reproduction
short circuit
skeletal system
slope
smog
sodium
soil profile
soil water
soluble
sonar
sound wave
species
specific gravity
spectroscope
spectrum
sperm
state of matter
static electricity
subscript
superconductivity
supersaturated
surface current
suspension
symbiosis
symmetry
symptom
synapse
synthesis reaction
synthetic element
taxonomy
temperate
terminal velocity
terminus
test tube
theory
thermal expansion
thermostat

thrust
titration
tolerance
trait
transfer
transfusion
transistor
translucent
transmutation
transparent
ultrasonic
ultraviolet ray
universe
unsaturated
vacuum
valence
valve
vapor
variation
velocity
vertebrate
vibration
visible spectrum
vocal cord
voltage
volume
warm-blooded
water cycle
water table
water treatment plant
watt
wavelength
wet cell
yeast
zoology
zygote

Section Seven

Culture

List 7.1. Seasons, Holidays, and Culture

The rhythm and rhyme of American culture comes alive through our shared experiences of seasons and holidays. Geographic and local customs add variety and color. Learning about seasons and holidays as they occur helps ESL/ELL students understand American popular culture, local events, media coverage, and more.

Discussing how each culture represented in the class treats universal elements—such as harvest—honors students' cultural traditions and shows how similar many customs are around the world.

In addition to holidays that mark seasons or public events in American history or culture, Americans, depending on their personal or family traditions, observe a number of festivals and historic days or periods marking significant events in their religions. Since the founding of the colonies that became the United States of America, the freedom to practice a religion of one's choosing has been a cornerstone of the country's culture. As immigrants from different parts of the world arrived in the United States, they brought their religious traditions with them. According to the 2007 *CIA World Fact Book*, the current population is approximately

52 percent Protestant
24 percent Roman Catholic
2 percent Mormon
1 percent Jewish
1 percent Muslim
10 percent other religions
10 percent no religious affiliation

In general, Christian holidays commemorate events in the life of Jesus Christ, Jewish holidays are remembrances of events in Jewish history, and Islamic holidays mark events in the life of Muhammad. Kwanzaa is a Pan-African holiday observed by many African Americans and individuals of African descent worldwide. It celebrates African culture, family, and community.

The lists that follow are organized by seasons and include major secular and religious holidays that are commonly celebrated in the United States. Key associated vocabulary, including colors, activities, weather, and idioms are also listed.

Teaching Ideas for Holidays and Seasonal Words

Integrating cultural information into weekly lesson plans helps ESL/ELL students acclimate and understand U.S. culture. Here are some ideas on how this information can be included in your instructional programs:

- Calendar study (lunar and solar calendars)
- History lessons (timelines, historical figures and events)
- Current events
- Map study
- Search-a-word (word recognition)
- Spelling lists and spelling bees
- Word wall helpers for writing assignments
- Graphs and charts
- Vocabulary study (related vocabulary and idioms)
- Art lessons (icons, decorations, painting, sculptures, crafts)
- Research projects
- Science lessons (seasonal changes, climate differences, growing cycles, astronomy)
- Newspaper reading lessons
- Speaking and presenting (skits and plays, panel discussions)
- Economics lessons (budgeting and spending)
- Interviews with family members about holiday significance
- Journal writing
- Poetry lessons

List 7.2. Fall (Autumn) Holidays and Seasonal Words

Months: September, October, November

Fall begins with the autumnal equinox, when the time between sunrise and sunset is equal to the time between sunset and sunrise (twelve hours). The equinox occurs at a moment in time, not for an entire day. It usually occurs on September 22 or September 23.

autumn	corn maze	soccer
cool	costume	standard time
crisp	daylight savings time	state fair
chilly	end of vacation	sweaters
morning fog	falling leaves	time change
black	football	trick or treat
brown	goblin	turkey
gold	harvest	uniforms
orange	harvest festival	witches
red	harvest moon	World Series
yellow	hay ride	yams
apple dunking	home improvement projects	Labor Day
apple picking	Indian summer	Patriots' Day
leaves	leaf peeping	Rosh Hashanah
foliage	light jackets	Yom Kippur
back-to-school shopping	long sleeves	Ramadan
backpacks	masks	Eid al-Fitr
barn dance	masquerade party	Columbus Day
black cats	new friends	Veterans Day
block party	new school year	election day
canning	pumpkins	Halloween
cider	pumpkin pie	All Saints' Day
corn husks	raking leaves	Thanksgiving

Labor Day   Labor Day has been celebrated on the first Monday of September since 1894 and honors the achievements of American workers and the American labor movement. It is often marked by parades and picnics. It also signals the end of summer. In many states, the school year begins the Tuesday or Wednesday following Labor Day. Labor Day is a national holiday and government agencies and banks are closed.

assembly line, benefits, child labor laws, contract, economy, employment, full-time, guilds, heath care, hourly, industrial age, innovation, jobs, labor, lockout, management, migrant workers, minimum wage, negotiation, outsource, parade, part-time, patents, pay, pickets, productivity, research, robots, salaried, salary, seniority, sick days, strike breaker, strike, taxes, trade agreements, undocumented workers, unemployment, union, vacation days, wages, work hours, work week, workers

Patriots' Day   In 2002, by presidential proclamation, George W. Bush designated September 11 as Patriots' Day. It is also called America Remembers Day. This day honors and remembers the more than three thousand innocent people killed in the terrorist attacks on the bright, clear morning of September 11, 2001. Terrorists hijacked commercial airliners and crashed into the twin towers of the World Trade Center in New York City; the Pentagon building in Washington, D.C.; and a field in Shanksville, Pennsylvania. Flags are flown on Patriots' Day.

act of war, Al-Qaeda, attack, bravery, collapse, command post, debris, emergency services, financial district, fire department, first responders, Freedom Tower, fundamentalist, Ground Zero, heroes, hijack, international, landmark, lower Manhattan, Manhattan, martyr, memorial, Middle East, Mohammed, New York City, radical, skyscraper, smoldering, suicide bombers, symbolic, terror, terrorists, Twin Towers, Wall Street, war, war on terror, World Trade Center, 9-1-1, 9-11-01

Rosh Hashanah   Rosh Hashanah is one of two High Holy Days (the other is Yom Kippur) and the first day of the new year on the Jewish calendar. It occurs in September on a date determined by the lunar calendar. For example, the year 5771 will begin on September 9, 2010, and the year 5772 will begin on September 29, 2011.

Rosh Hashanah is a festive day on which, as most Americans do on January 1, most Jews reflect on the past year and make resolutions to improve in the new year. Most Jews go to the synagogue as part of their Rosh Hashanah observance.

Note that Rosh Hashanah actually begins the evening before the calendar date because the Bible reference to the beginning of time starts in the evening, followed by day.

calendar, festival, High Holy Day, New Year, reflection, resolution, Rosh Hashanah, synagogue

Yom Kippur   Yom Kippur is one of two High Holy Days (the other is Rosh Hashanah) and occurs nine days after Rosh Hashanah. It is also called the Day of Atonement. As part of their atoning for misdeeds of the past year, most Jews fast for twenty-five hours, do not work, and attend a service at their synagogue. The fasting is usually preceded by a large meal the day before. Visiting others, asking for forgiveness for misdeeds, and giving to charities are also part of the preparation for the Yom Kippur services.

Note that Yom Kippur begins at sundown on the evening before the calendar date, because the Jewish day starts in the evening, followed by day.

Some Jews also observe this day by not wearing fragrances of any sort, bathing, wearing leather shoes, or engaging in sexual activities. Some wear white to symbolize their purity after repenting for their sins.

Ark, atonement, cantor, charity, fasting, forgiveness, incense, misdeeds, oaths, pledge, prohibit, repentance, resolve, scrolls, shofar, sins, sundown, Torah, transgression, Yom Kippur

Ramadan and Eid al-Fitr   Ramadan is the ninth month of the Islamic calendar and for Muslims around the world it is a time of fasting, prayer, and gathering with family and friends. Ramadan usually begins in September and ends in October. The date is set by a committee that observes the moon; thus it may fluctuate by a day or more depending on the weather conditions.

According to Islamic tradition, Muhammad received the Quran from heaven during the month of Ramadan, and because the Quran gives direction for one's life, the month is a special time for reflection and prayer using the teachings of the Quran. Many Muslims spend more time at their mosques during this month than during the rest of the year.

Muslims fast from sunup to sundown and break their fasts each evening before visiting family and friends. During this time, and especially toward the end of the month, Muslims make charitable contributions to the poor and mend relationships that have suffered during the year. The donations to the poor are often of food and are known as *sadaqah al-fitr*, or the "charity of fast-breaking." This charity is meant to ensure that all have means to join the celebration at the end of Ramadan.

At the end of the month, the three-day festival of the Breaking of the Fast, or Eid al-Fitr, is celebrated. It is a joyous time filled with feasting, gift-giving, and visiting with family and friends. Many Muslims decorate their homes with lights and wear new clothes to celebrate. The first day of Eid al-Fitr begins with special prayers at a mosque or other location, followed by travel to festive dinners with relatives and friends.

As-salaam alaykum (peace be with you.), *Wa alaykum as-salaam* (and peace be with you also), Allah, charity, contemplation, dates, Eid al-Fitr, *Eid Saeed!* (Happy Eid!), fasting, Five Pillars of Islam, guidance, mosque, Quran, Ramadan, sundown

Columbus Day   On August 3, 1492, with the approval of the Spanish Court, Christopher Columbus left Spain and traveled west hoping to find a shorter route to India. On October 12, after ten weeks at sea, crew aboard Columbus's ship the Pinta sighted land an island that is part of what is now known as the Bahamas. Believing he had found India, he named the native people he encountered Indians. Columbus's discovery marked a new era of exploration and set the stage for the migration of Westerners to the New World over the next several centuries.

Columbus Day has been celebrated with parades and festivals since 1792. The commemoration is a good time for students to review the early history of the New World, including native cultures and civilizations. Because Columbus was from Italy, many Italian-American neighborhoods and organizations sponsor celebrations in his honor.

Amerigo Vespucci, armada, Aztecs, barrels, captain, cargo, cartographer, charts, circumference, circumnavigate, Columbus Day, compass, crew, currents, discovery, exploration, fleet, galleys, globe, Incas, indigenous people, journal, latitude, longitude, maps, measurements, merchants, native, Native Americans, navigate, Nina, Norsemen, Pinta, provisions, sailing, Santa Maria, seafaring, sextant, silk, spice trade, telescope, the East, the Orient, trade routes, trade winds, voyage

Halloween   Originally, Halloween was the beginning of the centuries-old celebration of All Saints' Day on November 1. All Saints Day honors both the well-known and the common people who have lived good lives and are now thought to be in heaven. The day is celebrated by the Catholic and Anglican churches. The night before, October 31, All Hallows Eve, is now known as Halloween. The date coincides with an ancient pagan celebration in which the lord of the dead calls forth the evil spirits to walk about this one evening before the souls of the saints arrive the next day.

In the United States, the idea of evil or saintly people is hinted at by the phrase "trick or treat," which children, dressed in costumes, say when they knock at neighbors' doors to collect a payment of candy or coin to ward off having tricks played against them. In our time, Halloween has lost all religious significance and is now associated with the fun of dressing in costumes, going out trick-or-treating in the neighborhood, and collecting a cache of candy. Some historians believe that the celebration of Halloween became popular in the late nineteenth century because it was brought over to the United States by the large number of immigrants from Ireland and Britain who arrived during the 1840s and 1850s. Pagan symbols, including witches, black cats, and gourds, are still used for decorations.

black, black cats, broomsticks, caldron, candy, candy corn, character, cobwebs, corn husks, costume party, costumes, face painting, fairies, frightening, ghosts, ghoul, gourds, Halloween, Halloween parade, haunted, haunted house, hay bales, jack-o'-lantern, makeup, masks, monsters, orange, prank, pumpkins, scary, skeletons, spiders, spirits, witches

Election Day   Election day is held annually for local and state elections. Every fourth year there is a national election day to choose the president of the United States.

Polling places, where registered citizens go to vote, are in publicly accessible buildings such as schools, church auditoriums, libraries, and town halls. Flags are flown on election day.

Fifteenth Amendment, Nineteenth Amendment, ballot, ballot question, campaign, campaign headquarters, campaign promises, candidate, capitol, chads, concession speech, dark horse, delegates, Democrats, early returns, elect, electoral college, electorate, exit polling, franchise, governor, Green Party, identification, inaugural ball, Inauguration Day, Independents, legislature, mayor, nomination, nominations, oath of office, platform, political party, polling place, polls, recount, red-white-and-blue bunting, referendum, representative, representative democracy, Republicans, right to vote, run for office, slogan, swearing-in, tally, third party, too close to call, touch-screen voting machines, town council, victory speech, vote, voter registration, voting district, voting machines, ward, women's suffrage

Veterans Day   November 11, 1918, marked the end of World War I. To honor those who had served in the war, the anniversary of that day of armistice (laying down of arms/weapons) was set aside as a national holiday. Over the years it has come to be the day that we honor all veterans who have served in the U.S. armed forces.

On this day the president places a wreath at the Tomb of the Unknowns in Arlington National Cemetery to honor those who do not have a final named resting place. Veterans Day is typically celebrated with parades honoring those who served and are serving in the armed forces, including those in reserve units. It is a national holiday, and schools and government buildings and services are generally closed. It is a day when Americans fly their flags.

twenty-one-gun salute, Air Force, anniversary, Arlington National Cemetery, armed forces, armistice, arms, Army, Bronze Star, bugle, cemetery, Coast Guard, commemoration, Distinguished Service Cross, draft, draft dodgers, duty, enlist, fly a flag at half mast, fly over, honor guard, honorable discharge, indebted, Marines, military, military honors, National Guard, Navy, patriotism, pay tribute, Purple Heart, reserves, resting place, sailor, selfless, Semper Fidelis, servicemen, servicewomen, Silver Star, soldier, taps, Tomb of the Unknowns, ultimate price, veteran, wreath

Thanksgiving In 1620, the Pilgrims landed at Plymouth, in what is now Massachusetts. The harsh winter and rocky soil made living conditions very difficult. Without the help of the Indians they would not have survived. In the following year, having been taught how to plant crops, hunt, and survive in the new land, they reaped a bountiful harvest. In thanksgiving and friendship, they invited the Native Americans to a harvest feast. According to accounts in letters written by Pilgrims present at the first Thanksgiving, the feast included shellfish, turkey, corn, cider, cabbage, onions, fish, and pumpkin.

What we think of as Thanksgiving Day did not become an American tradition until 1863 when President Abraham Lincoln established the day of Thanksgiving. The celebration was moved to the fourth Thursday in November by President Franklin D. Roosevelt in 1939.

Cape Cod, clams, cultivate, feast, God-fearing, harsh weather, harvest, maize, mashed potatoes, Massasoit, Mayflower Compact, Mayflower, Native Americans, oysters, Pilgrims, Plymouth, pumpkins, Puritans, religious freedom, Samoset, settlement, strict, tribe, turkey, Wampanoag, yams

List 7.3. Winter Holidays and Seasonal Words

Months: December, January, February

Winter begins with the winter solstice, that is, when the sun is in the lowest part of the sky. Winter solstice occurs at a moment in time, not for an entire day. It usually occurs on December 21 or December 22.

cold	boots	jackets
freezing	caroling	Lincoln's Birthday
frigid	Christmas	Mardi Gras
ice	coats	Martin Luther King Jr. Day
snow	fireplace	Kwanzaa
sleet	furnace	New Year's Day
snowstorm	gift giving	New Year's Eve
slush	gloves	Muharram
blizzard	Groundhog Day	Eid al-Adha
black ice	Hanukkah	President's Day
gray	hats	skiing
brown	holiday spirit	snowboards
white	holidays	Washington's Birthday
baking	ice hockey	
basketball	ice skate	

Hanukkah (or Chanukah)   Hanukkah is the Jewish Festival of Lights. It usually occurs in December. More than two thousand years ago, the Syrian army had taken over the Jewish city of Jerusalem and was using its Temple to worship the Greek god Zeus. The Jewish Maccabees forced the Syrian army out and before the temple could be used for Jewish prayers it had to be rededicated. As part of the rededication, the lantern of the "eternal flame" was relit. However, there was only enough oil to last one day and a new supply of the special oil was not expected to be available in time to keep the flame burning. Miraculously, the flame burned for eight days! In memory of this miracle, Jews light candles on a menorah, one for each of the eight days.

During Hanukkah, children play with a four-sided spinner called a dreidel. On each side is the first letter of one of the words in the phrase "great miracle happened here" (*shin, hey, gimel, nun*). A variety of games are played with the dreidel, and children win gold foil-wrapped chocolate coins call *gelt*.

The observance also features special holiday foods, many of which are cooked in oil, including potato latkes, that is, potato pancakes made from shredded potatoes, onions, and flour.

In many Jewish families, small gifts are given during the holiday, one on each night. The gift-giving takes place after the ritual lighting of the candles.

candles, Chanukah, dreidel, Eternal Flame, Festival of Lights, gelt, gimel, Hanukkah, *hey,* Jerusalem, lamp oil, latkes, Maccabees, menorah, miracle, miraculous, *nun,* potato pancakes, rededication, *shin,* Temple

Hajj and Eid al-Adha   Islamic holy days shift eleven days earlier each solar year, so they are not fixed. The last month of the Islamic year is a time when Muslims from around the world make the Hajj, a once-in-a-lifetime pilgrimage, or journey, to the holy city of Mecca. During this time, about two million people go to Mecca and perform the rituals of prayer and symbolic acts. A three-day festival celebrated by Muslims worldwide begins at the end of the Hajj.

This celebration is called Eid al-Adha and is the Festival of Sacrifice. It commemorates the obedience of the prophet Abraham to Allah's (God's) instruction to sacrifice his son Isaac. According to the Bible and other religious writings and beliefs, Allah substituted a lamb for Abraham's son, sparing his life because Abraham had been willing to sacrifice so much for his faith in and love of Allah.

As part of the celebration, lambs, goats, and other animals used for meat are slaughtered and cooked, and most of the food is distributed to the poor or others outside the family. This shows symbolically that Muslims are willing to give what they have to others to do the will of Allah, and that they recognize that all they have comes from the bounty and blessing of Allah. Muslims also attend prayers at their mosque and exchange gifts and holiday greetings with family and friends.

Allah, Eid al-Adha, Hajj, Inshallah (*Insha'Allah*), Mecca, mosque, obedience, pilgrim, pilgrimage, ritual, sacrifice, slaughter, spare, stoning the devil

Christmas Day, Christmas Holidays   Christmas is both a Christian holiday and a secular holiday period. As a Christian holiday, it celebrates the birth of Jesus Christ in a manger in Bethlehem. From these humble beginnings, Jesus Christ rose to become a religious leader and is acknowledged as a holy man and a prophet by many religions. Christians believe he is the Messiah, the Son of God, who was sent by God to save the world. Most religious historians agree that December 25 is not the actual or even likely date of the birth of Jesus, but it was set by Pope Julius I and coincided with and replaced the pagan traditional holiday of the winter solstice.

As a secular holiday period, the Christmas season is characterized by friendship and goodwill, generosity toward others, family gatherings, reconciliation with others, peace-seeking, and celebration.

The holiday season starts immediately after Thanksgiving and lasts until about two weeks after Christmas. Many traditions now associated with Christmas came to the United States with immigrants from other countries, and several have their roots in non-Christian festivals or lore.

Christmas cards. The first known Christmas cards were designed in 1843 by artist John C. Horsely for an English businessman named Sir Henry Cole. The cards were requested as a time-saver because Cole was too busy to write individual letters to each of his relatives and business associates. A few years later, Richard H. Pease, who owned a variety store in Albany, New York, printed and sold the first cards in the United States. Inexpensive postage helped Christmas cards catch on as U.S. expansion resulted in families being apart at holiday time. Now, e-mail and e-cards convey holiday greetings around the world in seconds.

Santa Claus. The jolly gift-giver popularized in the 1822 poem by Clement C. Moore, "The Night Before Christmas," had his beginnings as a real person—a religious man named Nicholas—in Myra, Turkey, in the fourth century. Nicholas was a bishop and is often shown wearing his red cape, long white beard, and tall bishop's mitre (a type of hat).

He was a good and generous man who cared deeply about children. The feast of St. Nicholas, December 6, was celebrated with acts of charity and gift-giving. Nicholas was known and loved throughout Europe. Settlers from Amsterdam, Holland, brought him to New Amsterdam, which is now New York. By the seventeenth century, his Dutch name, Sint Nikolaas, evolved into Santa Claus as American settlers began to speak English.

Gift-giving. Gift-giving during the Christmas holiday season has several roots. It is first associated with the gifts that the Three Wise Men, or Three Kings, gave to the infant Jesus. And Santa isn't the only one who gives gifts during the holiday season. Depending on your culture, you could be waiting for a visit from Père Noël, Christkind, Mikulás, the Christ Child, Babbo Natale, Julenissen, Ded Moroz, Father Christmas, Hoteiosho, La Befana, or the Three Kings.

Christmas trees. There are several competing explanations for the origins of the Christmas tree. All of them, however, are rooted in Germany. In the eighth century, St. Boniface was working to convert pagan Germanic tribes who worshipped oak trees and decorated them for the winter solstice. He is said to have cut down a huge oak that was the object of worship, and in its place a fir tree grew. The evergreen became a symbol of Christianity, and the tribesmen decorated it in honor of Christmas, which was celebrated at about the same time of year. In the Middle Ages, a popular play told the story of Adam and Eve in the Garden of Eden. A fir tree was hung with apples and the play ended with the prophecy that a savior would come to bring hope and salvation to the world. Another explanation holds that Martin Luther put candles on a fir tree to recreate the beauty he saw as the stars twinkled between the branches of fir trees when he looked at the sky. Prince Albert, a German, brought the Christmas tree tradition to England in 1840 when he married Queen Victoria. Later, German immigrants continued the tradition in their new American homes.

Mistletoe. This evergreen was used in winter solstice celebrations by the Druids two hundred years before Christ's birth. It was believed to have magical and curative powers because it does not need to be planted but simply grows on other trees. This symbiotic relationship signified peace and harmony. Kissing under the mistletoe symbolizes acceptance and joining together. Scandinavians also associate mistletoe with a goddess of love.

Holly. The use of mistletoe, a pagan symbol, was frowned on by the early Christian church, which suggested replacing it with holly as a decoration for the Christmas holiday. Holly was considered an appropriate symbol because it was evergreen; its sharp-edged leaves and red berries were symbolic of Jesus' crown of thorns and blood.

Poinsettias. This beautiful plant came to us from Mexico, where its leaves were thought to symbolize the star of Bethlehem. The Aztecs called it Cuetlaxochitl and made a red-purple dye from its leaves. It is also referred to as the Crown of the Andes in some South American countries. The first U.S. ambassador to Mexico, Joel Poinsett, brought the plant to the United States in 1828, and it has continued to grow in popularity and variety.

Yule log. The word *yule* originally came from the Middle East and means "infant." Some Germanic tribes, including the Anglo Saxons, who settled in what is now northern Europe, celebrated winter festivals called Yule as early as the thirteenth century to encourage a bountiful birthing of new livestock in spring. As part of the celebration, large logs were sprinkled with oil and salt and then lit. Each spark that came from the log was thought to represent a birth to come. While the logs burned, prayers were said to protect the house from evil spirits. Over time, the Yule log became associated with Christmas Eve and was often used as a decoration. By the late 1800s, a rolled cake decorated to look like a yule log became popular.

Advent, angels, Bethlehem, caroling, centerpiece, charity, choir, Christian, Christmas cards, Christmas carols, Christmas stocking, Christmas tree, crèche, decorations, garland, generosity, gift-giving, gift wrap, goodwill, Happy Holidays, holly, joy, manger, Merry Christmas, Messiah, mistletoe, poinsettia, prophet, reindeer, religious, Rudolph, sack, Santa Claus, savior, Secret Santa, sleigh, snowmen, toy trains, tree-lighting ceremony, tree lights, tree ornaments, tree skirt, winter solstice, wrapping paper, wreath

Kwanzaa   Kwanzaa is an interfaith African American holiday established in 1966 by Dr. Maulana Karenga to promote seven principles that support family, community, and culture for African Americans and Africans throughout the world.

Each of the seven principles, called *Nguzo Saba* in Swahili, is highlighted on one of the seven days of the holiday. These principles are Umoja (unity), Kujichagulia (self-determination), Ujima (collective work and responsibility), Ujamaa (cooperative economics), Nia (purpose), Kuumba (creativity), and Imani (faith).

A special candleholder called a *kinara* holds one black candle in the center and three red and three green candles on either side. Each day the candles are lit by first lighting the black candle and using it to light first a red candle, then a green one, alternating until on the seventh day all candles are lit. As each day's candle is lit, a person of honor says something about the principle it represents; then a Unity Cup is passed around and everyone takes a sip. Afterward, the candles are extinguished.

On the last day, which is also New Year's Eve, the celebration becomes more lively and family and friends gather to mark endings and beginnings.

Seven symbols are used in the celebration and are displayed in a place of honor: a woven mat, the unity cup, harvested crops (fruits or vegetables), the kinara, seven candles, corn (one ear for each child in the family), and gifts.

Kwanzaa is a cultural celebration, not a religious observance. It's founder is a professor in the Department of Black Studies at California State University, Long Beach.

ancestors, collective work and responsibility, cooperative economics, creativity, Dr. Maulana Karenga, faith, harvest, kinara, Kwanzaa, legacy, Native Americans, Nguzo Saba, purpose, self-determination, seven principles, Swahili, symbol, unity

New Year's Eve   New Year's Eve, December 31, is a celebration of the year just ending. It is a night for parties and socializing with family and friends. Traditionally, at midnight partygoers blow horns, ring bells, and throw confetti to bid goodbye to the old year and to welcome the new one. In Times Square in New York City, thousands of people gather to witness the dropping of the New Year's Eve ball. During a countdown, a large glittering ball is lowered down a pole atop one of the city's well-known buildings as people in the street cheer, sing, make noise, and throw confetti. At midnight, Americans wish one another a happy, healthy, and prosperous New Year. This event is televised worldwide.

auld lang syne, ball-dropping, champagne, counting down, kissing at midnight, make a toast, New Year's Eve party, noisemakers, streamers, stroke of twelve, Times Square

New Year's Day   On New Year's Day, Americans typically make resolutions, or promises to themselves, to do or not do certain things, with the intent of self-betterment.

behavior, contemplate, examine, fresh start, hangover, headache, overdo it, promise, reflection, resolutions, self-improvement

Muharram   Muharram is Islamic New Year and marks the beginning of the Islamic religious calendar, which counts time from the year Muhammad left Mecca to go to Medina (622 CE). His journey from Mecca to Messina is called the *Hegira*. In 2009 it will be 1430 AH (anno Hegira, or in the year of the Hegira).

The date of Muharram is determined using a lunar calendar. The holiday begins at sundown on the evening before the calendar date.

Unlike the American celebration of New Year's Eve, Muharram is a quiet day spent in prayer and reflection.

Martin Luther King Jr. Day   Dr. Martin Luther King Jr., an African American clergyman, was born on January 15, 1929, in Atlanta, Georgia. His life's work was dedicated to nonviolence and civil rights. He led a March on Washington on August 28, 1963, to draw attention to civil rights. More than two hundred thousand people attended. His speech that day—"I have a dream"—is one of the most famous in the civil rights movement. He is credited with helping pave the way for the Civil Rights Act of 1964, which made discrimination illegal. In 1964, at the age of thirty-five, he was awarded the Nobel Prize for Peace. In 1968 he was assassinated by James Earl Ray, a career criminal.

Dr. King's birthday is commemorated on the third Monday in January.

advocate, affirmative action, bias, civil rights, Civil Rights Act of 1964, desegregation, discrimination, hate crime, marchers, nonviolent, protest, protest march, resistance, segregation, sit-in, slavery, voting rights, We Shall Overcome

Inauguration Day   Inauguration Day is January 20, every four years. It follows the election of a president on election day the previous November. On Inauguration Day, on the steps of the Capitol in Washington, D.C., the elected president and vice president take their oaths of office and are sworn in. The inauguration marks the orderly transfer of power from one president to the next. The president's first speech is thought to set the tone of the administration and usually outlines priorities for the coming years.

Chief Justice, Constitution, declaration, defend, domestic policy, first lady, foreign policy, "Hail to the Chief," inaugural ball, inaugural parade, make an oath, oath of office, preserve, protect, swearing in, take an oath

Ground Hog Day   Ground Hog Day is celebrated on February 2. On this day, crowds gather on Gobbler's Knob, a wooded area outside of Punxsutawney, Pennsylvania, for a sign of whether winter will be over soon or there will be another long period of cold. They wait to see whether the groundhog, Punxsutawney Phil, will see his shadow when he comes out of his den. If the weather is bright and clear, he will see his shadow and there will be another six weeks of winter. If the weather is not bright, spring will come early. It's easy to remember with this little rhyme:

> If Groundhog Day is bright and clear,
> Six weeks of winter, we'll still bear.

This folksy celebration comes to us from German immigrants who settled in Pennsylvania. In Germany and many other parts of Europe, Candlemas Day is also observed. On that day, priests bless candles and distribute them for use in the remaining dark days of winter. This custom came from earlier times when the pagans celebrated the time between winter solstice and the spring equinox. The conquering Roman army brought the custom to northern Europe.

burrow, crisp, customs, extended, folklore, forest ranger, gamekeeper, gathering, groundhog, handed down, hiking, immigrants, overcast, park ranger, shadow, tradition, trails, wintry, wooded

Lincoln's Birthday   Abraham Lincoln was born in Kentucky on February 12, 1809. He was a storekeeper, country lawyer, and representative who later became the sixteenth president of the United States. He was president from 1861 until April 15, 1865, when he died after being shot by John Wilkes Booth at the Ford Theater in Washington. Lincoln is most often remembered for his speeches at the dedication of the Gettysburg military cemetery—the Gettysburg Address—and for the 1863 Emancipation Proclamation, which set free those who were enslaved in the Confederate States. His actions during the Civil War are considered to have preserved the Union.

Lincoln is remembered on his birthday and on Presidents' Day, which honors both Lincoln and Washington.

abolish, abolitionist, assassinate, beard, burial ground, cemetery, Civil War, compromise, Confederacy, conscription, crisis, debate, devotion, emancipate, enlist, forefathers, four score and seven years, freedom, gaunt, Gettysburg, gunshot, hallowed, hill country, Honest Abe, honorable, landowner, lanky, lawyer, plainspoken, plantations, proclamation, recruit, regiment, Republican Party, resting place, rural, sharecropper, slavery, statesman, stovepipe hat, theater, Underground Railroad, Union, volunteer

Valentine's Day   February 14 is the feast of St. Valentine, a Christian bishop and martyr. Multiple stories link St. Valentine to notions of love. In one story, the emperor declared that soldiers should not be permitted to marry and Valentine was jailed for continuing to perform marriage ceremonies for the young men and the women they loved. In another story, he fell in love with his jailer's daughter and, before he was executed, sent her a love note signed "from your Valentine." He died on February 14, 269. In 496, the Pope declared his day of martyrdom to be his feast day. By the 1600s, Valentine's Day was widely observed as a day to celebrate love. According to the Greeting Card Association, by the 1700s, tokens of affection and notes were exchanged by friends and lovers in all social classes. In the 1800s, with improvements in printing and the postal service, mass-produced Valentine cards became popular. Ester Howland is credited with selling the first mass-produced cards in the United States. The association reports that approximately one billion Valentine cards are sent each year.

attraction, attractive, be crazy about someone, be mine, bouquet, box of chocolates, boyfriend, celebrate, champagne, commitment, committed, cupid, exchange, fall in love, get engaged, girlfriend, go on a date, going out, have a crush on someone, have a date, head over heels, heart, heartfelt, in love, lacy, perfume, long-stem roses, love at first sight, love letter, lovely, make a date, mushy, pink, red roses, red, romance, romantic, secret admirer, sentimental, token of affection, Valentine, Valentine card

Presidents' Day   George Washington's birthday used to be celebrated as a national holiday. In 1971 a law went into effect changing the date it would be celebrated from February 22, Washington's actual birthday, to the third Monday in February. This was done to simplify the employment calendar for federal workers and to give them some three-day weekends. Officially, the day commemorates Washington, but over time it has come to be called Presidents' Day, and most states and individuals honor both Washington and Lincoln on this date.

Washington's Birthday   George Washington, the first president of the United States, was born on February 22, 1732. Washington, a Virginia farmer, surveyor, and statesman, was appointed commander of the Continental Army. Later he served as the presiding officer at the continental convention. He was unanimously elected as first president of the United States. His birthday has been celebrated as a national holiday since the last year of his presidency. The traditional holiday is celebrated on his birthday. The national holiday is celebrated on Presidents' Day, the third Monday of February.

army, Battle of Trenton, Continental Army, crossing the Delaware River, declaration, general, gentleman farmer, independence, integrity, landowner, Minute Men, presidency, Red Coats, representative, statesman, surveyor, tell a lie, territory, wealthy

St. Patrick's Day   Patrick was born around 385 AD, the son of Romans who were living in Britain and overseeing the Roman holdings. As a teenager, he was kidnapped and taken to Ireland as a slave to tend sheep. During his time there, he learned to speak the Irish language and learned about the Druids and pagan customs. As a young man he escaped and returned home to Britain. He became a priest and later a Bishop and returned to Ireland in 433 to convert the pagans and replace the Druid cults with Christian believers. His knowledge of the language and his love of the Irish people from the time of his youth helped him reach the people and establish churches and monasteries all over Ireland. It is said he used the three-leaf clover as a means to teach about the Holy Trinity—a Christian belief of one God with three manifestations: the Father, the Son, and the Holy Spirit. He died on March 17, 461.

In Ireland, St. Patrick's Day is a national holiday. In the United States, it is a widely celebrated secular holiday. The first observation of the holiday in the United States took place on March 17 in 1737 in Boston. The first St. Patrick's Day parade in New York City occurred nearly 250 years ago in 1766. Modern parades draw more than 150,000 marchers from all over.

It's not surprising that St. Patrick's Day is so popular. According to the U.S. Census Bureau, more than 34.5 million U.S. residents claim to have Irish ancestors. This is almost nine times the population of Ireland, which has about 4.1 million residents. About 24 percent of Massachusetts residents are of Irish heritage, about twice the national average.

believer, canonize, church, conversion, convert, Druids, Emerald Isle, enslaved, Ireland, kidnapped, miracle, missionary, monasteries, monks, overseer, pagan, parish, preached, priest, Roman colony, Roman Empire, sacrifices, saint, salvation, Scotland, sheep, shepherd, slavery, snakes, staff, three-leaf clover, tribes, worship, worshipers

List 7.4. Spring Holidays and Seasonal Words

Months: March, April, May

Spring begins with the spring equinox, when the time between sunrise and sunset is equal to the time between sunset and sunrise (twelve hours) The equinox occurs at a moment in time, not for an entire day. It usually occurs on March 20 or March 21.

warm	chicks	baseball
breezy	new life	lacrosse
showers	gardens	field hockey
pink	planting seeds	track
yellow	seeds sprouting	spring break
lavender	waking up from hibernation	April Fools' Day
light green	snow melting	income tax due date
flowers bloom	kite flying	Easter
trees grow leaves	hiking	Passover
tips	bicycle	Mawlid al-Nabi
crocuses	skateboard	May Day
bunnies	outdoors	Mother's Day

April Fools' Day   April Fools' Day dates back to France in 1582 AD. At that time, Pope Gregory XIII made corrections to the calendar started by Julius Caesar. These changes were needed because the solar year is not exactly 365 days long. As a result of the corrections, in order to catch up with the natural occurrence of the equinoxes and seasons, in 1582 ten days were deleted from the calendar and October 4 was followed immediately by October 15. Another change was to move New Year's Day from March 25 to January 1. These changes were adopted by most Catholic countries. Frenchmen who forgot the New Year's change were teased and pranks were played on them. Not all countries made the change to the Gregorian calendar in 1582. The date of the New Year's holiday, however, spread throughout Europe. Britain and her colonies, including what is now the United States, did not adopt the date reckoning of the Gregorian calendar until 1752, when September 2 was followed immediately by September 14 in order to catch up. The Gregorian calendar is now used all over the world. We correct the calendar every four years by adding a leap day in February.

calendar, confuse, embarrass, fool, fool's errand, Gregorian calendar, harmless fun, jest, jester, Julius Caesar, leap year, Pope Gregory, prank, solar year, tease

Mawlid al-Nabi   Mawlid al-Nabi commemorates the birthday of the Prophet Muhammad, the founder of Islam. The date fluctuates because the Islamic calendar uses lunar observations to mark the beginning of each month.

The life of Muhammad and the meaning and importance of his teachings are the focus of the day.

Arabic, Hegira, Islam, Koran, Mecca, Medina, Middle East, Muhammad, Muslim, Quran, *rasul* (messenger), *risala* (ideology), theologian

Easter   Easter is a major Christian holiday and is considered to be Christianity's most important religious observance. It commemorates the resurrection of Jesus Christ. The forty-day period before Easter is called Lent and is a time of reflection and sacrifice. The last week of Lent is called Holy Week. Holy Thursday observes the Last Supper, a Passover meal that Jesus ate with his apostles. Good Friday commemorates the day that Jesus was crucified. Easter Sunday marks Jesus' rising from the dead in fulfillment of scriptural promises of redemption. Easter is celebrated on the first Sunday after the full moon on or after March 21, the vernal equinox. Ash Wednesday, which begins the Lenten period, is forty-six days before Easter.

Easter is considered a time of rebirth and its timing at the beginning of spring replaced a number of pagan rites of spring and rebirth. Christians generally celebrate by going to church services and spending time with family.

The secular celebration of Easter focuses on new life and new beginnings. People dress up in new, colorful clothes and stroll the avenues and boardwalks. The Easter Bunny brings children baskets of candies. Families dye boiled eggs as signs of new life about to hatch. Flowers and plants are given as gifts. Chocolate bunnies and colorful jelly beans are common.

apostles, bloom, bunny, Calvary, chick, chocolate bunny, chocolate, color Easter eggs, colorful, crocuses, crucifix, crucifixion, dye Easter eggs, Easter basket, Easter bonnet, Easter egg hunt, Easter parade, eggs, finery, give up for Lent, Good Friday, green, hard-boiled eggs, holy day, Holy Thursday, hyacinths, jelly beans, Jesus Christ, Lent, new life, pink, purple, rabbit, rebirth, redemption, renewal, resurrection, rise from the dead, salvation, savior, spiritual, springtime, stroll, Sunday best, tulips, yellow

Passover (Pesach)   Passover commemorates the Exodus, or leaving, of the Israelites (Jews) from Egypt, where they had been held in slavery. It occurs on a night of the full moon, usually in April, but occasionally in late March, and lasts seven or eight days, depending on the branch of Judaism.

Note that Passover actually begins the evening before the calendar date because the Bible reference to the beginning of time starts with the evening followed by day.

A *seder,* the ritual dinner of Passover, is usually celebrated on the first and second days of the holiday. The ritual usually takes place in homes and focuses on retelling the story of the Exodus by reading from the Haggadah. A seder plate of symbolic foods is also part of the ritual meal, with each food representing aspects of slavery or freedom. Matzo, an unleavened bread, for example, represents the poverty of the slaves; bitter herbs (often horseradish) represent the bitterness of being enslaved; a sweet paste called *charoset* represents the mortar the Israelites used to build with bricks; and dipping vegetables (celery or potatoes) in salt water represents both freedom and the tears of sorrow during captivity. The seder also includes a ritual drinking of wine and a question-and-answer sequence used to teach children why this night is different from other nights.

beef brisket, bitter herbs, captivity, charoset, commemorate, deliverance, Egypt, Exodus, gefilte fish, Haggadah, hard-boiled egg, Israelites, kosher, lamb, leavened, matzo, matzo ball soup, Messiah, mortar, Passover, pharaoh, plagues, ritual, roasted, salt water, seder, seder plate, shank bone, slavery, unleavened

Arbor Day   The word *arbor* comes from Latin and means "tree." In the United States, Arbor Day was first celebrated in 1872 in Nebraska and resulted in the planting of nearly one million trees that year. The holiday, started by conservationist J. Sterling Morton, is dedicated to conservation and the preservation of forests and trees. Many Arbor Day celebrations involve the planting of trees to beautify and preserve healthful environments in cities and towns. Each state sets its own date for a statewide Arbor Day, on the basis of climate conditions. The national celebration has been observed on the last Friday in April since 1970.

arbor, bark, beautify, berries, birch, broadleaf, carbon dioxide, clusters, conifers, conservation, cypress, deciduous, deforestation, dogwood, elm, environment, Environmental Protection Agency, environmentalists, erosion, evergreens, fir, flowers, foliage, forests, fruit, green space, hemlock, leaves, life cycle, magnolia, maple, needles, nutrients, nuts, oak, open spaces, oxygen, palm, pine, pinecones, plant, poplar, preparation, preservation, redwood, replenish, shed, soil, spruce, tree, wash away

May Day (May 1)   May Day has its roots in the pagan celebration of Beltane, which honored Bel, the Celtic god of the sun. The celebration was marked by feasting, dancing around a May pole with ribbons, singing, and drinking. It also marked the end of winter and the first planting of the fields.

In the United States, May Day has also been a national day of prayer since 1775, when the Continental Congress set it aside for this purpose during the process of establishing a new nation. Several presidents since then have also proclaimed days of nonsectarian prayer and reflection. In 1952, President Truman and the Congress passed a resolution for an annual day of prayer. In 1988, President Reagan signed a law making the first Thursday of May a National Day of Prayer.

Note: In some countries, May Day honors workers in much the same way as our Labor Day does.

ancient, antiwar, church, dancing, ecumenical, fertile, fertility, festive, interfaith, laborers, May pole, mosque, nonsectarian, pacifist, pagan, peace, prayer, reflection, self-determination, streamers, strike, synagogue, temple, workers

Mother's Day   After Anna Jarvis's mother died in 1908, Anna wanted to establish a secular day for honoring mothers. She wrote letters to prominent people asking for their support. In response, two ministers, one in West Virginia and one in Philadelphia, dedicated Sunday, May 10, to mothers. Anna Jarvis provided carnations, her mother's favorite flower, to parishioners at one of the churches. The idea quickly caught on and by 1914 Congress passed a resolution making the second Sunday of May the official Mother's Day. It is now celebrated in countries throughout the world.

adopt, adoptive mother, biological mother, birth mother, birthstone jewelry, birthstone, bond, breakfast in bed, center of the family, flowers, godmother, grandmother, heritage, lineage, maternal, matriarch, mother, mother-in-law, nurture, pregnant, prenatal care, restaurant reservation, selfless, sentiment, single mother, stepmother, surrogate, tribute

Memorial Day   Memorial Day, celebrated on the last Monday in May, is a national holiday that originally honored those who died in the American Civil War. It has become a day to honor all women and men who died in wars in service to the United States. Memorial Day is celebrated with parades, tributes to war heroes, flags and flowers placed on military graves, and patriotic speeches.

The day is also considered an unofficial start of the summer season. Many parks and recreation facilities open on the holiday. Many towns and families have picnics, fireworks, and games. U.S. flags and red-white-and-blue bunting are visible in every town.

admiral, Air Force, antiwar demonstrations, armed forces, battalion, bunting, captain, combat, corporal, domestic, draft dodger, draft, enlisted, flags, fleet, garrison, general, gunnery sergeant, invasion, lieutenant, lottery, major, Marine, memorial, military, monument, overseas, platoon, private, rank, sailor, salute, sergeant, servicemen, stationed, tickertape parade, Tomb of the Unknowns, veteran

List 7.5. Summer Holidays and Seasonal Words

Months: June, July, August

Summer begins with the summer solstice, that is, when the sun is in the highest part of the sky. Summer solstice occurs at a moment in time, not for an entire day. It usually occurs on June 20 or June 21.

hot	commencement	pick-it-yourself
humid	farewells	picnic
hazy	farms	pools
thunderstorms	Father's Day	promotion
dust storms	festivals	sailing
drought	fishing	shells
red, white, and blue	Fourth of July	summer jobs
yellow	free time	swimming
orange	graduation	theme parks
white	graduation day	vacations
multicolored	hammock	waves
air conditioners	hot air balloons	weddings
beach	ocean	

Father's Day   According to the U.S. Census Bureau, Mrs. Sonora Smart Dodd of Spokane, Washington, came up with the idea for a day to honor fathers in 1910 while listening in church to a sermon on Mother's Day. For Mrs. Dodd it was her father, William Smart, who had been the family's center and had sacrificed much to raise his daughter and five sons after his wife died in childbirth. She proposed a Father's Day to complement the establishment of Mother's Day two years earlier, and town leaders and newspapers picked up on the idea. A date in June was selected because Mr. Smart had been born in June and some time was needed to prepare for the first celebration. The commemorative date did not become official, however, until 1972, when President Richard Nixon signed a law that made the third Sunday in June the permanent commemorative date for Father's Day.

adopt, adoptive father, biological father, birth father, child support, collect call, father, father-in-law, godfather, good provider, grandfather, guidance, hardworking, sentiment, heritage, inheritance, lineage, paternal, patriarch, role model, sperm donor, stepfather, support

Independence Day   Independence Day marks the date of the signing of the Declaration of Independence in 1776. It is celebrated on July 4, although the first Independence Day was celebrated in Philadelphia on July 8, 1776, when the declaration was read aloud publicly.

Fourth of July celebrations include family picnics and outings to beaches and parks; parades; the flying of flags; concerts; the wearing of red, white, and blue; political speeches; the singing of patriotic songs; and fireworks displays.

barbeque; beach blanket; beach chair; beverage; chili; concert; cooler; delight; firecrackers; fireworks; folding chair; gas grill; grill; hamburgers; hot dogs; iced tea; independence; liberty; patriotic; pickles; picnic; potato salad; red, white, and, blue; ribs; sparkle; Statue of Liberty; steak; street fair

List 7.6. Month-by-Month Commemorative Dates

Holidays and other notable commemorative dates are wonderful opportunities to introduce bits of Americana into morning activities and classroom conversations. They are also great topics for small group research online or in the library because informative books and sites are available at all reading levels and most have significant visual icons to assist learning. Use the commemorative dates as themes for integrating art and writing, for dramatic reading of related poetry, and for service projects. An excellent online resource for information about what happened each day in America's history can be found at http://memory.loc.gov/ammem/today/today.html. For lists of events that happened on a particular day worldwide across time, visit http://www.historynet.com/today_in_history.

The holidays in italics are considered national holidays; public and financial institutions and government services (courts, government offices, schools, banks, stock exchanges, and so on) are generally closed on these days.

January

January 1	*New Year's Day*
January 8	Elvis Presley's birthday (1935)
January 13	First radio broadcast
January 15	First Super Bowl game (1967)
January 15 or third Monday in January	*Martin Luther King Jr. Day*
January 20, following the election of a president	*Inauguration Day*

February

All month	Black History Month
February 2	Groundhog Day
February 12	Abraham Lincoln's Birthday
February 14	Valentine's Day
February 22	George Washington's Birthday
3rd Monday of February	*Presidents' Day*

March

All month	Women's History Month
March 2	Dr. Suess's birthday
March 14	Pi (π) Day
Second Sunday in March	Daylight savings time begins
March 17	St. Patrick's Day
March 19	Iraq War began (2003)
March 30	First pencil patented (1858)

April

April 1	April Fools' Day
Varies by state; most in March or April	Arbor Day
April 9	U.S. Civil War ended (1865)
April 15	Income taxes due
April 22	Earth Day

May

First week of May	PTA Teacher Appreciation Week
May 1	May Day
Second Sunday of May	Mother's Day
May 14	Jamestown settled (1607)
Wednesday and Thursday of Memorial Day week	National Spelling Bee finals
Last Monday of May	*Memorial Day*

June

June 4	First Pulitzer Prizes awarded (1917)
June 5	Apple II computer debut (1977)
June 10	Ballpoint pen patented (1943)
June 14	Flag Day
June 17	Watergate Day (1972)
Third Sunday of June	Father's Day

July

July 1	First TV broadcast (NBC, 1941)
July 4	*Independence Day*
July 10	Telstar first satellite TV (1962)
July 20	First moon landing (1969)
July 29	NASA established (1958)

August

August 1	Francis Scott Key's birthday
August 6	First atomic bomb dropped (1945)
August 7	First satellite picture of Earth (1959)
August 26	First televised baseball game (1939)
August 29	Hurricane Katrina hits United States (2005)

September

First Monday of September	*Labor Day*
First Sunday after Labor Day	National Grandparents Day
September 11	Terrorist attack on United States (2001)
September 14	Greenpeace Day
September 15–October 15	Hispanic Heritage Month
September 17	Citizenship Day
September 24	National Book Day

October

All month	Diversity Awareness Month
October 12 or second Monday of October	*Columbus Day*
October 23	Mole Day (6.02×10^{23})
October 24	United Nations Day
October 31	Halloween

November

All month	Native American Heritage Month
November 1	National Family Literacy Day
First Sunday in November	Daylight savings time ends
First Tuesday after first Monday of November	Election Day
November 11	*Veteran's Day*
Week before Thanksgiving	Children's Book Week
Fourth Thursday of November	*Thanksgiving Day*

December

December 1	Basketball invented (1891)
December 5	Walt Disney's birthday
December 10	UN Human Rights Day
December 17	Wright Brothers' first flight (1903)
December 25	*Christmas Day*
December 31	New Year's Eve

List 7.7. Flag Pledge and Patriotic Songs

Everyone recognizes the "Stars and Stripes" as the American flag and the symbol of our country. The American flag has thirteen alternating red and white stripes and, in the top left corner, fifty white stars on a field of blue. There is one star for each state in the Union.

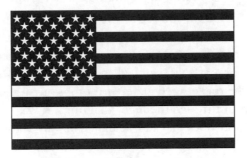

The stars are a symbol of the heavens and the lofty goals to which human beings aspire. The stripes symbolize rays of light. Red is for bravery and valor, white is for purity and innocence, and blue is for justice and perseverance.

The Pledge of Allegiance

According to the U.S. Printing Office, the Pledge of Allegiance was published in 1892 in celebration of the four hundredth anniversary of Columbus's discovery of the New World. It was first used in public schools and was officially adopted by Congress in 1942. The phrase *under God* was not part of the original pledge but was added by Congress in 1954. The U.S. Code states that when the Pledge is being made, all present should be standing and facing the flag with their right hand over their heart. Men should always remove their head covering, unless it is worn for religious reasons.

The Pledge of Allegiance

I pledge allegiance
to the Flag
of the United States of America,
and to the Republic
for which it stands,
one Nation
under God,
indivisible,
with liberty and justice
for all.

National Anthem

An anthem is a hymn of praise or loyalty. "The Star-Spangled Banner" is the United States national anthem. It was written by Francis Scott Key during the War of 1812. Two years into the war, on September 1814, Key was on a ship in the Chesapeake Bay during the shelling of Fort McHenry by the British. After a day and night of bombing, in the morning Key awoke to see through the smoke that a large American flag was still flying. The sight of it moved him to write a poem to mark the bravery and perseverance of the American soldiers. The music that it was set to was originally a British tune. President Woodrow Wilson declared "The Star-Spangled Banner" our national anthem in 1916. This is the first stanza:

The Star-Spangled Banner

O! say can you see by the dawn's early light
What so proudly we hailed at the twilight's last gleaming.
Whose broad stripes and bright stars, through the perilous fight,
O'er the ramparts we watched, were so gallantly streaming.
And the rockets' red glare, the bombs bursting in air,
Gave proof through the night that our flag was still there.
Oh, say does that star-spangled banner yet wave
O'er the land of the free and the home of the brave?

America

Another widely known and often sung patriotic hymn, "America"—which is also called "My Country, 'Tis of Thee"—was written in 1832 by Samuel Smith. It is said that as he leafed through a German hymnal, he came across a patriotic song set to a melody he liked, so he wrote his own patriotic song for the same tune.

America

My country, 'tis of thee,
Sweet land of liberty,
Of thee I sing;
Land where my fathers died,
Land of the pilgrims' pride,
From every mountainside
Let freedom ring!

America, the Beautiful

In 1893, Katharine Lee Bates, a poet and college professor, traveled to Pike's Peak in Colorado. The view from the mountaintop inspired her to write "America the Beautiful." This song has an unusual history. The words have been sung to a number of melodies, including "Auld Lang Syne." There was once even a contest for music to be written for it, but none of the entries seemed just right. The music now used was written by Samuel Ward for a song called "Materna."

America, the Beautiful

O beautiful, for spacious skies,
For amber waves of grain,
For purple mountain majesties
Above the fruited plain!
America! America! God shed His grace on thee,
And crown thy good with brotherhood,
from sea to shining sea.

O beautiful, for pilgrim feet
Whose stern impassioned stress
A thoroughfare for freedom beat
Across the wilderness!
America! America! God mend thine ev'ry flaw;
Confirm thy soul in self-control,
thy liberty in law!

O beautiful, for heroes proved
In liberating strife,
Who more than self their country loved
And mercy more than life!
America! America! May God thy gold refine,
'Til all success be nobleness,
and ev'ry gain divine!

O beautiful, for patriot dream
that sees beyond the years,
Thine alabaster cities gleam
Undimmed by human tears!
America! America! God shed his grace on thee,
And crown thy good with brotherhood,
from sea to shining sea.

List 7.8. Government

The United States is a singular world power. Cable television and the Internet have helped U.S. presidents, the Congress, and some governors become known throughout the world. ESL/ELL students need to know more about the U.S. government than the views presented by the media. This list presents some of the terms commonly used in government and civics instruction.

U.S. Government

national government

federal government

country

nation

Democratic Republic

Capitol building

Capital of the United States

Washington, D.C.

District of Columbia

branches

checks and balances

separation of powers

executive branch

president

vice president

inauguration

oath of office

"Hail to the Chief"

head of state

commander in chief

first lady

first family

White House

State of the Union

Air Force One

Oval Office

line of succession

cabinet

departments

legislative branch

bicameral

Congress

House of Representatives

lower house

Peoples' House

Senate

upper house

representation

Speaker of the House

minority leader

President of the Senate

legislation

bill

veto

advise and consent

treaty

declaration of war

taxation

impeach

electoral college

congressional district

congressional committee

judicial branch

Supreme Court

associate justice

chief justice

unconstitutional

opinion

Supreme Court decision

Bill of Rights

Constitution of the United States

Library of Congress

Constitutional Powers of Congress

- To levy and collect taxes
- To borrow money for the country
- To provide for the common defense

- To provide for the general welfare of the United States and its citizens
- To regulate commerce between states and with other nations
- To coin and mint money and regulate its value
- To establish rules for citizenship
- To establish a postal service
- To establish roadway systems
- To raise and support armed forces
- To declare war
- To promote progress
- To define felonies
- To make laws necessary to carry out the power of Congress

State Government

governor	state representative
lieutenant governor	state senator
state bill of rights	statutes
state constitution	direct democracy
state capitol	referendum
statehood	recall
state departments	initiative
state income tax	licenses
state sales tax	contracts
state department of education	health
state teacher certification	education
state supreme court	common good
state legislature	criminal law

County and Local Government

county	city	municipal
freeholder	mayor	school districts
county executive	council	wards
Board of Chosen Freeholders	city executive	urban
county manager	town	suburban
commission	village	rural
township	borough	metropolitan area

List 7.9. States

The Thirteen Original Colonies and First States

Connecticut	New Hampshire	Rhode Island
Delaware	New Jersey	South Carolina
Georgia	New York	Virginia
Maryland	North Carolina	
Massachusetts	Pennsylvania	

State	Postal Abbreviation	Capital
Alaska	AK	Juneau
Alabama	AL	Montgomery
Arkansas	AR	Little Rock
Arizona	AZ	Phoenix
California	CA	Sacramento
Colorado	CO	Denver
Connecticut	CT	Hartford
Delaware	DE	Dover
Florida	FL	Tallahassee
Georgia	GA	Atlanta
Hawaii	HI	Honolulu
Iowa	IA	Des Moines
Idaho	ID	Boise
Illinois	IL	Springfield
Indiana	IN	Indianapolis
Kansas	KS	Topeka
Kentucky	KY	Frankfort
Louisiana	LA	Baton Rouge
Massachusetts	MA	Boston
Maine	ME	Augusta
Maryland	MD	Annapolis
Michigan	MI	Lansing
Minnesota	MN	St. Paul
Missouri	MO	Jefferson City
Mississippi	MS	Jackson
Montana	MT	Helena
North Carolina	NC	Raleigh
North Dakota	ND	Bismarck
Nebraska	NE	Lincoln
New Hampshire	NH	Concord
New Jersey	NJ	Trenton
New Mexico	NM	Santa Fe
Nevada	NV	Carson City
New York	NY	Albany
Ohio	OH	Columbus
Oklahoma	OK	Oklahoma City

State	Postal Abbreviation	Capital
Oregon	OR	Salem
Pennsylvania	PA	Harrisburg
Rhode Island	RI	Providence
South Carolina	SC	Columbia
South Dakota	SD	Pierre
Tennessee	TN	Nashville
Texas	TX	Austin
Utah	UT	Salt Lake City
Vermont	VT	Montpelier
Virginia	VA	Richmond
Washington	WA	Olympia
Wisconsin	WI	Madison
West Virginia	WV	Charleston
Wyoming	WY	Cheyenne

States (and D.C.) by Region

Eastern	States east of the Mississippi River
Western	States west of the Mississippi River
Northern	Connecticut, North Dakota, Delaware, District of Columbia, Idaho, Illinois, Indiana, Iowa, Kansas, Maine, Maryland, Massachusetts, Michigan, Minnesota, Missouri, Montana, Nebraska, New Hampshire, New Jersey, New York, North Ohio, Oregon, Pennsylvania, Rhode Island, South Dakota, Vermont, Washington, Wisconsin, Wyoming
Southern	Alabama, Arkansas, Florida, Georgia, Kentucky, Louisiana, Mississippi, North Carolina, Oklahoma, South Carolina, Tennessee, Texas, Virginia, West Virginia
Continental United States	All states except Alaska and Hawaii
East Coast	Connecticut, Delaware, District of Columbia, Florida, Georgia, Maine, Maryland, Massachusetts, New Hampshire, New Jersey, New York, North Carolina, Pennsylvania, Rhode Island, South Carolina, Vermont, Virginia
West Coast	California, Oregon, Washington
New England	Connecticut, Maine, Massachusetts, New Hampshire, Rhode Island, Vermont
Mid-Atlantic States	Delaware, District of Columbia, Maryland, New Jersey, New York, Pennsylvania
Midwest	Illinois, Indiana, Iowa, Kansas, Michigan, Minnesota, Missouri, Nebraska, North Dakota, Ohio, South Dakota, Wisconsin
Northeast	Connecticut, Delaware, District of Columbia, Maine, Maryland, Massachusetts, New Hampshire, New Jersey, New York, Pennsylvania, Rhode Island, Vermont
Northwest	Idaho, Montana, Oregon, Washington, Wyoming
Southwest	Arizona, California, Colorado, Nevada, New Mexico, and Utah

List 7.10. Common Names

Names are very important in all cultures and often have interesting stories behind them. Some surnames or family names are *toponyms*—based on the place where the family originated—for example, *Hill*. Others originated as a way to identify a father's children, as in *Williamson*. Some tell us an ancestor's occupation, for example, *Wright*. First names also have interesting meanings and histories. *Cassandra* comes to us from mythology; *Abraham*, from the Bible. Others such as *Felicity* and *Charity* are descriptors. Of course parents sometimes invent a child's first name, giving the name a unique sound or individuality.

The most common name in the world, according to a 2006 study by Yuan Yida of the Chinese Academy of Sciences Institute of Genetics and Developmental Biology, is the Chinese surname *Li*. It is also the most common last name in China, where more than 100 million people are named Li. (Visit http://www.chinapage.com/biography/lastname.html for more information about Chinese last names, including the "list of Hundred Names.") In the United States, according to census data, *Smith* is the most common family name. It is also one of the top-ranked names in other countries settled by persons of English ancestry, including the United Kingdom, Canada, Australia, and New Zealand. *Smith* references the occupation of a blacksmith and has variations in many countries and cultures worldwide, including Szmidt (Polish), Schmid and Schmitt (German), Smit and Smid (Dutch), Schmieder (Yiddish), and Smid (Slovak).

To find the rankings of more than a thousand names for the last one hundred years, go to http://www.ssa.gov/OACT/babynames. There are also many good sources for the meaning of names from around the world, including http://www.behindthename.com and http://www.babynamesworld.com

Common U.S. Family Names

1. Smith	21. Clark	41. Mitchell
2. Johnson	22. Rodriguez	42. Perez
3. Williams	23. Lewis	43. Roberts
4. Jones	24. Lee	44. Turner
5. Brown	25. Walker	45. Phillips
6. Davis	26. Hall	46. Campbell
7. Miller	27. Allen	47. Parker
8. Wilson	28. Young	48. Evans
9. Moore	29. Hernandez	49. Edwards
10. Taylor	30. King	50. Collins
11. Anderson	31. Wright	51. Stewart
12. Thomas	32. Lopez	52. Sanchez
13. Jackson	33. Hill	53. Morris
14. White	34. Scott	54. Rogers
15. Harris	35. Green	55. Reed
16. Martin	36. Adams	56. Cook
17. Thompson	37. Baker	57. Morgan
18. Garcia	38. Gonzalez	58. Bell
19. Martinez	39. Nelson	59. Murphy
20. Robinson	40. Carter	60. Bailey

61. Rivera
62. Cooper
63. Richardson
64. Cox
65. Howard
66. Ward
67. Torres
68. Peterson
69. Gray
70. Ramirez
71. James
72. Watson
73. Brooks
74. Kelly
75. Sanders
76. Price
77. Bennett
78. Wood
79. Barnes
80. Ross
81. Henderson
82. Coleman
83. Jenkins
84. Perry
85. Powell
86. Long
87. Patterson
88. Hughes
89. Flores
90. Washington
91. Butler
92. Simmons
93. Foster
94. Gonzales
95. Bryant
96. Alexander
97. Russell
98. Griffin
99. Diaz
100. Hayes

One Hundred Most Common Boys' Names as of 2006

1. Jacob
2. Michael
3. Joshua
4. Ethan
5. Matthew
6. Daniel
7. Christopher
8. Andrew
9. Anthony
10. William
11. Joseph
12. Alexander
13. David
14. Ryan
15. Noah
16. James
17. Nicholas
18. Tyler
19. Logan
20. John
21. Christian
22. Jonathan
23. Nathan
24. Benjamin
25. Samuel
26. Dylan
27. Brandon
28. Gabriel
29. Elijah
30. Aiden
31. Angel
32. Jose
33. Zachary
34. Caleb
35. Jack
36. Jackson
37. Kevin
38. Gavin
39. Mason
40. Isaiah
41. Austin
42. Evan
43. Luke
44. Aidan
45. Justin
46. Jordan
47. Robert
48. Isaac
49. Landon
50. Jayden
51. Thomas
52. Cameron
53. Connor
54. Hunter
55. Jason
56. Diego
57. Aaron
58. Owen
59. Lucas
60. Charles
61. Juan
62. Luis
63. Adrian
64. Adam
65. Julian
66. Bryan
67. Alex
68. Sean
69. Nathaniel
70. Carlos
71. Jeremiah
72. Brian
73. Hayden
74. Jesus
75. Carter
76. Sebastian
77. Eric
78. Xavier
79. Brayden
80. Kyle
81. Ian
82. Wyatt
83. Chase
84. Cole
85. Dominic
86. Tristan
87. Carson
88. Jaden
89. Miguel
90. Steven
91. Caden
92. Kaden
93. Antonio
94. Timothy
95. Henry
96. Alejandro
97. Blake
98. Liam
99. Richard
100. Devin

One Hundred Most Common
Girls' Names as of 2006

1. Emily	26. Kayla	51. Jennifer	76. Paige
2. Emma	27. Addison	52. Avery	77. Arianna
3. Madison	28. Victoria	53. Mackenzie	78. Ariana
4. Isabella	29. Jasmine	54. Zoe	79. Vanessa
5. Ava	30. Savannah	55. Riley	80. Michelle
6. Abigail	31. Julia	56. Sofia	81. Mariah
7. Olivia	32. Jessica	57. Maya	82. Amelia
8. Hannah	33. Lily	58. Kimberly	83. Melanie
9. Sophia	34. Sydney	59. Andrea	84. Mary
10. Samantha	35. Morgan	60. Megan	85. Isabelle
11. Elizabeth	36. Katherine	61. Katelyn	86. Claire
12. Ashley	37. Destiny	62. Gabrielle	87. Isabel
13. Mia	38. Lillian	63. Trinity	88. Jenna
14. Alexis	39. Alexa	64. Faith	89. Caroline
15. Sarah	40. Alexandra	65. Evelyn	90. Valeria
16. Natalie	41. Kaitlyn	66. Kylie	91. Aaliyah
17. Grace	42. Kaylee	67. Brooklyn	92. Aubrey
18. Chloe	43. Nevaeh	68. Audrey	93. Jada
19. Alyssa	44. Brooke	69. Leah	94. Natalia
20. Brianna	45. Makayla	70. Stephanie	95. Autumn
21. Ella	46. Allison	71. Madeline	96. Rebecca
22. Taylor	47. Maria	72. Sara	97. Jordan
23. Anna	48. Angelina	73. Jocelyn	98. Gianna
24. Lauren	49. Rachel	74. Nicole	99. Jayla
25. Hailey	50. Gabriella	75. Haley	100. Layla

List 7.11. International Proverbs

Proverbs, simple popularly used sayings, express a common perception or truth. Some came about due to particular events or circumstances, others reflect a cultural view of life and the human condition. Many are not meant to be taken literally, and some do not translate well into other languages. *Paremiology,* the study of proverbs, is a hobby for many and dates back at least as far as Aristotle. Many proverbs have been around hundreds of years and have a form in several languages and cultures.

Studying proverbs is an effective way for ESL/ELL students to share their cultural backgrounds and find ideas that are common across cultures. International proverbs make interesting content for a class bulletin board, for essay writing, for panel discussions, and for student presentations. Here is a *paremiography*—collection of proverbs—from around the globe.

A bird in the hand is worth two in a bush. (English)
A book is like a garden carried in the pocket. (Arabian)
A broken hand works, but not a broken heart. (Persian)
A closed mouth catches no flies. (Italian)
A courtyard common to all will be swept by none. (Chinese)
A friend in need is a friend indeed. (English)
A friend's eye is a good mirror. (Irish)
A healthy man is a successful man. (French)
A hedge between keeps friendship green. (French)
A leaky house may fool the sun, but it can't fool the rain. (Haitian)
A little too late is much too late. (German)
A lock is better than suspicion. (Irish)
A man does not seek his luck, luck seeks its man. (Turkish)
A man is not honest simply because he never had a chance to steal. (Yiddish)
A man should live if only to satisfy his curiosity. (Yiddish)
A new broom sweeps clean, but the old brush knows all the corners. (Irish)
A penny saved is a penny gained. (Scottish)
A promise is a cloud; fulfillment is rain. (Saudi Arabian)
A rumor goes in one ear and out many mouths. (Chinese)
A silent mouth is melodious. (Irish)
A son is a son till he gets him a wife, but a daughter's a daughter all of her life.
   (American)
A throne is only a bench covered with velvet. (French)
A trout in the pot is better than a salmon in the sea. (Irish)
After all is said and done, more is said than done. (American)
All is well that ends well. (American)
An enemy will agree, but a friend will argue. (Russian)
An hour of play discovers more than a year of conversation. (Portuguese)
As we live, so we learn. (Yiddish)
Begin to weave and God will give the thread. (German)
Better a red face than a black heart. (Portuguese)
Better late than never, but better never late. (American)
Better the devil you know than the devil you don't know. (English)
Better to light a candle than to curse the darkness. (Chinese)

Blood is thicker than water. (English)

Do not use a hatchet to remove a fly from your friend's forehead. (Chinese)

Don't bargain for fish that are still in the water. (Indian)

Don't insult the alligator until you've crossed the river. (Haitian)

Don't show me the palm tree, show me the dates. (Afghani)

Every cloud has a silver lining. (English)

Every garden may have some weeds. (English)

Fall seven times, stand up eight. (Japanese)

Flatterers, like cats, lick and then scratch. (German)

Fool me once, shame on you; fool me twice, shame on me. (Italian)

Friends are lost by calling often and calling seldom. (French)

God grant me a good sword and no use for it. (Polish)

Half a loaf is better than none. (American)

Haste makes waste. (American)

He that plants thorns must never expect to gather roses. (English)

He who gets a name for early rising can stay in bed until midday. (Irish)

He who has health has hope, and he who has hope has everything. (Arabian)

Hygiene is two-thirds of health. (Lebanese)

If a man be great, even his dog will wear a proud look. (Japanese)

If someone sweats for you, you change his shirt. (Haitian)

If you are planning for a year, sow rice; if you are planning for a decade, plant trees; if you are planning for a lifetime, educate people. (Chinese)

If you do not sow in the spring you will not reap in the autumn. (Irish)

If you make a habit of buying things you don't need, you will soon be selling things you do. (Filipino)

It is better to conceal one's knowledge than to reveal one's ignorance. (Spanish)

Keep a green tree in your heart and perhaps a singing bird will come. (Chinese)

Lower your voice and strengthen your argument. (Lebanese)

Many a friend was lost through a joke, but none was ever gained so. (Czech)

Men count up the faults of those who keep them waiting. (French)

Never ask God to give you anything; ask Him to put you where things are. (Mexico)

Never cut what can be untied. (Portuguese)

No matter how fast the poplar grows, it will never reach heaven. (Lebanese)

No time like the present. (English)

Nobody has ever bet enough on a winning horse. (American)

Nothing is as burdensome as a secret. (French)

Nothing is impossible to a willing heart. (American)

One cannot shoe a running horse. (Dutch)

One generation plants the trees, another gets the shade. (Chinese)

One of these days is none of these days. (English)

Only stretch your foot to the length of your blanket. (Afghani)

Put silk on a goat and it's still a goat. (Irish)

Success and rest don't sleep together. (Russian)

Talk does not cook rice. (Chinese)

The best armor is to keep out of range. (Italian)

The cobra will bite you whether you call it cobra or Mr. Cobra. (Indian)

The pencil of God has no eraser. (Haitian)

The rattan basket criticizes the palm leaf basket, but both are full of holes. (Filipino)

The work praises the man. (Irish)

There are twenty-five uncaught sparrows for a penny. (Afghani)

There is no shame in not knowing; the shame lies in not finding out. (Russian)

Time spent laughing is time spent with the gods. (Japanese)

Under capitalism man exploits man; under socialism the reverse is true. (Polish)

Vision without action is a daydream; action without vision is a nightmare. (Japanese)

What you see in yourself is what you see in the world. (Afghani)

When you drink the water, think of the well. (Finnish)

You can bring a horse to water but you cannot make him drink. (American)

You can't see the whole sky through a bamboo tube. (Japanese)

You'll never plow a field by turning it over in your mind. (Irish)

List 7.12. *Dichos:* Spanish Proverbs

Proverbs of all languages express a broad range of cultural ideas and wisdom. Most are not meant to be taken literally. Proverbs often have distinctive rhythms or rhymes that make them easy to remember. Many familiar English sayings have Spanish counterparts that are almost identical. Other Spanish *dichos* convey similar sentiments but use phrasing and words that express differences in culture as well.

The following *dichos* include some that are very similar to U.S. English proverbs and some that are unique to the Spanish language. Use them as part of your class discussion of how proverbs convey wisdom and culture.

Dichos	Meaning
Más vale tarde que nunca.	Better late than never.
Quien mucho duerme, poco aprende.	If you sleep much, you learn little.
No nació quien erró.	No one has been born who has not erred.
Los pájaros de la misma pluma vuelan juntos.	Birds of the same feather fly together.
En boca cerrada, no entran moscas.	In a closed mouth, no flies will enter.
El trabajo compartido es más llevadero.	Burdens shared are lighter.
Cuanto mas estudio, tanto más sabe.	The more you study, the more you know.
Consejo no pedido, consejo mal oido.	Unsolicited advice is poorly heard.
Del dicho al hecho, hay mucho trecho.	Between the word and the deed, there is a great gulf.
Donde hay gana, hay maña.	Where there's the desire, there's the ability.
El mal escribano le echa la culpa al la pluma.	The poor writer blames the pen.
Comida hecha, compania deshecha.	Food done, friends undone.
La salud es la mayor riqueza.	Health is better than wealth.
Con el tiempo y la paciencia se adquiere al ciencia.	With time and patience comes knowledge.
Donde hay humo, hay calor.	Where there's smoke, there's fire.
El que mucho habla, mucho yerra.	He who speaks much errs much.
En las malas se conocen a los amigos.	You can tell who your friends are in a time of trouble.
La palabra es plata, el silencio oro.	The word is silver, silence gold.
El amor todo lo puede.	Love will find a way.
Por el árbol se conoce el fruto.	By the tree the fruit is known.
De sabio poeta y loco, todos tenemos un poco.	We are all poets and fools sometime.
La verdad a medias es mentira verdadera.	Half the truth is often a whole lie.
El remedio puede ser peor que la enfermedad.	Sometimes the remedy is worse than the disease.
Querer es poder.	To want to is to be able to.
Mejor solo que mal acompañado.	Better alone than in poor company.
El dinero llama al dinero.	Money attracts money.

Dichos	Meaning
Dime con quien andas, y te dire quien eres.	Tell me who you walk with and you tell me who you are.
El que algo quiere, algo le cuesta.	Everything has its cost.
Los genios pensamos iqual.	Great minds think alike.
Las palabras se las lleva el viento.	Words fly on the wind.
Excusa no pedida, la culpa manifiesta.	He who excuses himself accuses himself.
Quien quiera saber, que compre un viejo.	If you seek wisdom, ask an old man.
La ira es locura, el tiempo que dura.	Anger is a short-term madness.
El tiempo lo cura todo.	Time heals all things.
Amigo y vino, el mas antiguo.	Friends and wine improve with age.
Hay mas felicidad en dar que en recibir.	It is more blessed to give than to receive.
La risa es el major remedio.	Laughter is the best medicine.
Quien compra ha de tener cien ojos; a quien vende le basta uno solo.	The buyer needs a hundred eyes, the seller only one.
Ha ropa tendida.	Walls have ears.
A diario una manzana es cosa sana.	An apple a day is the healthy way.
A falta de pan, buenas son las tortas.	If there's no bread, the cake will do.
A palabras necias, oidos sordos.	Let foolish words fall on deaf ears.
Persevera y triunfaras.	Perseverance leads to triumph.
¡Que pequeno es el mundo!	It's a small world!
Lo major es ser franco.	Honesty is the best policy.

List 7.13. Idioms Across Five Languages

Idioms with similar meanings can be found in many languages. Learning equivalent idioms in English helps students express themselves using familiar ideas and informal language. Here are some idioms that students may know in their first language.

English	Spanish	French	German	Chinese
all right	bien	c'est bien	zufreiden sein	ānrán wúyàng
at once	enseguida	tout de suit	gleich	lìkè
be in the way	estorbar	être de trop	im Wege sein	fáng ài
big deal	gran cosa	grande chose	grosse Sache	míng-ren
call up	llamar	téléphoner	anrufen	dǎ diàn-huà
catch on	darse cuenta	y être	berstehen	líjiě
cross out	tachar	barrer	ausstreichen	huà héngxiàn chuānguò
do over	rehacer	refaire	wiederholen	zuò zài
dream up	soñar	rêver	aufdenken	píngkōng xiǎngchū
drop out	dejar de asistir	quitter	verlassen	tuìchū
figure out	razonar	calculer	herausfinden	líjiě
fill out	llenar	remplir	ausfullen	biàndà
fool around	perder el tiempo	perdre son temps	Unsinn machen	yóudàng
get better	mejorar	aller mieux	besser werden	fùyuán
get off	apearse	descendre	aussteigen	xià
get on	montarse	monter	einsteigen	zài chuán shàng
get sick	enfermarse	tomber malade	krank werden	gǎn-mào
get up	levantarse	se lever	aufstehen	qǐlai
hand in	presentar	remettre	einreichen	yíjiāo
knock it off	dejar de	cessar immédiatemente	aufhoren	tíngzhǐ
let go of	soltar	lâcher	freilassen	shìfàng
lie down	acostarse	s'étendre	sich hinlegen	tǎng-xià
look at	mirar	regarder	ansehen	kàn
look for	buscar	chercher	suchen	zhǎo
make believe	pretender	prétendre	vortauschen	jiǎzhuāng
make sense	ser lógico	être logique	verstandig sein	yǒu yìyì
never mind	no importa	peu importe	schon gut	méiguānxi
on purpose	a proposito	exprès	absichtlich	gùyìde
on the whole	en general	en somme	im Allgemeinen	zǒngde lài kàn
out of order	descompuesto	ne pas fonctionner	ausser Betrieb	chū cùzhàng
over and over	repetidamente	sans cesse	immer wieder	fǎnfù
pick out	seleccionar	choiser	aussuchen	tiāo
put away	guardar	ranger	weglegen	fànghǎo
put off	aplazar	remettre	aufschienben	tuīchí

put on	ponerse	mettre	aufsetzen	chuānshàng
right away	inmediatamente	immédiatement	sofort	mǎ-shàng
run errands	hacer mandados	faire des courses	Besorgungen machen	gàn chàshi
sit down	sentarse	s'asseoir	sich hinsetzen	zuòxià
stand up	ponerse de pie	se mettre debout	aufstehen	zhàn-qi-lái
take off	quitarse	enlever	ausziehen	qǐfēi
take over	encargarse de	se charger de	ubernehmen	jiēren zhí wù
take turns	alternar	alterner	absechseln	lúnliú zuò mǒushì
talk over	discutir	discuter	besprechen	shāng liàng
think over	pensar	réfléchir	uberlegen	zǐxì kǎolù
throw away	botar	jeter	wegwerfen	làngfèidiào
tired out	exhausto	n'en pouvoir plus	ubermudet	píjuàn
try on	probarse	essayer	anprobieren	shi-chuān
try out	probar	essayer	jemanden halten fur	shi-yan
wear out	gastarse	user	abgetragen	shǐ mǒurén jīnpí-lìjìn

Section Eight

Teaching

List 8.1. ESL Standards

Standards for teaching English as a Second Language to pre-K through grade 12 students have been developed and disseminated by Teachers of English to Speakers of Other Languages (TESOL), a worldwide professional association with more than thirteen thousand members. TESOL sponsors a host of professional resources, including annual conferences, and has state affiliates. TESOL's three goals and nine standards are listed here. Visit the TESOL Web site at http://www.tesol.org to review the associated descriptors, progress indicators, and vignettes provided for grades pre-K to 3, 4 to 8, and 9 to 12.

- Goal 1: To use English to communicate in social settings

    Standard 1: Students will use English to participate in social interactions.

    Standard 2: Students will interact in, through, and with spoken and written English for personal expression and enjoyment.

    Standard 3: Students will use learning strategies to extend their communicative competence.

- Goal 2: To use English to achieve academically in all content areas

    Standard 1: Students will use English to interact in the classroom.

    Standard 2: Students will use English to obtain, process, construct, and provide subject-matter information in spoken and written form.

    Standard 3: Students will use appropriate learning strategies to construct and apply academic knowledge.

- Goal 3: To use English in socially and culturally appropriate ways

    Standard 1: Students will use the appropriate language variety, register, and genre according to audience, purpose, and setting.

    Standard 2: Students will use nonverbal communication appropriate to audience, purpose, and setting.

    Standard 3: Students will use appropriate learning strategies to extend their sociolinguistic and sociocultural competence.

List 8.2. Thematic Language Units

Language learning is facilitated when students are exposed to new vocabulary in context. Thematic language units, each focusing on its own discipline, provide a natural learning context and opportunities to integrate the same vocabulary and concepts into reading and language arts, social studies, math, science, and other subjects. The list of topics for units contains major content groups that contribute to core English vocabulary. The following example is based on *animals* and offers activities suitable for all grades and ages.

Instructional Activities in an Animal Theme Unit

Reading and Language Arts	Read nonfiction books about baby animals of all species, including books focused on a single animal (horses, cats, dogs, spiders, dinosaurs, fish, snakes, butterflies, and so on).	Vocabulary and concepts
	Read fiction about relationships between animals and their owners and about heroic animals.	Vocabulary and concepts
	View videos on both nonfiction and fiction topics.	Vocabulary, pronunciation, concepts
	Use key reading vocabulary for word study and structural analysis.	Roots, affixes
	Use animal-related vocabulary in sentences for grammar instruction.	Punctuation
	Use selections from reading-for-comprehension work.	Inferences
	Use readings to practice note-taking skills.	Study skills
	Work on Internet and library research skills to complete a Five-by-Five graphic organizer comparing five different mammals or five different species of fish.	Analysis
	Make podcasts or video spots on an animal of the student's choosing.	Presentation
Social Studies	Work on map-reading skills to plot where different animals are found.	Social studies, mapping
	Study the role of specific animals in different cultural and belief systems.	Social studies, world cultures
	Study how humans use animals for food, shelter, and producing wealth.	Social studies, economics
	Research the impact of pets on lives, culture, and the economy.	Social studies, psychology, world cultures, economics

Science	Study life cycles using the life cycle of a mammal from the readings.	Science, life cycle
	Study the habitat needs of different mammals and consider the effects of changes in the environment.	Science ecology, climates, data analysis
	Write poems about animals and their characteristics.	Language arts, poetry forms, poetry characteristics, concepts, vocabulary
	Write rap or chant about animals and their characteristics.	Language arts, rhythm and rhyme vocabulary, concepts
Math	Use animal-related vocabulary as the basis for word problems.	Math, application of computation trends
	Use research on animals and pets to develop data tables.	Math, data arrays, presentation, analysis
	Use animal data to develop charts showing frequency and change over time.	Math, data arrays, statistics trends
Art	Make animal masks, drawings, papier-mâché or clay figures, or other art projects.	Art: drawing, sculpture, painting, pottery

Ideas for Other Thematic Language Units

Civics	Divisions of government	Law and safety
	Elections and voting	Police, fire, and other services
	Municipal buildings	Officials in our city and state
Education	Levels of education	Types of schools
	Classrooms	School workers
	Subjects	Education and career links
Employment	Types of careers and jobs	Want ads—paper and online
	Resumes	Interviews
	Office life	Work routines
	Business correspondence	Applications and other forms
Family	Relationships	Names for family members
	Roles in the family	Ancestry and family trees
Food	Names of food	Names of meals
	Food preparation	Recipes
	Kitchen and table	Grocery shopping
	Nutrition	Eating out
Grooming	Getting a haircut	Cosmetics and grooming aids
	Impact of appearance	Taking care of your appearance
Health	Body parts	Illnesses, medical terms
	Medicines, pharmacy terms	Doctors, dentists, and health workers
	Medical tests and procedures	Making a doctor's appointment
	Hospitals and care centers	Dealing with health emergencies
Housing	Types of housing	Reading housing ads
	Terms of lease or purchase	Understanding contracts
	Background checks	Security at home
	Addresses and mail delivery	Utilities

Measurement	Sizes	Quantities
	Distances	Measurement tools
Money	Denominations and equivalents	Banks and services
	Opening accounts	Using ATMs, debit cards, credit cards
	Applying for credit cards	Applying for loans
Numbers	Ordinal	Cardinal
	Formats: decimals, fractions, and so on	Numbers we use: phone, ID, SSN, and so on
Time	Measuring time	Days of the week
	Months of the year	Seasons
	Holidays	Time idioms and formula dialogues
Repairs	Tradespeople (plumber, carpenter, and so on)	Common household problems
	Tools and supplies	Shop vocabulary
	Contracts	Do-it-yourself instructions
	Electrical systems	Plumbing systems
	Heating systems	Air conditioning systems
Clothing	Places to shop	Clothing and accessories
	Caring for clothing	Fabrics and styles
	Seasonal clothing	Shopping idioms
Social	Greetings	Making introductions
	Terms of respect	Etiquette
	Hospitality and visiting	Gestures
	Entertainment and leisure	Music, MP3s, recording artists, radio
	Video, movies, TV	Libraries, museums, galleries
	Newspapers, magazines, books	Games
	Friendship and dating	Using the phone
	Giving and receiving gifts	Social letter writing, sending cards
Sports and Hobbies	Names of sports	Sports equipment and uniforms
	Where sports are played	Sporting events
	Sports teams and activities	Names of hobbies
	Hobby equipment and supplies	Hobby associations, events
	Specialized sports vocabulary	Sport-related idioms and dialogues
	Hobby-related vocabulary	Hobby-related idioms and dialogues
Transportation	Modes of travel	Asking for directions
	Reading a map, directions	Hotels and other places to stay
	States and capitals, place names	Driving a car
	Highway signs and safety	Getting a driver's license
	Train and bus vocabulary	Reading train and bus schedules
	Buying train and bus tickets	Plane and ship vocabulary
	Reading plane and ship timetables	Buying plane and ship tickets
	Passports, visas, customs	Consulates and other government offices
	Subways	Bicycles and other transportation
Weather	Weather conditions	Seasonal weather
	Weather-related activities	Seasonal clothing, shelter issues
	Weather idioms and dialogues	Weather reports

List 8.3. Word Walls

Word walls (WWs)—lists of words or other information organized and displayed in the classroom—are mainstay teaching and learning tools for ESL/ELLs as well as general education teachers. They are indispensable aids for building vocabulary. They are also gentle, omnipresent memory boosters for students learning many new words and concepts at the same time. Develop WWs with your class over the school year and teach students how to use them to gain independence in speaking, reading, and writing English. WWs can be used in any grade and at any level.

Word walls support learning by

1. Showing the alphabetic principle
2. Providing exemplars for letter-sound relationships
3. Providing visual scaffolding for new words
4. Supporting students' independent writing efforts
5. Adding visual memory elements to word study and recall
6. Enabling analogy strategies for word recognition
7. Involving students in selecting words for study
8. Recording progress in word mastery through the year

To Construct a Word Wall

Post the letters of the alphabet on a large wall, leaving space beneath each letter. As students learn key vocabulary, write the words with bold black marker and cut them out to highlight their unique visual outlines. Back the words with colored paper to make them easier to view and distinguish. Post each word under the alphabet letter with which it begins. Once students are familiar with the WW, ask them which words from their lessons should be part of the WW; and after preparing the word for posting, ask them where the new word should be placed.

Other ways to arrange words on a WW include posting them alphabetically under a key word or using a content-related organizational scheme—for example, listing quantity words in size order.

Types of Word Walls

There are three types of word walls. The first type supports *speaking, reading,* and *writing* instruction; the second type helps build *content vocabulary;* and the third type provides *structure and process reminders.* Each type should be displayed separately. As you develop each type with your class, explain their different purposes and how they are used.

Speaking, Reading, and Writing Instruction

Begin a WW with students' first names or the words for items in the classroom. Use these familiar words to teach sound-letter relationships as well as to review the words as sight vocabulary. Add about five or more words each week that students have encountered in other subjects and that can be used as examples for the direct teaching of pronunciation, decoding, and spelling skills. Work with the list daily and include choral reading of the list to build automaticity and fluency. As you teach categories of words, create a separate WW for each.

Following are suggested WWs for speaking, reading, and writing:

The most frequently used English words
Phonograms
Irregularly spelled words
Cognates
Sight words from reading texts
Words learned on field trips
Language experience chart vocabulary
Adjectives
Colors
Family relationships
School-related words
Social interactions
Polite phrases
Compound words
Suffixes and prefixes and their meanings
Root words and meanings
Words taken from student writing

Content Area Vocabulary

WWs for content area vocabulary reinforce key words in themed units and help students enrich their schema for the topic. Include words from introductory activities such as viewing a video or listening to a story, or words introduced during a lesson. Add drawings or digital photos to provide visual cues. Repeated work with the words during content area lessons, in supplemental independent reading materials, and in daily or weekly writing builds fluency as well as conceptual knowledge.

Content area vocabulary WWs are often set up on bulletin boards or three-panel display boards at learning centers around the room. Add words from any math, science, social studies, health, music, career, technology, art, or other subject content studied or encountered. Remember to start with the subject, then together with students select the key words for your WW.

Structure and Process Reminders

Structure WWs help students self-check grammar, writing, punctuation, and spelling. Process WWs are reminders of steps that need to be completed. Consider structure WWs on irregularly spelled words, spelling rules, capitalization rules, punctuation examples, irregular plurals, conjugation of *be*, comparison of adjectives, phrasal verbs, noun-verb agreement, and pronouns. Consider process WWs on decoding a word, writing a letter, solving a problem, and using an online dictionary.

List 8.4. Conversation Starters

Making a statement or asking a question in a second language is not easy, but carrying on a conversation is more difficult because it requires listening, understanding, thinking, and production of words in the second language—all within seconds. An individual can control the processing and production time for reading and writing responses and can also look up unknown words in a dictionary and edit responses before making them public. Not so in conversations and discussions: these more difficult tasks require daily practice to develop needed skills and strengthen students' confidence and willingness to participate.

Plan daily conversation time around recently acquired vocabulary, school or holiday events, current affairs, or other natural topics. ESL/ELLs need to express themselves and practice newly acquired vocabulary. Opportunities to talk to one another about ordinary things and shared experiences meets this need. Avoid single-question assignments and those without goals. Such assignments fizzle out quickly.

Pair students rather than ask them to find a partner. Students selected last feel less confident; if you assign partners, everyone starts on an equal footing. Change pairs frequently to broaden linguistic experiences. There are several ways to pair students for conversation:

Have them pick an A or B card from a box, then partner the first A with the first B, and so forth.

Have them pick numbers from a box and then partner the two ones, the two twos, and so forth.

Call one name from the back-left side of the room, the other from the front-right side.

Have students in row one partner with students in row three, and so forth.

Assign partners from a list you read or post.

Devise other ways to pair students appropriately in terms of their age and language levels.

The following conversation starters introduce a topic and assign conversation goals for speakers A and B. If more than two persons are part of the group, double up on A or B goals.

Getting to School

A and B have the same goals. They tell each other how they get to school and ESL class—whether they walk, someone drives them in a car, they take a bus, and so on. They tell the names of the streets, what time they leave home, how long it takes, whether there is much traffic. They should be ready to tell the class whether their trips to school are similar or different and why they think so. They should also be ready to figure out who has the longest trip.

Classroom

A and B have different goals. A looks around the room and picks something out, then gives clues to B. A gives up to five clues. If B does not get it after five clues, then A wins. The winner picks an object and gives clues. Continue until one partner has six wins.

Family

A and B have different goals. A draws a picture with stick figures about B's family. To do this activity, A and B must discuss the number of people in the family, their ages, their relationships, and so on. If time permits, the partners may reverse roles and have B draw A's family according to A's description and answers to B's questions.

Pets

A and B have the same goals. A asks B questions to find out about the "best" pet that belongs to someone B knows. What kind of animal is it? Who has it? What does it look like? Why is it "best?" Where is it kept? What needs to be done to take care of it? At the end, each partner tells a little about the pet they chose as "best" and the class votes on the most interesting of the "best" pets presented by the pairs.

Birthday Cards

The teacher explains the use of birthday cards in the United States, then organizes the class into partners. A and B have the same goals: to talk about birthday cards and how their American use is the same or different from birthday greetings in their native countries. Would they like to give and receive birthday cards? Why or why not? What other ways do they celebrate friends' birthdays? At the end they should be ready to contribute to a brainstorm session on ways to celebrate class birthdays.

Sports

A and B have the same goals. They begin by picking a sport together and identifying ten things everyone should know about it. Next they practice reporting the list by taking turns adding and explaining one idea each. Finally they share the ten things with the class. If others picked the same sport, students must be ready to add from their list to the others' any of the information that is not reported.

Review

A takes the role of teacher, B takes the role of student. The "teacher" poses questions about a recently studied topic (weather, colors, numbers, money, safety, and so on) and the "student" answers. If the "student" doesn't know the answer, the "teacher" gives clues. After three clues, if the student-partner doesn't know the answer, the teacher-partner provides it. After seven minutes the pair switches roles and starts a new topic. Topics can be written on cards from which the "student" or "teacher" picks.

How Was Your Weekend?

A and B have the same goal. On Monday morning, students interview one another about what they did over the weekend. After seven minutes they report on what their partner did. The teacher makes notes about the activities and asks follow-up questions, including additional theme-related vocabulary.

Picture That!

A and B are competing. Each pair receives a picture with lots of details, for example, a giraffe at a zoo and part of its habitat. A and B take turns telling one another about the picture. They get one point for each sentence they say about a different aspect of the picture. For example, if A says, "It is at the zoo. This is a giraffe. It has spots. The grass is green. His neck is long," A earns five points. Ten to twelve minutes are allowed for the exercise.

Lost and Found

A and B have the same goal. The students discuss what to do if they lose their book, their wallet, their dog. After ten minutes the class discusses steps to take in each case. These steps are then written on newsprint and posted. One "lost" scenario is used for young students or beginners. High schoolers and adults can compare options.

Favorite TV Show

A and B have the same goal. The pairs discuss their favorite and least favorite TV shows and list the reasons they like or dislike them. At the end of the conversation, the students report on the data they have collected (tallied).

I Really Like That!

A and B have the same goal. The pairs discuss their favorite (or best) of a suggested topic, giving several reasons. Each partner questions the other about their choice to find out what attributes make it a favorite. At the end of the conversation, the class discusses which characteristics students felt were most important in picking a favorite (or best) from among many. This exercise can be done every week using topics as diverse as TV stars, backpacks, music, beverages, vegetables, zoo animals, dinosaurs, beaches, radio stations, malls, cars, and terrain.

List 8.5. Discussion Starters

Discussions, like conversation, are verbal interactions among two or more individuals. Common synonyms for *conversation—chat, talk,* and *exchange—*convey informality, personal, and viewpoint perspectives, while synonyms for *discussion—debate, deliberation,* and *considerations—*refer to more formal, thoughtful, and fact-based content. The art of discussion involves sharing facts, drawing conclusions, evaluating ideas, arguing a point, persuading others, choosing solutions, ranking options, and developing consensus. Academic and job success require effective discussion skills.

Once ESL/ELL students show some comfort with conversation and speaking in class, plan frequent paired, small-group, and whole-class discussions that deal with content area material. Use supported strategies for most of the content learning, but be sure that the answers to questions or the graphic organizers cannot be found simply by matching text or without discussion. Discussions should give students opportunities to work together to achieve a single goal, to work in opposition and contrast their answers, and to work to influence one another.

How Happy?

Introduce the idea of connotations for synonyms and give examples of the "strength"—a little to a lot—of a characteristic conveyed (for example: *giggle, laugh, guffaw*). Divide students into pairs or small groups. Give each group a key word and have them brainstorm three or more synonyms for their word. Next, have students cut out pictures (or download them from graphics files) that show the differences among the synonyms, and mount them on posters with labels. Have each team present their work to the class and explain the reasons they picked each graphic or photo. Note: it is helpful to review the list informally and provide guidance, if needed, about connotations so that the student presentations assist peers in gaining accurate knowledge of American usage.

Chapter Review

Assign pairs of students to work cooperatively on answers to end-of-chapter review questions. Have one student write out the answers to the even-numbered questions while the other student answers the odd-numbered questions. On the following day, using their completed lists, have the students quiz each other and provide copies of their answers to each other for independent study before a test.

Flow Chart

Have students work in pairs to design a flowchart showing the steps in a process they have studied. Examples of topics include getting a driver's license, cell division, how plants get water, making paper, the water cycle, making a peanut butter and jelly sandwich, getting dressed, making a mask, and making a salad.

Party Planning

As part of a unit on money and shopping, have small groups of students plan a budget for a sports or holiday-related party. Use grocery store circulars (paper or online) for prices, and give groups a budget limit. Have them include food, decorations, prizes, and entertainment in their plans and budgets. Then have the groups present their themed plans to the whole class to vote on which party they'd most like to attend.

Adding Up Ads

As part of a career awareness unit, have students working in pairs read newspaper or online help-wanted ads to identify five jobs that require mathematical knowledge and skills. Have them list the kinds of jobs, the tasks that are likely part of the jobs, and the type of math knowledge they would need. Look up average salaries for the jobs online. Have students present their findings to the whole class and discuss the range of jobs and tasks that are math related as well as the range of compensation for those who work in these jobs.

Story Map

Have pairs of students read the same short story and work together to create a story map using a drawing or visual concept application or markers and poster board. Then have the pairs present their work to the class, identifying the problem or central issue and describing how it is resolved.

Rubrics

Plan a whole-class discussion on rubrics and facilitate the brainstorming and discussion of criteria that will be used to evaluate the next assignment. Use questions to guide students both to explain and to persuade others, as well as to state beliefs and values.

Scruples

Provide a short scenario that demonstrates an ethical or legal problem. It can be presented either orally or in written form. Have small groups or pairs discuss the issue and propose one or more solutions and their rationale. For example:

- Two boys are fighting and an adult driving by sees them. Should the adult "interfere" and stop the fighting?
- A woman with three young children is leaving a food store. The woman's purse is open and a $20 bill falls out. You notice it on the ground. Is it okay to pick it up and keep it if she doesn't?
- You are playing a game with a friend when his phone rings. As he gets up to answer the phone, his game piece accidentally moves backward on the board, giving you an advantage. What should you do when he returns?
- Three people are in a car crash. They are in separate cars and are unrelated. One is a child, one is a middle-aged single person, and one is an old person. The ambulance arrives at the scene. Who should the paramedics check first?

News at Five

Have students write scripts for TV-style talk shows with three brief segments planned per week and alternating roles. Take the topics from online news outlets and include an international, national, and local story. Videotape the shows and, after airing them for the class, archive them on the class Web site.

Comic Strips

As part of a unit on the wisdom of proverbs, have pairs of students write and illustrate a comic strip that shows the wisdom of the proverb. The projects can be mounted and displayed in public spaces such as the hallway outside the classroom, or they can be included on the class Web site.

Campaign Press

Using any issue for which there are two or more well-defined positions, have students take a side and create campaign slogans, posters, and logos to persuade the rest of the class or school to their viewpoint. This activity can also be used to mount a one-sided campaign, such as to urge fuel conservation, healthy eating habits, exercise, savings accounts, seatbelt use, and so on. Have the students research the topic to pick key ideas and suitable design elements. The projects can be displayed around the school.

Word Problems

Have students in pairs develop word problems that fit a set of math equations. The students can be instructed to tailor their problems to different interest groups in order to focus on related vocabulary sets. The use of a set of equations and focused vocabulary requires more interaction than leaving the math and vocabulary up to the students. This activity can review both language and math at the same time.

Homework Helpers

Assign students to be study buddies. Have each buddy read and summarize the key ideas of a section of a chapter. Then have the students take turns presenting mini-lessons on their sections and give handouts to their classmates. Upload the written work to a shared workspace (or e-mail it to a single contact) and incorporate it into a study guide. For each section, have students also propose one or more quiz questions.

Debate

Brainstorm or assign students a debate topic. Place cards marked *affirmative* or *negative* in a box and have each student select a card to determine which side they will present during the debate. To be successful, students will also need to be familiar with the key arguments of the other side so they can refute them. After individual research is well under way (a few days or a week in most cases), have students on the same side form teams of two, three, or four to prepare the best arguments and a strategy for winning the debate. On the day of the debate, have each side alternate its presentation of the following: an introduction to the issue, key points in general, data from external sources (published, surveys, testimonials solicited, and so on), refutation of opponents' key points and data, and concluding remarks. Large teams can have each team member take one section; small teams can alternate roles. Another class or teacher can judge the debate. If more than one topic is assigned, the teams not involved in the first debate topic can judge the debate.

Legacy Newsletter

Have the whole class participate in planning a newsletter, including what articles should be included, the name of the newsletter, and who should write, edit, and lay out the newsletter. If this exercise is used near the end of the school year, the newsletter can be directed to students coming into the course and shared at the midpoint of the year. This timing allows current students to get advice from previous students, to see an exemplar of a newsletter as a prototype to the one they will produce, and to develop sufficient English skills to read and understand the newsletter. Some topics in legacy newsletters have included information about where to shop, favorite restaurants, online sites of interest, local places of interest to visit, and how to contact helpful community agencies.

Soap Opera

Have students write an episode of a soap opera about a current event, keeping the dialogue and action true to the characters from week to week. Each segment should take not more than six minutes for a dramatic reading.

Historical Times

As part of a history program, assign students to identify important ideas, influential people, and key events as they read each chapter. Discuss and vote on the most essential ideas, people, and events for each period and add them to a timeline posted across a wall of the classroom.

Characters Welcome

As a review of literature or reading, have students work in pairs to complete a five-by-five data organizer with information related to issues of interest. For example, have students work together to identify setting, theme, plot, characters, and turning point for five stories. The groups then compare entries for each element and defend their choices.

Video Director

Have students work in pairs with a video camera (a digital camera works if camcorders are not available) to capture images that represent ideas and make a video or photo dictionary. For example, students can identify different kinds of trees and capture images, including close-ups, of tree bark and leaves, and then do a voice-over identifying each variety.

List 8.6. Helping Students with Audience Recognition

Communication takes two—a speaker and a listener, or a writer and a reader. Effective communication, whether spoken or written, means that the audience—the listeners or readers—understands the message. To help listeners and readers get the message, we speak and write with the audience in mind, changing the level of formality, explicitness, and vocabulary to suit the audience and the circumstances. When we adapt the message to different audiences, we are changing the *register* of the language. Before speaking or writing, consider the following:

- The age of the audience
- Your social relationship
- Their knowledge of the subject
- The subject itself
- The purpose of the communication

Age of Audience

Children's knowledge of language and of the world is limited, and their ability to deal with complicated information is not well developed. When speaking or writing to children, use a narrative style with common words and basic sentence structures. Keep the message simple and brief.

An older, more mature audience has a full command of language and a broad understanding of the world. Adults can understand complex information if it is clearly presented. When communicating with adults, use explicit vocabulary. Vary sentence structure, including both simple and complex sentences. The message may draw on commonly known or experienced phenomena; it may be detailed. Lengthy messages must be organized in order to be easily understood.

Social Relationship

There are many types of social relationships, including those between parents and children, among family members, between teachers and students, between an employer and employees, between individuals and those in authority, between individuals and those in religious or other respected positions, among friends, between spouses, between strangers, and between older and younger persons.

The relationship between the speaker and listener, or writer and reader, affects several aspects of the communication. It determines the level of respect that needs to be conveyed, and the degree of familiarity and shared experiences that can be relied on. These factors determine the greeting, tone, structure, vocabulary, level of detail or completeness, appropriateness of slang or jargon, and suitability of personal referents.

Knowledge of Subject

Estimate how much the audience knows about the subject by considering their age and education, their employment, and their social status. Sometimes personal background, such as where they grew up or their ethnicity, will help the speaker estimate the audience's level of knowledge of a subject. That knowledge will determine the level of detail and explanation that are necessary, as well as the type of vocabulary that is suitable.

Subject Matter

Subject matter covers a range from common to uncommon, serious to humorous, technical to general, scientific to affective, and so on. Subject factors will help determine what vocabulary, tone, and level of detail to use.

Purpose of Communication

Communication has a purpose: to tell a story, to ask a question, to give directions, to share a joke, to make a request, to exhort, to show affection, and so on. The purpose affects the tone, vocabulary, and structures.

Audience Errors

The audience errors of nonnative speakers of English are often the result of cultural transfer or language instruction. When students transfer the rules for registers from their native language and culture to American English, the results may be inappropriate. For example, what might be perfectly acceptable for a target audience in Spain may be too formal, too flowery, and too indirect in the United States.

Language instruction also plays a part in some students' audience errors. For example, when ESL instruction focuses heavily on conversational elements, students are left without knowledge of more formal and academic vocabulary and grammar structures. When language instruction is focused on "book" work—grammar, academic vocabulary, and reading—students are left with little knowledge of colloquial expressions, idiomatic usage, and informal grammatical constructions.

Some activities that help students develop a proper audience sense include role-playing, rewriting dialogue or other material to suit different audiences, and comparing written and spoken samples addressed to different groups.

List 8.7. Activities for Developing Auditory Skills

Sound Flash

Ask students to listen carefully to the beginning sound of the word you are about to say, then to listen to the beginning sounds of other words. Have students hold up either a *yes* or *no* response flashcard after each word to show whether it has the same beginning sound as the target word—for example: *dig, dad, bed, dark, dinner.* After students can recognize the target sound in the initial position, repeat the activity for the sound in the final and medial positions.

Sound Switch

Ask students to pay attention to the beginning sounds of a series of words that you will read to them. Direct them to raise their hands when they notice that you have switched to a word that begins with a different sound. Read at least four words with the same sound before introducing one with a different initial sound.

Same or Different?

Ask students to listen as you read pairs of words and to indicate whether the two words are the same or different. Students may respond orally or by holding up *same* or *different* flashcards. Train students' auditory discrimination by beginning with gross differences and working down to minimal pairs. For example: *house/hat, pin/bin.*

Imposter

Have students listen as you say groups of three words, two of which are the same, one of which differs by only one sound. Ask the students to show which word was different by holding up a flashcard with the number 1, 2, or 3 on it. For example: *pat, pit, pit* (1).

Repeat After Me

Present a target sound in isolation, then as the initial sound in a word. Have students listen and repeat the sequence. Continue the exercise with several words for each target sound. For example: /p/ *Pete,* /p/ *pet,* /p/ *pack,* /p/ *pitch.*

Rhyme Time

First, have students listen to and repeat pairs of rhyming words, then have them suggest additional words that rhyme with the pairs.

Speed Recognition Game

The object of the game is to hear the target initial sound each time it is used. Scores represent the number of times students miss the word. Zero is a perfect score. To play, announce the target sound, then read a list of twenty-five words with the target-sound words randomly interspersed. Read at a moderately fast pace. Students may make hatch marks on paper to keep track. Keep students' scores and challenge them to improve when the game is played again.

Hide and Seek

Present a target sound and groups of three words, one of which contains the target sound in the initial, medial, or final position. Ask students to indicate which word has the target sound by circling the number 1, 2, or 3 on an answer sheet. For example: /t/ *by, tie, lie* (2); /t/ *wait, wade, wake* (1).

Close Calls

Give students a worksheet of word pairs for problem contrasts. Read one of the paired words and have them circle it on the worksheet. For example: *they/day (day); then/den (then).*

Starts with

In a rapidly paced exchange, say a word aloud and have students respond with the letter used to spell the initial sound of the word. Repeat the activity for the final sounds.

Flash Spell

Give students sets of flashcards on which are printed the spellings of sounds. Direct students to hold up the card that spells the sound they hear at the beginning, end, or middle of the words you will read.

Spell/Write Bee

Read a list of words aloud and have students write them down. In each exercise, give up to thirty words to review five sound/spelling correspondences. Repeat the exercise by having individual students spell the words orally.

List 8.8. Activities for Developing Aural Skills

Pick a Pic

Direct students to listen to the word that you will say and to mark the picture on the answer sheet that shows the item named. Use words that target sounds learned and require auditory discrimination of contrasts. For example: *man/pan, hat/bat, sun/run.*

Class Keys

Direct students to listen to the directions you will give and to follow them on the answer sheet. Introduce school-related vocabulary by demonstrating each action on the chalkboard or an overhead projector screen. For example:

> Put an X....
> Underline the....
> Draw a line....
> Connect....
> Circle the....
> Fill in the space below....

Show Me a Pen

Give students sets of twelve concept cards that show pictures of words with problem contrasts—for example, *a lamp/a ramp, a lake/a rake.* Direct students to arrange the concept cards face up on the desk and ask them to point to or pick up the picture of the objects you say. Tell students to "show me a _____," filling in the names of the pictured objects.

Simon Sez

Play the children's game Simon Sez, eliminating children from the game as they make errors following the directions. Use the game to teach parts of the body, items of clothing, position words, action verbs, gesture words, and expression words.

Captions

Ask students to listen as you read a sentence, then to mark the picture on their answer sheets that matches the sentence. For example, the pictures may depict a girl petting a dog and a girl feeding a dog, and the sentences could be *Mary pet the dog* and *Mary fed the dog.*

Happy Endings

Direct students to listen as you read the beginning part of a sentence and possible endings. Tell students to indicate on their answer sheets which of the endings best completes the sentence. Provide four choices. Begin with simple sentences and one-word completers, then go to more complex sentences. Sample sentence: *Tom hit the _____.* Sample words: *chair, book, ball, key.*

What's It All About?

Direct students to listen as you read them a story. Read a brief passage of five sentences, then ask students to listen to and pick from four choices the word that best tells the topic of the passage. Have students mark the corresponding number on their answer sheets.

Van Gogh?

Tell students to follow your directions and complete a drawing. Give simple directions to focus on lines, spaces, shapes, dimensions, and position words. For example:

Draw a triangle. Draw a long line over the top of the triangle. Be sure the line and the triangle touch. What did you draw? (A see-saw.)

Draw a rectangle with a four-inch top and bottom and two-inch sides. On top of the rectangle, at the left corner, draw a one-inch-high triangle. On top of the rectangle, at the right corner, draw a line up at an angle. Under the rectangle, at the right and left corners, draw one-inch circles. What did you draw? (A baby carriage.)

What Do You Think?

Direct students to listen as you read them sentences and to mark on their answer sheets whether the sentences are true or false. Intersperse the correct sentences with sentences that are logically inconsistent. For example: *The young lettuce asked for some milk. The student drove his book home to study.*

Dictation

Use the dictation format to practice sound and symbol associations, auditory discrimination, juncture sensitivity, and aural comprehension of words and sentences.

For sounds and words: Tell students to listen as you say a sound and a word that begins with that sound, such as /p/ *pet* (listen to the word). Then have them listen a second time and write the spelling for the sound (word). Finally, have them listen a third time to check their answers.

For sentences and passages: Direct students to listen to the sentence or passage and write it verbatim. Read it three times: first, read the passage through at a moderate, conversational pace; next, read it slowly, breaking it into meaningful phrases of no more than five words each; finally, read the passage through at a moderate pace. Students should write the passage during the first two readings and check their work during the final reading.

Getting the Facts

Have students listen as you read a passage, then ask them questions about details in the passage. Answers can be multiple choice, yes/no, or short statements.

Information, Please

Read a passage aloud to the class and have the students ask you questions about the action or information in the passage. As an alternative, students can write questions about the passage.

News Report

Select a narrative passage that describes an event. Direct students to listen and fill in their answer sheets with the *who, what, where, when, why,* and *how* of the story.

List 8.9. Activities for Developing Oral Skills

Pretty Perfect Pronunciation

Present a group of words with the target phoneme in the initial position and have students repeat the words after you. Read them clearly but without exaggeration or distortion. Use of a rhythmic choral response will aid students in learning new sounds and allophones within words. Tape-record the lists of words so that students can practice them independently. Repeat the exercise with the phoneme presented in the final position, then in the medial position.

A Big Pig

Practice the pronunciation of problem phonemes using contrast pairs. Direct students to listen carefully and repeat after you as you read the pairs. For example: b/p *bade/paid, bin/pin, big/pig, bet/pet.*

Give Yourself a Hand

Teach students to recognize differences in stress by having them clap out the rhythm of their English names. Use a loud clap for the accented or stressed syllable or syllables, and a soft clap for the unaccented or unstressed syllable or syllables. For example: MA-ry, ma-RIE, ED-ward, THOM-as, JENN-i-fer, JOHN-ny.

Cadence Drills

Give students lists of words that have the same stress patterns. Model the correct stress pattern for sample words, then direct students to read them aloud in unison. Have the students repeat the list until they develop a natural cadence for reading the various stress patterns. Use single-syllable words, two-syllable words with the accent on the first syllable, two-syllable words with the accent on the second syllable, and so on.

Sentence Tunes

Model the correct stress patterns for a series of similar sentences—statements, open questions, tag questions, yes/no questions, and so forth—then have students read them aloud. Repeat the exercise until students develop a natural cadence.

Mother Goose and Company

Use limericks, nursery rhymes, and short poems to teach and provide practice in American English intonation patterns. Recite them in choral groups and individually. Use proverbs and popular song lyrics for older students.

Stressed Cloze

Give students ten written sentences, each with a blank space where a word has been deleted. Above the blank, show the stress pattern of the missing word. Use markings the students are familiar with from their texts, such as dots in descending size, or dashes and accent marks. Give three answer choices, each syntactically and semantically correct but only one matching the stress pattern. Have students choose the one that matches the pattern. For example: Put the jar in the - ' - - -.

cabinet   refrigerator   closet

Charades

Prepare a set of charades cards with active verb phrases. Ask a student to pick a card and act out the verb phrase. Have members of the class guess what the student is doing. Set a three-minute time limit per charade. Guesses should be stated in complete interrogative sentences, such as, *Are you making a bed? Are you kneading dough?* This activity can be done as a team game, with points for correct answers within the time allowed.

Puppet Theater

Have students use masks, puppets, and props to practice dialogues related to social and other situations.

Role Life

Have teacher and student or student and student take on roles and act out various scenarios from everyday situations. For example, the teacher can be a bank teller and the student a customer who wants to cash a check; or the student can be injured and ask a passerby (another student) for directions to a hospital or help finding a doctor.

Show and Tell

Ask students to bring something into class and give a brief (three-minute) oral presentation about it. Suggest that students select items related to hobbies or culture. Preparation should include the learning of appropriate vocabulary, and consideration of how to present new material to the class. Visual aids (charts, demonstrations, pantomimes, and so on) may be helpful.

Ms. Manners

Have pairs of students pick a card at random from a set of concept cards that show people engaged in situations that normally require standard dialogue. Then have them act out the scenes in front of the class. Give the students a few minutes to organize and rehearse. Use this exercise to review vocabulary, develop fluency, and practice social skills.

Simon Sez

Use this children's game to review vocabulary, gestures, imperative structures, and many active verbs. Select a student to be Simon. The rest of the students are to follow Simon's directions only when they are preceded by the statement "Simon sez." Direct them to use words from a specific category, such as body parts, emotion words, or actions.

Take a Hike

Use this word game to develop fluency. The game requires students to chain nouns alphabetically. To begin, say, "I'm going to take a hike and I'm taking an [A word]. The next person says, "I'm going to take a hike and I'm taking a [B word]," and so on, until someone is unable to think of an appropriate word in alphabetical sequence. To help keep things going while students' vocabularies are still limited, supply a word when they cannot. The pace of the game should be brisk.

Tie One On

Use this word game to review and reinforce vocabulary in a specific category, such as food or sports. Using the food category, begin by having one student say a food word (such as *cake*), then have a second student say another word from the same category (such as *hot dogs*), followed by a third student saying another food word (such as *cheese*), and so on, until a student cannot think of a food word or makes a mistake. The next student begins the cycle again by announcing the new category and first word. The game should be played at a fast pace.

Tennis-Elbow-Foot

This word game practices fluency and association. To begin, have one student say a word, a second student say a related word, a third student say a word related to the second word, and so on until the student next in turn cannot think of a related word or makes a mistake. The words in a cycle must be related but do not have to be from the same category. For example: *knit, weave, basket, ball, bat, cave, mountain, Alps, Europe.* The game should be played briskly.

Telephone Chain

Use this children's game to encourage students to improve their pronunciation skills. To play, a message is whispered from one person to the next through a chain of ten persons. The tenth person repeats the message aloud. Teams can compete to see which one gets the message through with the least "interference."

Take Two

Divide the class into small groups. Select one person in each group to be the director. The director directs groups of two to four students in acting out written skits using stage directions and directions for movement, gesture, tone, attitude, characterization, and so on. Have the groups put on the skits for one another.

Twenty Questions

Select photographs or drawings of nouns that are in the students' vocabulary. Have a student pick one of the photographs without showing it to the class. Then have members of the class take turns asking questions about the item—for example: *Is it bigger than a book? Is there one in this room? Is it expensive?* The student must answer yes or no. The questioning continues until someone can guess the item or the class has reached twenty questions. This exercise develops fluency, vocabulary, grammar, and listening comprehension.

Salesmanship

Have students select a product or service and "sell" it to the class. Have them create poster ads, charts comparing their product with the competition, and a sales pitch. Have them make their sales presentations to the rest of the class.

Headline News

Divide the class into three-person reporting teams. Have one team each week (more often if your schedule permits) prepare a five- to seven-minute news feature on an approved topic. Focus on issues in independent living such as employment, banking, insurance, health issues, or social services. Have the team members meet and work out an outline of the topic, decide on the distribution of research work, research and write assigned parts, and edit one another's work. Have the team present its report orally. The use of graphs and other visual aids should be encouraged.

Talk Show

Have students prepare background information on a given current events topic. Have one student act as the talk show host and lead a panel discussion and question-and-answer period. Select four students for the panel and have each give a brief prepared presentation. Have the rest of the class participate in the question-and-answer session as the audience. If possible, videotape the show and share it with other classes. To prepare for the activity, show the class a taped TV talk show and focus students' attention on format, personal interactions, and vocabulary used.

Ask Me Again

Do a rapid oral drill in which each student is asked a different question but using the same structure. For each question type, give one or two model questions and answers before asking students to respond. Ask questions that have these types of responses: yes or no, yes or no with a restatement, yes or no with a counterstatement, yes or no with a partial statement, yes or no with a synonymous statement, a short answer (one word or phrase), or a complete sentence.

Backing Up

Practice intonation patterns by using a backward buildup drill. A backward buildup begins with the last word in a sentence; then, in each repetition, the preceding word is added. This method maintains the correct intonation pattern throughout the multiple repetitions. For example: *John got an A on the test today.*

> today.
> test today.
> on the test today.
> an A on the test today.
> got an A on the test today.
> John got an A on the test today.

Changing Your Tune

Divide the class into groups of three and present a situation. Have the first group role-play the situation as originally stated. For the second group, change the context and have them alter their register, manner, and so on while preserving the storyline. Change the context for each group. Example situations: asking one's brother for a loan, asking a banker for a loan, asking one's father for a loan, asking a stranger on the street for a loan.

TV Times

Send for the transcript of one of the class's favorite television sitcoms and rehearse the lines of the show with a cast selected from the class. Present a reading of the show to the class.

Exhausting Your Options

This exercise should be done as a game. Have all of the students stand. Then ask the first student a question, such as, *Where did you go yesterday?* After the student answers, repeat the question for the next student, and so on, continuing until a student cannot respond with a new answer and sits down. Then change the question and continue to play until only one student remains and is declared the winner.

Between the Lines

Have students listen to a taped dialogue. Ask the students questions that go beyond the literal meaning of the conversation. For example: *Why did Mary react the way she did when Tom told her what happened? How do you think Mary felt? What was Tom trying to do? Did Tom do the right thing? How would you have handled the problem?*

Career Plans

Have students, one at a time, tell the class what they want to do on their first (or next) job. They should identify the type of work, say something about what it entails, and explain why they want to do it. They should also tell what skills are needed to do the job and how they plan to prepare for it if they don't already have the skills.

List 8.10. Activities for Grammar Instruction

Sentence Flips

Select two sets of concept cards—nouns and active verbs. Place the two sets face up and side-by-side. Ask students to look at the noun-verb pair and tell, in a complete sentence, what the two cards show. Go through the card sets using three substitution patterns. First, flip through the verb set and create sentences with the first noun and each of the verbs, then the second noun and each of the verbs, and so on. Second, reverse the pattern and flip through the noun set. Third, flip the cards from both sets, creating a totally new sentence each time. Use singular and plural nouns to give practice for number agreement.

Markers

Present noun phrases that show the correct use of *a/an* and explain the rule. Present one of the noun phrases in a model sentence and direct students to replace the target word, in brackets, with a new word. This can be done as a written or an oral exercise. For example:

I bought [a book] on Tuesday.

| vase | orange | purse | umbrella |

Yes It Is/No It's Not

Present model pairs of positive and negative statements. For example:

| It is snowing. | It is not snowing. |
| It is raining. | It is not raining. |

Then read a positive sentence (such as, *It is foggy*) and ask students to respond with its negative form (*It is not foggy*). Responses may be made by the whole class or by individual students. Repeat the exercise using alternate forms of the negative:

| It is raining. | It isn't raining. |
| It is raining. | It's not raining. |

Repeat the exercise presenting the negative form and having students respond with the positive. For example:

| She doesn't have a pen. | She has a pen. |

Question

Present model pairs of a statement and its question form. For example:

| It is snowing. | Is it snowing? |
| It is raining. | Is it raining? |

Then read a statement and have students give the question form. Responses can be made by the whole class or by individuals.

Time-Lapse Pictures

Show students sets of three related pictures depicting an action about to happen, in progress, and obviously already occurred. Describe the pictures as you show them. For example, if the first picture in the set shows a boy on a diving board about to dive into a pool, say, "The boy will dive into the pool." For the second picture, with the boy in the air, say, "The boy is diving into the pool." For the last picture, showing the boy descending into the depths of the pool, say, "The boy dove into the pool." After presenting an example, have students supply the sentences as you show them other sets of action in time sequence.

Timeline

Create a timeline marked in hours, days, or years and show when several events occurred. Include a mark for the present and marks for events that will occur in the future. Ask the students questions about the relative time of the events and direct them to respond in complete sentences. Examples based on a timeline of John's day:

Did John leave home before or after breakfast?	John left after breakfast.
When will John meet Jim?	John will meet Jim after school.

Learning One's Place

Using word cards and a pocket board, arrange the cards to show proper sentence word order, including the placement of adjectives and adverbs, negatives, and question words. Have students practice the structures by replacing word cards to make new sentences in proper order.

Condensed Thoughts

Give students a pair of sentences and have them condense the ideas of both into one, taking care to make all correlative changes for number, subject-verb agreement, and so on. For example:

Are they in the library? Are they studying?	Are they studying in the library?
The dress is too big. Jean cannot wear it.	The dress is too big for Jean to wear.

Meaningful Mates

Give students two columns of basic sentences and a list of conjunctions. Have students make as many meaningful sentences as possible by joining a sentence from column A with one from column B using the contractions.

Compare and Contrast

Present two items that share some characteristics, such as a chair and a table. Have students write statements using *and* or *but* to compare and contrast the items. For example:

The chair has a seat but the table has a top.
The chair has a back but the table has no back.
The chair has four legs and the table has four legs.

Sub Drill

Give the students sentences with proper or common nouns and direct them to replace the nouns with pronouns. In the beginning of the drill, cue the response; later, do not cue the response. For example:

Billy has the notebook.	he	He has the notebook.	it	He has it.
The teacher has the book.		She has the book.		She has it.

Keeping It Straight

Select a passage of 200 to 250 words that includes pronouns and other anaphora. Direct students to circle all the words that refer to the same person or thing. For example:

John Wills was on a new job. The detective always had interesting work to do. When he met his client at the office, something told John it would be more interesting than usual.

Reflexives

Present the reflexive pronouns in pairs with the personal pronouns: *I/myself, you/yourself,* and so on. Have students repeat each pair. Present a model sentence—*I painted the desk by myself*—then a cue—*she.* Direct students to make the replacements needed by the cue: *She painted the desk by herself.* Continue with each reflexive pronoun and several model sentences.

More or Less

Present a graph or pictograph comparing six things, such as the numbers of people who like six different candies. Ask students questions using vocabulary for inequalities, equality, and comparisons. For example: *Which candy is liked by the most people? The least? Which candies were liked more than X? Which candy was liked more than X but less than Y?*

Do You Agree?

Have students select a topic and conduct an opinion survey on an issue, then create simple graphs or pie charts comparing responses. Have students write a report of the results using the vocabulary for inequalities, equality, and comparisons.

Wishful Thinking

Provide practice for the conditional tense by having students complete the following sentences:

> If I had an X. . . .
> If I were to win the lottery. . . .
> If I had only known. . . .
> If I hadn't seen the car. . . .
> If I hadn't been late. . . .

When I Was a Child. . . .

Have students write their autobiographies paying careful attention to the proper use of past tenses, sequence, and transition words.

Crystal Ball

Ask students to "look into the crystal ball" and write about the lives they will have in the next five years. Direct their attention to the use of the future tense, sequence, cause and effect, and transition words.

It's the Law

Direct students to compose a set of rules for one of the following: the kitchen, the classroom, good citizenship, being a good neighbor, or being a good friend. Attention should be given to imperative structures and modals.

Gotcha

Prepare a text of 200 to 250 words, embedding errors of one grammatical type, such as improper pronoun use or tense shifts. Have students read the text and then edit it to correct the errors. Tell them the number but not the type of errors that are in the passage.

Ripple Effects

Use a moving slot substitution to practice correlative changes required by a replacement word. Present a sentence and cue the word that will be used as the substitute. Vary the slot in the sentence for the substitution. For example:

	Carol has a white cat.
dog	Carol has a white dog.
we	We have a white dog.
brown	We have a brown dog.
two	We have two brown dogs.

Expansion

Present a basic sentence and cue students to make additions. Have students repeat the complete expanded sentence after each cue. For example:

	The girl swims.
young	The young girl swims.
gracefully	The young girl swims gracefully.
in the pool	The young girl swims gracefully in the pool.

List 8.11. Activities for Vocabulary Development

Introducing

Introduce vocabulary by presenting the object and the spoken word together. Use the actual object, pantomimes, demonstrations, gestures, series pictures, photographs, or other means to show the meaning of the target word. After saying the word three times, ask the students to repeat it after you. Then use the word in a sentence or meaningful phrase. Choral repetition should precede individual response.

Not So Basic

When introducing basic vocabulary, show students several examples of the target concept. For example, if the target word is *dog,* show pictures of several different sizes, colors, and breeds of dogs. This step eliminates inappropriate associations. After students learn the target word, review the examples and, for each one, add a word for the differentiating characteristic. For example: *black* dog, *tan* dog, *black and white* dog, *small* dog, *large* dog.

All Sorts

Select twenty vocabulary words from a single lexical group and four appropriate descriptive categories. Create a chart using the categories for column headings and the vocabulary words for the rows. Direct students to put an X in each category that describes the vocabulary words. For example:

Vocabulary	Categories Male	Female	Old	Young
father	X			X
girl		X		X
child				X
grandmother		X	X	

Word Maps

Introduce sets of related vocabulary, defining each word as you present it. Engage students in a discussion of the relationships among the words. Create semantic maps by writing the words on the chalkboard and showing, by placement and connecting lines, the relationships among the words presented. Common descriptors, such as category names, may be added to the map for detail.

Mix-Up

Give students several pairs of mixed-up sentences and have them repair and rewrite them. The errors should be lexical. For example: I was so hungry I went to sleep. I was so tired I had dinner.

Cognate Review

Give students lists of words that are cognates in English and their native language. Select cognate concepts and terms that are already understood by the students in their native language. Read the English word of the pair and have the students repeat it after you. Help them recognize spelling conversion patterns such as: *tion/cion* and *ly/mente.*

Content Cognates

Prepare a grammar review or other structure-centered class around a content area and use cognates to make the lesson a natural presentation of language in context. The use of cognates results in a more mature level of language than what usually occurs with the limited high-frequency vocabulary of prepared lessons, particularly in the early stages of language learning. This activity will help students make the transition to English-only content area instruction.

Want Ads

Teach job-related vocabulary by presenting job titles along with job descriptions and lists of qualifications as they would appear in a newspaper advertisement. For example:

> Wanted: Auto mechanic to tune engines, change oil, change filters, and fix flat tires. Must know how to use a jack, socket wrench, gauges, and other tools.

Crossword Puzzles

Have students complete crossword puzzles to review the definitions and spelling of new vocabulary words. Weekly crosswords can be habit forming and a painless way to continue to review vocabulary and spelling.

Descriptors

Have students cut out several newspaper and magazine ads for target items such as vacations, banks, stereo equipment, and cars. Have students make a chart and for each item list the adjectives or other descriptive language used in the ads. Discuss the similarities and appeal of descriptors for each item. This activity helps students with connotation and with categorizing words (for example, *scientific, glamorous, safety, lighthearted*).

Synonyms and Antonyms

Give students a list of word pairs and have them indicate whether they are synonyms or antonyms. An alternative activity is to present two columns of words—in column A, the target words; in column B, the synonyms or antonyms. Have students match the two columns.

Word Search Puzzles

Have students do word search puzzles that contain the target vocabulary words for a current lesson or words from prior vocabulary lessons. This activity helps reinforce students' visual memory of the words and their spellings.

Survey

Develop a survey of students' hobbies and extracurricular activities. For each item, have students indicate how often they participate: always, often, sometimes, rarely, never. Have students tabulate the results. Distribute the results and direct individual students to report on the participation rate for a particular hobby or activity. For example, five out of eight people watch TV often, two out of eight people watch TV sometimes, and one out of eight never watches TV.

Subject Pictionaries

Create a specialized "pictionary" for a content area by mounting titled drawings or pictures on three-by-five or five-by-eight prepunched index cards and arranging them alphabetically in a card binder. Have students use the pictionaries to learn the vocabulary and to look up a word and its spelling.

Really?

Give students a list of sentences, many having embedded lexical errors, and direct them to indicate whether the sentence is true or false. For example:

The cat studied for a geometry test.   T/F

The fisherman caught a tuna.   T/F

The sunny weather was annoying.   T/F

Flash

Pair students—an advanced student with a beginner—for word-recognition flashcard drills. Have the advanced student show the beginner the picture of the object and say the word, which the beginner repeats. Flashcards with the written form of the word can be used for word-recognition drills if the concept is already known. The pace should be brisk. As an alternative, students at the same level of skill can be paired and take turns drilling each other. When both students are stumped by a word, they should put the card aside for teacher assistance.

Mirror, Mirror

Pantomime new vocabulary words and say them. Have students mirror your actions and repeat the words. After you have introduced and repeated a few words and feel that the students are fairly comfortable with them, speed up the pantomimes and repeat them in random order.

Object-Article Card Drills

Review vocabulary and appropriate articles using concept cards. Deal a set of concept cards face down to all players. Begin by turning over the top card on your pile (for example, a cat) and saying, "I have a cat." The student to the right then turns over his or her card and says, "I have a/an [object]." Students should continue in turn until all cards have been used. Correct for articles and partitives. Points can be added to a score for correct responses and subtracted for errors.

Charades

To review vocabulary, have students pick a card with a vocabulary word written on it and gesture, pantomime, or otherwise dramatize the word. Have members of the class guess the word. This is a good team game.

Mix and Match

Teach basic Latin and Greek prefixes, suffixes, and root words. On a worksheet, have students match words in column A that are based on these elements with the definitions provided in column B.

Content Quick

Begin as early as possible to introduce groups of related vocabulary words in regular drills. Use pictures, concept cards, and so on.

Examples at the word level: *map, ocean, Christopher Columbus, ships, Indians, America.*
Examples at the sentence level:

> Christopher Columbus had a map.
> Christopher Columbus had three ships.
> Christopher Columbus saw the ocean.
> Christopher Columbus saw the Indians.
> Christopher Columbus saw America.

Use of content words throughout the language learning experience helps students make the transition to appropriate grade-level texts.

Cloze in the Gaps

Have students practice recognizing and spelling new vocabulary words by completing cloze passages. In the beginning, give students the list of vocabulary words for the exercise to ensure correct spelling.

Clued in

Give students a list of related words that have connotative information on an event or circumstance and direct the students to group the words that go together best. For example:

For store and school scenarios: cashier, desk, chalk, hangers, dressing room, dictionary.

For restaurant scenarios: waitress, musicians, chef, coat hook, tablecloths, plastic-covered menu, candles, paper napkins, a counter, a takeout sign.

Close Relatives

Develop a chart on the chalkboard or overhead that shows the adjective, noun, adverb, and verb forms of the same root word. Help students form generalizations about the forms. For example:

Adjective	Noun	Adverb	Verb
sad	sadness	sadly	to sadden
happy	happiness	happily	to be happy
sick	sickness	sickly	to sicken

Very Punny

Use puns or jokes to help students learn multiple meanings and connotations of words. There are many pun books available commercially. Humor should be a regular part of the instructional plan. It makes classwork fun, and it motivates students to attend carefully to word meaning.

Shades of Meaning

Give students lists of words dealing with the same trait, characteristic, and so on and help them arrange the words on a continuum from least to most. For example:

smirk, chuckle, giggle, laugh, belly laugh

mist, drizzle, rain, downpour, deluge

Five-by-Fives

Make copies of the five-by-five grid (see List 8.22) and prepare a set of category cards (for example, animals, parts of the body, places, school subjects, people) and a set of alphabet letters (not including *Q, U, X, Y,* or *Z*). Ask a student to pick five category cards and read them to the class. Have students write the category names in the five spaces across the top of the grid. Ask another student to select five alphabet cards and read them aloud. Have students write the letters in the five blocks in the left column of the grid. Allow the class three to five minutes to fill in the grid with appropriate words. For example, if one of the categories was animals and the letters were B, M, L, C, and G, the column under the heading *animal* might be filled in with the words *bear, mouse, lion, cat,* and *giraffe.*

'Tis the Season

Pick a season and have students compete to see who can write down the most words that have some relationship to the season. The students must be able to state a relationship if challenged. For example:

> *Spring:* rain, crocuses, baseball, jelly beans, mud, buds, warm, sweaters

As an alternative, give the students a list of fifty words and the name of a season and have them circle the words that relate to the season.

List 8.12. Activities for Improving Writing Skills

Pen Pals

Have students write letters to one another without knowing their pen pal's identity. Randomly assign each student a number, then have students draw numbers out of a hat to pick a pen pal. Suggest that first letters be autobiographical and include information about the students' hobbies and other activities.

May I?

Collect the addresses of government agencies, businesses, and other groups that offer free information booklets and samples. Many addresses, including those for institutions, businesses, and agencies providing curriculum-related giveaways, are available online. Have students write letters asking for an item they would like to receive. Stress letter format and address components.

Class News

Help students launch a class newspaper. Include standard news features dealing with current events, a school events feature, a cultural feature, study advice, and so on. In the beginning it may be necessary to provide substantial support for the newspaper, but as students' skills develop they can take on writing assignments, editing, formatting, and so forth.

Favorite People

Have students write fan letters to their favorite television or movie stars or athletes. In the letters, students may express their opinions, compliment the individual, ask for a photograph, and so on.

Picture This Competition

Give students a basic two-word sentence such as, *Boys play.* Then have students add modifiers, including adjectives, adverbs, and adjectival and adverbial phrases, to the basic sentence. Students can compete individually or in small groups to see who can create the greatest number of sentences in ten minutes. For example:

> Boys play.
> The older boys play tubas.
> The tall boys play basketball.
> The young boys play with blocks.

News Flash

To keep students abreast of the news, have them write a news flash when a special or unusual event occurs. A news flash is similar to a language experience chart. The students contribute information and dictate the story. The teacher writes the story out on newsprint or, if possible, types it into a word processor. Copies are made and distributed. When the story is completed, read each sentence to the group and have them repeat the reading as you point to the words. After two or more repetitions, distribute individual copies of the news flash. This activity introduces topical vocabulary in high-interest areas and helps link students to important events around them.

No Telegraph Today

Give students several pages from a major newspaper and ask them to rewrite the headlines into complete, correct sentences.

You're in the Headlines

Have the students write headlines for ten important events in their own lives.

House Party

Have students write directions from school to their homes or to their favorite restaurants or parks. Attention should be given to direction vocabulary, sequence, and proper names (streets, place names).

Gist

After students have practiced an oral dialogue, have them write a paragraph that tells the gist of the dialogue.

What's Going On?

Give students concept cards that depict people engaged in activities or situations. Ask the students to write as much about the picture as they can.

Travel Agent

Provide timetables for buses, trains, and taxis, and a chart of the time it takes to travel between destinations by each mode of transportation. Have students plan an itinerary for a trip from one city to another. Give conditions, such as *can't leave before 8 A.M. or arrive after midnight*, or *shouldn't have more than a one-hour stopover in any single place.* Students should work in pairs to practice travel vocabulary. The itinerary should be written out in a specified format. Attention should be given to abbreviations, logical connections, sequence, proper nouns, and punctuation.

Reporter

Have students conduct oral interviews, take notes, and write an article on the person they interviewed. Students should not report on the person who interviewed them.

Graduation Party

Have the students work in small groups to write a proposal for a graduation party. Have the students decide on a theme for decorations, a price per person, the type of site, the dinner menu, and the type of entertainment. Provide a how-to-plan-a-party brochure from a caterer, a phone book, travel and dining books, and newspaper ads for caterers and restaurants. Have students prepare a proposal with options, giving a brief narrative description of the affair including suitable sites with names, addresses, costs per person, benefits, and so on. The research for the proposal should be done using the materials supplied; however, advanced classes may be required to make one or two phone calls for price-per-person estimates. The proposals should follow a specified format. Provide a worksheet or short sample.

There Ought to Be a Law

Have students write essays on a pet peeve or a matter of serious concern. The essay should focus on problem and solutions or cause and effect. Topics might include alternative energy sources, pollution of the oceans and rivers, seatbelts on school buses, drug sales, street crime, homelessness, and unemployment.

Outlines

Select well-constructed passages of 200 to 250 words from a content area text at an appropriate reading level. Give students copies. Working with the whole group, teach students to select the key ideas for an outline by crossing out information that is not important or by underlining or highlighting the important information. Once students can identify the key ideas, they can develop the outline with minimal assistance.

Scenes from a School

Distribute photographs of activities that take place at school. The scenes should cover the ordinary (such as cafeteria lines) and the special (such as graduation). Have students select a picture and write a story about the event.

Advice Column

Have each student write a letter to "Dear Gabby" for advice and sign the letter with a pseudonym. After the letters are put into a box, have each student pick one out and answer it. Then put the answers back in the box and distribute them in a "mail call." Have students read the replies aloud. This can be done as a humorous exercise or with some seriousness.

Diamante

Have students write *diamantes,* or diamond-shaped poems. In this poetic form the writer goes from one idea to its opposite in a very organized way. The first line is a noun. Line two has two adjectives that describe the noun. Line three has three verbs that end in *-ing* and are related to the noun. Line four is the transition line. It has four nouns. The first two relate to the original noun. The second two relate to an opposite noun that will be named in line seven. Line five has three *-ing* verbs related to the noun in line seven. Line six has two adjectives related to line seven, and line seven is the noun that is the opposite of line one. For example:

summer

hot, sunny

swimming, playing, sailing

picnics, vacation; school, holidays

sledding, skiing, studying

cold, snowy

winter

What Characters!

Distribute cartoons or several frames of a comic strip that have empty dialogue balloons. Have students write in the dialogue or captions.

Note: there are several commercially available sets that are great fun.

One, Two, Three

Give students sets of directions for common activities, such as making a sandwich or washing dishes. The directions should be out of order and mixed up. For example, one direction in making the sandwich might be to spread mayonnaise on the lid instead of on the bread. Give no more than eight steps for each activity. Have students rewrite the directions in proper order and with logical connections. Note: the mix-ups add interest to the activity and require students to do more than simply recopy sentences. Fixing the inconsistencies will require making correlative changes.

Stolen Property

Have students fill in an insurance form for a claim based on a hypothetical break-in at their home. Attention should be given to the special terms of the report, the narrative about the incident, and the need for accuracy.

Fender Bender

Have students fill in a police report about a hypothetical car accident. Give attention to special vocabulary, the narrative about the accident (sequence, cause and effect, who did what, and so on), and the need for accuracy.

List 8.13. Taste and Touch Lessons

Taste and touch words are difficult to describe but easy to experience. Assemble a selection of common foods (no peanuts or other foods known to cause allergic reactions, please!) that have different characteristics and divide them into very small portions. Prepare a graphic organizer for students to complete as they engage in taste tests. Provide an exemplar for each category. For example, using a salt shaker, shake a bit of salt into each student's hand and have them taste *salty*. Then, spooning from a sugar bowl, give each student a taste of *sweet*. Next, have the students work in pairs to taste test a number of foods and complete the graphic organizer.

Redo the exercise adding texture words, for example, *sweet* and *smooth* or *sweet* and *crispy*. Engage students in conversation about likes and dislikes, and have them name other foods that fit into each category. On a word wall, identify an exemplar for each characteristic on the basis of students' suggestions and experiences during the taste tests.

Taste and Texture Words

sweet	salty	sour	bitter
smooth	crunchy	mushy	hard
chewy	juicy	crispy	dry
sticky	flakey	brittle	soft
light	dense	lumpy	jellied

Plan a touch test for students to experience various textures in nonfood items. Gather a variety of items with different textures and enclose each in a numbered cloth pouch. Provide students with a "guess list" graphic organizer that they fill in to identify the texture and the item. Give points for each correct answer. Use common household items.

Touch Words

hard	soft	spongy	smooth
rough	dented	bumpy	gritty
sharp	feathery	hairy	furry
rocky	textured	bristled	tacky
silky	nappy	polished	glassy

List 8.14. Journaling

Self-expression through writing is a goal of all language arts instruction. Many teachers find that journaling helps ELLs to develop confidence and competence in expressing their views in English. Journal writing differs from other writing experiences in key ways: It is personal, not public, writing. There are no right or wrong answers. Journals are not graded or corrected. They can be embellished with drawings and doodles, photos and scrapbook findings. Each one is different.

There are two types of journals. The most common type is like a diary. Students make entries daily or weekly and record their thoughts and ideas about their experiences. The second type is a dialogue journal, in which the student and teacher write notes back and forth. Either one may ask a question, make a comment, or share a thought.

The process is simple. All that is needed is a ruled blank book for writing in and time set aside for making entries. Begin journaling by asking students to respond to the question or theme of the day. Entries may be tied into recent vocabulary lessons or shared experiences. Here are some topics to get you started:

Favorite colors	Best friend
What I like about school	What I like about winter
Where I live now	A game I enjoy
Things that are big	Things that are small
Things that are yellow	A place I want to visit
Favorite food	Something I want to learn
My family	Favorite actor
Dogs or cats	Today's weather
Songs I like	Things that grow
Things that make me happy	Favorite subject at school
Favorite TV show	Something I do well
Things that are funny	Favorite sport
Car I would like to own	My brother or sister
Things to do on the weekend	Ways I help at home
Things I am thankful for	Do I like school?
Things I do after school	What I would buy with $100
Why be nice to others?	Things I don't like
My grandparents	Best snack in the world
Why I like summer	The best holiday
A poem I like	What I had for lunch
What I learned today	Things that are scary
Good things for breakfast	What I look like
Things that are cold	Good bugs and bad bugs

List 8.15. Interviewing

Interviewing is a great way to develop ELLs confidence in speaking English to others, because students can plan the questions they will ask and have some control over the conversation. In addition, if the interviews are on topics related to areas they have already studied, they are likely to have listening and writing knowledge of the core vocabulary. Armed with an audio recorder, any information that is missed can be captured later by replaying the interview and, if necessary, getting some help from another student or a teacher. In addition to providing students with listening and note-taking experience, interviewing helps them to hone their writing skills, including their use of subject-related idioms. Their work can be gathered and shared in a class report, newsletter, Web site posting, or "book."

Here are some guidelines to give to your budding journalists:

- Make an appointment with the person you are going to interview, determining starting and ending times and location.
- Let the interviewee know what you will discuss so that he or she will have time to consider the questions. Provide either a written list or a verbal summary. Knowing the questions in advance reduces anxiety.
- Ask the interviewee whether it will be okay to record the interview. If you would like to take the person's photo, ask for permission first.
- Prepare an interview form that provides space for note taking under each of the questions and that is organized in a logical order. Be sure to leave space for additional comments.
- Formulate questions that get at the five *W*s and *H* (*who, what, where, when, why, and how*); these are the basics for any article or report. Also plan to ask if there is anything else the interviewee wants to add; this often elicits some excellent details that "make" the story.
- Be on time for your interview appointment and be prepared. Make sure your audio recorder is working (check the batteries!) and bring your own pen and interview forms.
- Start by introducing yourself and thanking the person for agreeing to be interviewed, then get down to business.
- Ask one question at a time and allow the person to respond. Don't rush the speaker.
- If you need more information, ask the person to "tell me more about that."
- If you want to check a fact, ask a yes/no question, for example, *Were you born in Taiwan?*
- Practice asking the questions with a friend so you are comfortable saying the words.
- Think about the topic before the interview and about what kinds of answers you might hear. This will help you relax and recognize key ideas and write them quickly.
- Enjoy the time you are spending getting to know what someone else thinks or what they have experienced. Smile and make eye contact with your subject to let them know they are doing a good job and to help them feel comfortable too.
- At the end of the interview, thank the interviewee for his or her time and for sharing ideas and information. Tell the person you appreciate his or her help with your project.

Here's a list of interview topics to get you started:

What is different about the food you have here compared to the food you had in your old country?
How is shopping for food different here?
What new foods have you tried in the United States?
What foods are prepared when you celebrate a special occasion or holiday?

When did you begin school?
What was your first teacher like?
Tell me about your first school.
What was your favorite subject in school?

What kind of work do you do?
How did you decide to do this?
Who taught you how to do your job?

What do you like about the work you do?
How many brothers and sisters do you have?
Where are they now?
What kinds of work do they do?
How does your family stay connected to one another?

How did you feel the first time you were in an airplane?
How do you feel about flying now?
If you could fly anywhere tomorrow, where would you go?
Why did you choose there?

What do you think about the shows on TV?
How have they changed in the last ten years?
Which show do you think is the best for children?
How can parents use TV to help their children understand the world?

Where do you get information about your town?
Who do you contact when you have a question or problem in your town?
How are law enforcement officers viewed by people in your community?
What can local officials do to promote positive community feelings?

What positive effects has technology had on your family?
What concerns do you have about technology?
How do you use the Internet in your personal life?
Where did you learn to use the Internet?

How did you choose your career?
Who was an important influence on your choice?
What do you like about your career?
What advice would you give to someone just starting in the same job?

What sport do you like to play?
What makes it fun or exciting to play this sport?
When did you learn to play?
Tell me about the most exciting time you had playing this sport.

What do you think is the most amazing invention of the last one hundred years?
Why is it amazing?
How does it make a difference?
What are your concerns about its use?

Who do you think is a real modern-day hero?
What did this person do that made him or her a hero?
What are some of the characteristics that make someone a hero?
How can we encourage young people to be heroes?

List 8.16. Surveys

Surveys gather information from a group of people about topics of interest in order to learn something about the group. To survey members of a group, a set of questions are asked and their answers are organized into categories. The organized information is referred to as *data*. It helps the surveyors to understand the group and the topic. Using surveys in ESL/ELL classes achieves three goals: it helps students learn about the topic and the group, it gives them experience working with data to make decisions, and it familiarizes them with this very popular data-gathering process so they can be good consumers of survey data published in the media and other places.

As a getting-to-know-you exercise and to introduce key vocabulary, start with simple in-class surveys and post the results on a bulletin board. If you are working with very young children, use squares of paper with students' names written on them to indicate their response in the appropriate column. The tally number can then be written at the bottom of each column of responses to show students that each person's response, or "vote," counted toward the total.

Here are some suggested survey topics to try:

Our eyes: brown, blue, green, hazel
Favorite ice cream flavor: chocolate, vanilla, strawberry, rocky road, butter pecan
Favorite color: yellow, green, blue, red, orange, purple, brown, white, black
Favorite season: fall, winter, spring, summer
Pets we have: dog, cat, fish, bird, guinea pig, hamster, none
Animals we like: lion, elephant, tiger, horse, monkey, deer
Things we like to do: swim, play ball, ride a bike, read a book, draw pictures
Our brothers and sisters: none, one, two, three, four, five, more than five
Sports we like: soccer, baseball, football, hockey
Lunch food we like: hamburgers, macaroni and cheese, sandwiches, chili
Things we like to drink: water, milk, tea, coffee, soda, lemonade, iced tea
Favorite subject: math, English, science, social studies, physical education, music, art
Musical instruments we like: drums, guitar, piano, flute, trumpet, violin, organ
Where we were born: North America, South America, Central America, Africa, Europe, Asia, Australia, Middle East
Seeing clearly: no glasses, eyeglasses, contact lenses
Distance from home to school: one block, two blocks, three blocks, four blocks, five or more blocks
Breakfast today: cereal, rice, eggs, toast or bread, donut or cake, no breakfast, other breakfast

List 8.17. Strategies for Inclusive ESL/ELL Classrooms

Many instructional activities can be modified to meet the needs of students with disabilities. According to the U.S. Department of Education's Nineteenth Annual Report to Congress on the Implementation of the Individuals with Disabilities Education Act (IDEA), 95 percent of all children with disabilities are served in regular schools. This number includes ESL/ELL students who have been identified as having a disability. While students' individualized education plans (IEPs) provide academic goals, appropriate teaching strategies help children meet them. The following strategies have been shown to be effective when teaching English language arts to a wide range of special needs students in inclusive classrooms. Use them in conjunction with the instructional activities provided throughout this book.

- Match the modality of instruction to the student (for example, large print, Braille, or audiotaped versions for low-vision students).
- Observe students in individual, paired, small-group, and whole-class activities and note which environment maximizes their engagement and success.
- Help students track their success using different strategies to accomplish a frequent task or assignment (such as learning new spelling words) and discuss which strategy worked best.
- Review students' IEPs to identify areas of strength, and develop instructional activities that use them to advantage.
- Use error analysis as a basis for planning instruction and practice activities.
- Maximize time on task by simplifying and creating standardized procedures so that time is spent on the learning activity, not on giving and interpreting directions.
- Make connections explicit or ask leading questions to help students make links and transfer learning to similar but new situations.
- Provide ample response time and let students know it's okay to take time to think in order to decide on an answer; discourage guessing as a way to "get it over with."
- Focus first on accuracy, then on speed and fluency.
- Practice reading high-frequency words, key words, and other target words until students reach automaticity. This will enable them to use their energy on comprehension and not allow time lag and decoding struggles to interfere with meaning.
- Use direct instruction and modeling to demonstrate desired learning behavior.
- Provide immediate and clear feedback with an informing, neutral tone.
- Pace instruction so that learning is achieved and skills are practiced, and move on before students become bored.
- Use task analysis with students to show how to break down complex tasks into smaller components that allow students to focus their attention, recognize important sequences, learn subskills, and then reconstitute the tasks.
- Use structured, guided practice, gradually moving students from fully supported to fully independent work.
- Use echo or choral reading to help students pace reading and use inflection to support understanding.
- Use group response methods (such as having students hold up a response card marked yes or no to answer questions) to keep the active learning level high for all students and to enable scanning of the responses to track individual students' learning.
- Give both oral and written directions. Post the directions on the board or in another prominent location. Keep the language simple, number the steps, and use rebuses or flowcharts to show steps graphically.

- Use cues or prompts to guide students' work. For example, underline or color code the key element or elements, or provide a template for organizing the task.
- Use a visual thesaurus to show how words' meanings are related.
- Use concept mapping to help students organize what they know about a concept.
- Use tables and other graphic organizers to show similarities and differences.
- Use K-W-L charts to help students plan and evaluate their learning. Before reading, have students identify what they already know about the topic and list this information under the *K* heading. Next, have students identify what they want to learn from the reading selection and list this information as questions or topics under the *W* heading. Later, after reading, have students list what they learned under the *L* heading and compare their learning to their want-to-learn goals.
- Extend the amount of time provided, reduce the amount of work (number of pages, examples, items, words), or both to reduce stress and focus attention on positive outcomes.
- Provide informative feedback for correct answers to reinforce the use of an effective strategy, as well as for incorrect answers to show how the answer could have been found.
- Permit students to draw and tape a narrative, instead of writing a response, if spelling and writing are challenges.
- Provide advanced organizers, including questions for students to "read and find out."
- Teach decoding skills, high-frequency words, and frequently used word parts (prefixes, suffixes, and root words) directly. Research shows that a code and skill approach is more successful than literature or whole language approaches with students who have learning difficulties.
- Provide word walls to remind students of key words and their spellings.
- Teach related words and their spellings after the key word is learned. For example, *cat, cats* or *make, made.* Once children learn a word and want to use it, they should not be limited to the singular or present forms. Showing the changes that occur for number and time in relation to spoken language helps students recognize spelling and grammar patterns.
- Use computer-based programs for individualized practice and reinforcement.
- Use interest inventories and book circles to encourage independent reading.
- Provide texts at different readability levels on the same subject so all students can study and contribute to a themed interdisciplinary unit.
- Use different types of art to respond to a piece of literature or word study. For example, have students create colorful mobiles of words based on the same root word, or use finger painting to show how a poem made them feel.
- Engage students in word play daily. There is no limit to the number of puns, jokes, puzzles, games, odd phrases, and interesting words and idioms that can be used.
- Read to the class every day, if possible. Not only is it enjoyable but you can model fluent reading and interest.
- Incorporate research into each week's lessons. Introduce and teach related skills (key words, indexing, alphabetical order, types of resources, evaluating sources, note taking, and so on) as part of the process.
- Create a language-rich classroom where books, magazines, newspapers, the Internet, craft directions, journals, word walls, favorite authors, and other language artifacts engage students' interests and imaginations as well as help them become proficient readers and independent learners.
- Pair older students with younger ones (sixth graders and second graders, for example) for reading enrichment and reinforcement activities.

List 8.18. New Literacies

What are new literacies? They are reading and writing activities that are different from traditional uses of reading and writing. Traditional uses of literacy are books, letters (correspondence by mail), reports, and so forth. New literacies include such things as reading and writing e-mail, instant messaging, posting in chat rooms, working collaboratively using a wiki, and manga (words and cartoons).

New literacies are important because traditional literacies are in steep decline. A U.S. Census Bureau survey for the National Endowment for the Arts found that literature reading in the United States went from 57 percent of the population in 1982 down to 47 percent in 2002, with no end in sight as younger adults read far less than older adults. However, many adults and students spend hours each day reading and writing at their computer. In addition, the number and sales of specialized magazines are up. As the general population moves toward these new literacies, so also will the ESL/ELL population. The new forms require less extended reading and provide visual clues, making them appealing to English language learners. They are also part of the emerging culture, and they bridge gaps of time, distance, and fluency. The following list will help you become familiar with these forms. Because these new literacies are developing rapidly, the Internet is the best source for up-to-date information on them.

Blogs or Weblogs

Open commentary and reviews written and posted on the Internet by users of items, Web sites, or just about anything. Blogs can contain annotated links (to other Web sites), are generally journal-like, and may reference hybrids of products, sites, and services.

E-mail

Written communications to an individual or a group on the Internet, often with a very informal writing style. E-mail may use emoticons such as :-) (a happy face turned sideways) to show pleasure, or acronyms such as IMHO (in my humble opinion).

Gaming

Terminology used in video console games, computer games, and Internet-mediated games.

Manga

Written communications that rely either heavily or partly on pictures. The Sunday comics are manga, but so are more sophisticated adult cartoons, such as pages that contain real or imaginary pictures with written text placed in various parts of the illustration. Some manga can be read in a nonlinear fashion, whereby the reader decides which part to read first. Manga can be fictional or storylike, or realistic, as in maps and mechanical illustrations.

Wiki sites

Collaborative online environments that allow visitors to the Web site to add and edit information. *Wiki* is an acronym for *what I know is*.

Metazines

Zines about zines.

Web pages

A Web site's information is displayed on Web pages. Most Web sites provide more information than can be viewed on one page, so the information is divided into linked Web pages. Schools, companies, and many individuals and organizations have Web sites.

Zines

Online magazines for children and adults, both professionally and volunteer written, fiction and nonfiction, illustrated and unillustrated.

List 8.19. Test-Taking Strategies

All students benefit from direct instruction on strategies to help them perform their best in different types of testing situations. State and national assessment requirements may create additional pressure for ESL/ELL students to perform well on standardized tests. The following strategies have been found to be helpful in reducing stress and maximizing scores. Many are also appropriate for chapter, unit, midterm, and final exams.

General

- Recognize that testing is a normal part of schooling. While you are learning, take notes, highlight your texts, complete homework, and read and discuss the new information with the intention of understanding and remembering it. These activities are all part of studying. If you do them regularly, you will need less preparation for a test.
- Ask your teacher what will be on the test and review that information, paying more attention to areas that you did not remember as easily as others.
- Don't wait until the last minute to study. Try to finish studying in time to go to sleep at your regular time. Being overtired will make it difficult to do your best.
- Eat breakfast on the day of the test. Being hungry can be very distracting. Avoid sugary foods.
- Plan to arrive early. You need time to compose yourself, get your pen or pencils out, and prepare mentally for the test. Rushing in, or arriving late, will raise your stress level and it will take time for your body to relax enough to focus your attention.
- Be sure you have everything you need with you, including your test registration materials, your photo ID (a school ID, driver's license, or passport may be required), pencils and erasers, pens, and approved calculator (if appropriate), and tissues.
- If you have a choice of seats, sit where you will not be distracted. For example, don't sit near the door, or right in front of the proctor's desk. Don't sit under the heating or air conditioner vent; it may be noisy or create an uncomfortable climate—too warm or too cool—for doing your best.
- When you receive the test, look it over if you are permitted and find out what kinds of questions (true-false, matching, multiple choice, essay, short answer) it contains. Knowing what to expect and deciding which part to do first gives you some feeling of control.
- Ask the teacher or proctor how many points each question is worth and how much of the score is determined by each section's results. For example, there may be only two short essay questions at the end, but they may be worth 25 points each, or half the points for the test, while fifty true-false questions may be worth only one point each. This information helps you plan how much time to spend on each section of the test.
- If possible, do the easiest section or type of question first. This will give you more time to spend on the harder parts, and help you relax.
- Notice that as you answer questions you begin to remember many other things. This additional information may be helpful for later sections of the test.
- Budget your time. Allow sufficient time for questions worth the most points. If the test has several timed sections, consider how much time you have for each section. How many questions do you need to complete by the midpoint of each period? Check your progress and adjust your speed if you are behind.
- Listen carefully to the directions. Standardized tests have very specific and strict rules. If you do not follow the directions, you may encounter problems. For example, in some testing situations you will not be able to ask any questions, leave the room, or sharpen a

pencil once the test has begun. If you do not follow the directions, the proctor may take your test booklet and ask you to leave.

- Don't worry if you don't remember something immediately; move on. Your memory may be helped by information in another question.
- Do not talk to anyone or look at others' test papers or booklets. This may be considered cheating.
- Do not engage in any form of cheating. Cheating on tests can have serious consequences.

Objective Tests (Multiple Choice, Matching, Fill-in-the-Blank, Short Answer)

- Ask the teacher or proctor if there is a penalty for guessing. If there is no penalty and you don't know the answer, you may be able to eliminate some of the choices and guess the correct answer.
- Read the test directions and questions carefully. Underline important directions, such as *choose one, briefly,* or *all that apply.* Watch for qualifiers like *sometimes, always, all, none, never, all of the above,* and *none of the above.*
- Answer the questions you are sure about first. If you don't know an answer, put a mark in the margin so you can find the question easily when you go back to it. If you know that one or more of the answers are definitely wrong, cross them out. This will save time when you go back to think about the remaining choices.
- If you are using a machine-scored bubble sheet, check to be sure you are filling in the correct line for each question, especially if you skip one or more.
- If you are having difficulty with a question, look for grammar (number, gender, tense) or context clues. If all the answers seem OK, pick the one that seems more generally correct. Read the question with each alternative answer. The correct answer may seem to make more sense, even if you can't explain why.
- If the test has a matching section, read all the choices before you begin to complete the section. Match the items you are sure of first. Avoid changing an answer. One change may require several others. Ask your teacher if you can use the same answer more than once.
- If the test has a fill-in-the-blank or short answer section, look for clues in the question and use a word or words with appropriate tense, gender, and number. Read the completed statements to make sure they sound correct. Sometimes the teacher will provide clues by making the blank lines fit the length of or number of letters in the answer.
- If you have time left, check over the exam. Change an answer only if you can think of a good reason to do so. Generally your first answer is correct.

Essays

- Read the directions before you begin. Do you have to answer all of the questions? Are there required and student-selected questions?
- Mark the key direction words that tell you what you are to do in the essay:

analyze	create	distinguish
apply	criticize	draw conclusions
assess	define	enumerate
categorize	demonstrate	evaluate
cite evidence	describe	explain
classify	develop	express
compare	diagram	formulate
construct	differentiate	generalize
contrast	discuss	identify

illustrate	provide	state
interpret	rank	subdivide
judge	rate	suggest
justify	react	summarize
label	rearrange	support
list	reason	tell
organize	recommend	trace
outline	relate	transform
paraphrase	restate	translate
predict	review	utilize
propose	solve	weigh
prove	specify	why

- Many essay questions have multiple parts. Number the parts so you don't forget to answer all of them.
- If you do not understand the question, ask your teacher before you begin. Sometimes your question will be helpful to other students who also do not understand the question.
- Briefly outline your answer before you begin to write. Refer back to the question to be sure your answer is focused on it.
- Transforming the question into the introduction is often a good way to start. For example, if the question is, *Discuss the three forms of matter,* you might begin with *The three forms of matter are. . . .* Then, after listing them, write about each one.
- Essays should have an introduction, development, and a conclusion. They should include relevant details. Most essays require factual information rather than your personal opinion.
- Short essays usually present an idea and support it with examples and factual details.
- Allow some time at the end to proofread your essay for spelling and grammar, to make sure you answered all the parts of the question, and to check that you used the appropriate vocabulary.
- If you are running out of time, quickly outline the answers to the remaining questions. List the information you would normally put in paragraph form. Many teachers will give some credit for the information, even if the essay is not well developed.

Quantitative Tests
- Read the questions or examples carefully to be sure you know what is being asked.
- Show all of your work, not just the answers. You may receive partial credit for how you worked out the answer even if you make a careless calculation error and end up with the wrong answer.
- For multiple-choice questions, estimate the answer and see which choice is closest to your estimate.
- Check to see that your choice has the correct unit of measure, not just the correct numbers.
- Prove your work by working the problem backward.
- If you are missing information, you may have to add another step and compute the missing information. Reread the question first.
- Sometimes information you do not need is included in the problem. Writing an equation will often help determine what is needed and what is not.

List 8.20. Bingo Blank

The bingo game is used with all ages and abilities and for many instruction and review purposes. Select at least thirty words or symbols and have students randomly pick twenty-four to use to fill in their card. Put the cards with the words or symbols on them into a box. Pick one card at a time and call it out. Have students cover the space on their card that contains the word selected. The first student who covers all words in a straight line across, down, or diagonally calls out "bingo" and wins if their words are verified.

List 8.21. Fill-in Event Calendar

Events, to-do lists, holidays, numbers 1 to 31, days of the week, and months of the year can be practiced by filling in group and personal calendars. ESL/ELL students can use this blank calendar to track important dates in school, sports, and their personal lives.

Month of						
Sunday	Monday	Tuesday	Wednesday	Thursday	Friday	Saturday

List 8.22. Five-by-Five Data Organizer

Human understanding is based on the characteristics that something both has and does not have. Children, for example, notice that there are many similarities between small dogs and cats—both are animals with fur and pointed ears and can be playful pets. But dogs bark and cats meow. The distinguishing feature—what makes them different—is as important as all the shared characteristics. When learning new concepts, linking the new to what is already known through trait comparison, or learning about several things at once by contrasting features, helps ESL/ELL students. In a five-by-five data organizer, write features or traits you are looking for in the first column and the name of five objects at the head of the remaining five columns. As information is gathered from books, lectures, online research, videos, interviews, and other sources, fill in the cells. A completed five-by-five is a great study guide and serves as notes without requiring students to write full sentences. Five-by-fives are also excellent scaffolds for note taking. For younger students, use only the first three columns and first three rows.

		Object				
		A	B	C	D	E
Trait	1					
	2					
	3					
	4					
	5					

Section Nine

Assessment

List 9.1. Language Assessment Guidelines

A variety of assessments are used to make decisions about English language learners and programs for English language learning. Recent changes in federal and state regulations have placed increasing emphasis on nationally normed standardized assessments. School district testing and evaluation plans are evolving to meet these new requirements for placement, progress, and performance data, and to provide better information about the effectiveness of programs.

In addition to the standardized measures, which provide information about students' language performance in relation to a sample population, less formal instruments, including portfolios and assessment materials linked to texts, are helping teachers make decisions about students' competencies, instructional needs, and progress. The following list shows the types of assessments used for each purpose. See List 9.7: Tests for Assessing English Language Learners, for descriptions of commercial tests that are commonly used for many of these purposes.

Assessment Purpose	Assessment Type
Student eligibility for program	Standardized placement tests
	Standardized oral interviews
	Standardized language competency tests
	Standardized academic achievement tests
Student instructional needs	Diagnostic tests
	Criterion-referenced tests
	Textbook pretests or level tests
	Oral interviews
	Observation checklists
	Student work samples (audiotaped, written)
Student learning progress	Academic achievement tests
	Diagnostic pretests and posttests
	Textbook pre- and posttests or level tests
	Oral interviews

	Criterion-reference tests
	Observation checklists
	Student portfolio of work samples
Student eligibility to exit program	Standardized placement tests
	Standardized oral interviews
	Standardized language competency tests
	Standardized academic achievement tests
Program effectiveness	Standardized language competency tests
	Standardized academic achievement tests
	Textbook pre- and posttests or level tests
Program pacing	Oral interviews
	Observation checklists
	Student portfolio of work samples
	Textbook pre- and posttests or level tests
Instructional materials selection	Diagnostic tests
	Standardized language competency tests
	Observation checklists
	Criterion-referenced tests
Instructional time allocation	Diagnostic tests
	Standardized language competency tests
	Observation checklists
	Criterion-referenced tests

List 9.2. Assessing Language Proficiency

Language proficiency is the ability to communicate effectively in a target language using context-appropriate structures and content, including accurate vocabulary. To be proficient in English, the speaker must integrate many aspects of English sound and symbol relationships, grammar and syntax, knowledge of idioms and vocabulary, cultural expectations, and more. Methods used to assess students' language proficiency provide opportunities to demonstrate this integration in addition to demonstrating basic abilities to communicate. The following list provides a variety of options.

Cloze procedure for written passages
Select a written passage of approximately 250 words. It may deal with functional, sociocultural, or curriculum content. Delete every fifth or seventh word. Direct students to read the passage silently and write in the missing words. To make this task less difficult, provide a list of words from which to choose. To make the task more difficult, provide a longer list of words including less accurate synonyms so that students have to make more nuanced choices to complete the passage correctly.

Cloze procedures for aural passages
Select a passage of approximately 150 words. It may deal with functional, sociocultural, or curriculum content. Delete every fifth or seventh word. Present the passage to the students, either by reading it aloud or by having them listen to an audio recording of it. Ask the students to select and mark the words that best complete the passage from choices provided on an answer sheet. As an alternative, provide a numbered answer sheet that corresponds to the number of deleted words. Ask students to supply appropriate words to complete the passage.

Dictations
Select a thematic passage of 100 to 150 words. Direct students to listen to the passage and then write it verbatim. Read the passage three times: first, at a conversational pace; next, slowly, breaking the passage into meaningful phrases of no more than three to five words each; and finally, at a moderate pace.

Dramatizations by individuals or groups
Select a topic for dramatization (see List 8.2: Thematic Language Units for suggestions). Prepare a script incorporating related vocabulary, gestures, movements, actions, and props. Have the students learn the script and perform the dramatization for the class. Intermediate or advanced students may also be asked to develop the script or to do an extemporaneous dramatization on a given topic.

Formula dialogues
Create a set of cue cards that present different social or functional language situations, for example, asking for directions to the supermarket or introducing a friend, Tom, to Uncle Chuck. Have pairs of students pick a card from the set, prepare for two minutes, and then engage in the cued formula dialogue.

Listen and respond
Select a passage of 200 to 250 words and audiotape it or read it aloud to the students. Direct the students to listen to the passage and then answer open-ended questions about the content or meaning of the text. As an alternative, direct the students to write the answers to the questions or to write a summary of the passage.

Read or listen and respond

Select a passage of 200 to 250 words. Direct the students either to read the passage or to listen to it as it is read aloud or presented on an audio recording. Then have them respond to multiple-choice questions. Use all combinations of presentation and response modes: written text and aural or oral questions and answers, aural text and aural or oral questions and answers, written text and written questions and answers, aural text and written questions and answers.

Prepared narrative

Ask students to research a self-selected or assigned topic and prepare an oral presentation of between three to seven minutes. Encourage the use of visual aids, including charts and graphs.

Paraphrase recognition

Select passages of between 100 and 150 words each and develop paraphrased versions of varying quality for each passage. Ask students to select the best paraphrase for the material from the choices given. Use all combinations of presentation and response modes: aural material and aural choices, aural material and written choices, written material and aural choices, written material and written choices.

Story retelling

Ask students to read or listen to a story of between 200 and 250 words and then retell the story. The stories should have functional, sociocultural, or curricular content. Gist recall, not verbatim, is required.

Storytelling

Ask students to prepare and then tell a story, either factual or fictional.

Structured interview

Interview the students using a prepared set of questions on target topics. Develop a checklist of language features to note in the students' responses.

Translations

Direct students to translate written passages of varying lengths from their native language into English. The passages may deal with functional, sociocultural, or curriculum content.

List 9.3. Assessing Auditory and Aural Skills

Auditory skills are related to the ability of the ear to hear meaningful sounds. In language learning, auditory skills include the trained or culturally acquired ability to recognize the sounds that belong to a particular language, and the ability to discriminate among similar sounds within the language. Aural skills are related to the ability of the student to listen to and understand spoken messages. The following activities provide many options for assessing both auditory and aural skills.

Methods for Assessing Students' Auditory Skills

Sound-contrast recognition in words
Ask students to listen carefully as you read aloud groups of two or three words. Tell them to indicate whether the words in the groups are the same or different by circling *same* or *different* (*S* or *D*) on their answer sheets. Use minimal contrasts. Examples: *sit/set, sit/sit/sit, set/sit/sit.*

Sound-contrast recognition in sentences
Ask students to listen carefully as you read pairs of sentences aloud. Tell them to indicate whether the pairs are the same or different by writing or circling *same* or *different* (*S* or *D*) on their answer sheets. Use minimal contrasts. Example: *Did she get it?/Did she pet it?*

Target-sound discrimination in word pairs
Tell students to listen carefully to the initial sound of the word you are about to say, then to listen to pairs of words. Ask them to write or circle *yes* or *no* (*Y* or *N*) on their answer sheets to indicate whether the pairs of words have the same initial sound as the target word. Use the same method for medial and final sounds.

Target-sound discrimination in word groups
Tell students to listen carefully to the initial sound of the word you are about to say, then to listen to the initial sound in each of the next four words. Ask them to indicate whether the other words have the same initial sound as the target word. Example: *bit—Ben, bug, pit, bat.* Students may respond: by writing or circling *yes* or *no* (*Y* or *N*), by raising their hand when the initial sounds are the same, or by holding up a card that says *same* or *different*. Use this method also to assess sound recognition in the final and medial positions.

Rhyming word recognition
Ask students to listen carefully to the ending sounds as you read pairs of words and to write or circle *yes* or *no* (*Y* or *N*) on their answer sheet to indicate whether the pairs rhyme.

Sound and spelling association and recognition
Direct students to listen to word parts, words, word pairs, or word groups as you read them aloud. Tell them to circle the matching items on their answer sheets. Prepare multiple-choice answer sheets with four choices.

Sound and spelling association and production
Direct students to listen to the words you read aloud, then to write the words. Begin by using words with target sounds presented first in the initial position, then in the medial and final positions.

Sound and spelling discrimination

Ask students to listen as you read a series of three words aloud, then to cross out on an answer sheet with four words per item the word they did not hear. The exercise can also be done using word parts, word pairs, or phrases.

Methods for Assessing Students' Aural Skills

Vocabulary

Direct students to listen as you read a word and then to mark the matching picture on their answer sheet.

Aural understanding and pictorial match

Direct students first to listen as you read a short passage and then to mark the picture on the answer sheet that matches the passage just read. Begin with simple noun phrases (*the happy baby*) and verb phrases (*hit the ball*). Repeat the exercise with simple sentences followed by brief passages of up to five sentences.

Aural comprehension and sentence completion

Direct students to listen as you read the beginning of a sentence and a set of possible endings. Ask the students to indicate on their answer sheet which of the endings best completes the sentence. Provide four choices.

Aural understanding of main idea or gist

Select a passage of between one hundred and two hundred words. Direct students to listen to a passage, then to select the best title for the passage from choices you read to them. As an alternative, ask students to select the main idea or gist statement from the choices presented either orally or visually on an answer sheet.

Aural comprehension to complete a task

Direct students to listen carefully and then follow your directions. Begin with a single but specific task (*raise your right hand*), then move on to a sequence of steps for the completion of a task.

Simon Sez

Play Simon Sez and incorporate key direction vocabulary (*first, second, left, right, up, down, in, on, close, open,* and so on) into Simon's orders. Winners may serve as Simon for subsequent rounds of play.

Logical predictions

Select a passage of between 150 and 250 words. Ask students to listen to the passage and to three additional statements, then to select the statement that best tells what is most likely to happen next in the story.

Paraphrase recognition

Select brief passages of up to 150 words and construct three single-sentence paraphrases for each. Direct students to listen as you read each passage and the three statements. Ask them to select the statement that is closest in meaning to the passage.

Factual understanding

Ask students to listen as you read a set of brief statements. Tell them to indicate on their answer sheets whether each statement is true or false (*T* or *F*).

Logical understanding.

Direct students to listen carefully as you read a statement containing an error. Tell them to state or write the correction for the statement. Example: *Eli slept in his book [bed].*

List 9.4. Assessing Oral Language Skills

Oral language includes both one-way and interactive speech. In one-way speech, the speaker addresses an audience, as in a formal presentation or lecture, and little, if any, reply is expected. During interactive speech, each speaker reacts to the other and is guided by the other's cues. The partner, in turn, is responsive to what is said and tailors the reply accordingly. Interactive speech is the most common type of oral communication. The following methods will help you evaluate both kinds of oral language.

Audio recordings

At the beginning of an instructional program, course, or semester, record all students individually as they state their names and the date of the recording, read a prepared target-level passage, and tell a story on an assigned topic. At intervals during the instructional program, follow the same procedure, using the same passage and assigned topic. Compare progress over time. Permit students to review their recordings and make self-assessments of their improvement.

Five-by-Five

Use a five-by-five graphic organizer to arrange information and compare and contrast five ideas, events, characters, or objects. Have different students explain the relationships, similarities, and differences.

Self-assessment by interview or questionnaire

Depending on students' competency, develop and use a structured interview or questionnaire to find out what they feel are their language strengths and needs. A K-W-L format indicating what students feel they *know, want* to learn, and have *learned* can also be used. With less competent language users, pointing to smiley or frowning faces in response to questions and using pictures to show context can be helpful. For example:

I can speak English	With friends	☺	☹
	At home	☺	☹
	At school	☺	☹
	At the bank	☺	☹
	At my job	☺	☹
	In math class	☺	☹
	At soccer practice	☺	☹
I understand English	In school	☺	☹
	At the grocery store	☺	☹
	On the radio	☺	☹
	On TV	☺	☹
	On the phone	☺	☹
	At the airport	☺	☹
	When one person talks	☺	☹
	When people are talking to each other	☺	☹

Giving directions

Have a student give directions orally to another student for the completion of a simple assigned task, such as making a sandwich. Intermediate or advanced students may give directions for tasks requiring the use of technical or advanced vocabulary and multiple steps, such as mixing a solution for a science class.

Extemporaneous narrative

Direct the student to select from a set of topic cards and prepare a brief oral presentation. Allow five minutes of preparation for a three-minute narrative; ten minutes of preparation for a five- to seven-minute narrative. Students may make and use an outline or brief notes.

Twenty Questions

Prepare sets of twenty questions on single topics and ask individual students to respond to each. Use a moderate pace for the question-and-answer protocol, and vary the types of questions asked (yes/no, tag, open-ended, negative, opinion, comparison, and so on).

Paired discussion

Direct pairs of students to discuss an event or situation. A photo may be provided as a stimulus. No preparation time is permitted.

Paired decision making

Direct pairs of students to engage in a discussion that leads to making a decision. For example, provide the pair with newspaper ads for three stereo systems and ask them to discuss the features and prices of each and determine the best buy.

Impromptu storytelling

Direct students to prepare and then tell a story. The story should be original and creative. Encourage the use of gestures, movement, and props.

Cued storytelling

Have students select a story cue card showing an event in progress. Tell them to describe what is happening in the picture and then make up and relate a suitable ending for the story.

Oral report

Direct students to research a self-selected or assigned topic and prepare a presentation of between three and seven minutes. Encourage the use of visual aids, including charts and graphs. Advanced students should speak on a complex situation or idea.

Travelog

Have students collect information, photos, and travel materials about their native country or a country of interest to them; assemble the information and graphics using presentation software; then present the travelog orally or by incorporating a voiceover into the electronic presentation.

Open-ended interview

Interview each student individually for ten to twenty minutes. Ask leading questions and provide continuation prompts so that the conversation is extended and permits at least some topics to be exhausted before moving on to new ones.

Story mapping

Using an appropriate software application, have students first create a story map for a story they have read, then present the story electronically, explaining the elements and how they flowed in the story.

Structured interview

Interview each student individually using a prepared set of questions on target subjects. This approach is especially useful for assessing vocabulary related to specific subjects or situations.

Role-play

Direct pairs of students to role-play on assigned topics. For example, have one student ask the other for advice on selecting an affordable restaurant.

Dramatization

Select a topic for dramatization and direct a small group of students to prepare a script incorporating dialogue, gestures, movement, and props. Have the students practice and perform the dramatization.

Reading aloud

Select passages of various types (narrative, instructive, poetry, technical) and have individual students read them aloud.

Poetry

Have students prepare poetry, rhymes, or riddles and recite them aloud to the class.

Story retelling

Direct individual students to listen to a tape-recorded story of between 200 and 250 words and then retell the story in their own words. Gist recall, not verbatim recall, is required.

List 9.5. Assessing Reading Comprehension

When assessing the reading comprehension skills of ELLs, consider methods that highlight vocabulary, idiomatic expression, register, and connotation. These elements may pose more difficulty to ELLs than to native speakers of English. Keep in mind students' frustration and their instructional and independent reading levels when constructing assessments and using the results.

Cloze procedure for comprehension. Select a written passage of approximately 250 words that deals with functional, sociocultural, or curriculum content. Delete every fifth or seventh word. Ask students to read the passage and fill in the missing words. As an easier alternative, direct students to fill in the missing words from choices presented on the answer sheet. For a more difficult task, include synonyms in the list of suggested words so that students have to pick the most appropriate one for the context.

Coherence recognition. Create written passages in which you embed words, phrases, or sentences that do not fit the meaning of the whole. Direct students to read the passages and circle the misfit words, phrases, or sentences.

Gist recognition. Select a passage of between one hundred and two hundred words. Ask students to read the passage and then select the best title, main idea statement, or summary statement for the passage. Provide four choices for each item.

Logical predictions from reading. Select written passages of between 150 and 250 words. Direct students to read each passage and its four additional statements and then select a statement that best represents the most likely next occurrence for each passage.

Paraphrase recognition. Select a passage of up to two hundred words and create four related statements, one of which is a paraphrase of the passage. Direct students to read the passage and statements and select the statement that best paraphrases the passage.

Factual comprehension. Select a written passage of between 200 and 250 words. Prepare a set of detail or factual questions related to the passage. Direct students to read the passage and questions and then select answers from the choices provided.

Inferential comprehension. Select a written passage of between 200 and 250 words. Prepare a set of inference or analytical questions related to the passage. Direct students to read the passage and questions and then select answers from the choices provided.

List 9.6. Assessing Written Language Skills

Written language proficiency has two components: vocabulary and structure. The more extensive the students' vocabulary, the better able they will be to express their ideas. Structure refers to grammar, punctuation, and other rules. When assessing vocabulary, be alert for students who have not progressed beyond literal meanings of words; they will have difficulty with idioms, synonyms, register, and tone. When assessing structural knowledge, look for students who overgeneralize an English language element (for example, using *childrens* as a plural) or apply a grammatical structure from their native language to English.

Methods for Assessing Vocabulary Knowledge

Definition
Show students pictures from a set of target objects or concepts and have them write the name and a definition for each picture. This exercise can be used with advanced subject-area vocabulary as well for as the most basic concepts. As examples, create a set of pictures that shows lab equipment, cell-division sequences, or molecular structure; or create a set of pictures showing basic items of clothing.

Vocabulary matching
Give students a set of pictures of objects or concepts and a set of words that name each picture. Direct students to match the pictures with the correct words.

Naming
Direct students to write the appropriate vocabulary word when shown pictures or visual representations of the words.

Classifying concepts
Ask students to arrange into meaningful categories words presented on flash cards, then to copy the words onto paper and label each category. Use twenty to thirty flash cards at a time. For example:

transportation	car	bus	train	bike	skateboard
people	happy	angry	tired	old	thin
job titles	waiter	teacher	baker	teller	priest
buildings	school	theater	post office	deli	factory

Distinguishing meaningful categories
Give students a worksheet on which words are presented in groups of five, including one word that does not share the relationship of the other four. Have students cross out the words that do not belong and replace them with appropriate words.

Matching definitions
Prepare a worksheet with target words listed in the left column and their definitions listed in a different order in the right column. Have students match the words to their correct definitions.

Multiple-choice definitions
Prepare a worksheet that presents target words with four possible definitions. Have students select and circle the correct definitions.

Recognizing antonyms and synonyms

Prepare a worksheet on which the target words are presented and paired with another word, either an antonym or a synonym. Have students indicate, by writing *A* or *S* on the worksheet, whether the pairs are antonyms or synonyms.

Supplying antonyms and synonyms

Have students write either antonyms or synonyms for a set of target words listed on a worksheet.

Analogies

Direct students to fill in the missing word in a series of analogies. Vary the difficulty of the analogy format. Test knowledge of part and whole, antonyms, synonyms, cause and effect, size, use, and so on.

Cloze procedure for vocabulary

Select a passage of 200 to 250 words and delete target words, either specific vocabulary words or word types. Direct students to fill in the missing words in the passage.

Interpreting idioms

Provide students with a list of idioms and idiomatic expressions and ask them to provide paraphrases of the meaning.

Vocabulary editing

Provide a worksheet of sentences containing target vocabulary words used either correctly or incorrectly with respect to the meaning of the words. Have students edit the incorrect usage by changing either the word or the context.

Multiple-meaning words

Provide students with a list of multiple-meaning words (homonyms). Direct them to write sets of sentences that show the correct use of each word in its various contexts.

Using context clues

Select a passage of 200 to 250 words and replace key words with nonsense syllables. Direct students to read the passage and replace the nonsense words with appropriate words.

Semantic mapping

Provide students with sets of related words and have them create semantic maps showing the relationships among the words.

Methods for Assessing Knowledge of Language Structure

Sentence order

Select ten sentences of appropriate difficulty for the students. Take the words of each sentence and rewrite them in a randomly ordered list, removing punctuation and capitalization. Give students the lists and have them re-create the sentences with proper word order, punctuation, and capitalization.

Cloze procedure for grammar

Select a passage of 150 words and delete those that fit a grammatical type, such as possessive pronouns. Have students complete the passage by writing in the missing words. Example: *Arthur, Jill, and John gave the girl _____ coats.*

Editing

Develop a written passage of 150 to 200 words that includes embedded errors in grammar, spelling, punctuation, word order, and capitalization. Direct students to edit the passage correcting all errors.

Embedded choice

Develop a written passage of 200 to 250 words that includes several embedded choices focused on grammar or mechanics. Have students cross out the incorrect words so that the final version of the passage is coherent and correct. Example: *Jack and John took (his/their) books to the library. (They/We) gave (it/them) to the librarian.*

Expansion

Develop a written passage of 200 to 250 words that includes several embedded word cues. Direct students to insert suitable words into the passage according to the cues. Example: *The (adjective, adjective) man walked (adverb) (preposition) the barn.*

Variations on a theme

Select a passage of approximately one hundred words. Direct students to rewrite the passage to change the voice from active to passive, the tense from past to future, the subject from third person to first person plural, and so on. Some basic passages can be used to test all standard transformations.

Literal translations

Give students passages in their native languages and ask them to translate them into standard American English. Select brief passages on a variety of topics so that different grammatical patterns and vocabulary are required.

Registers

Direct students to rewrite a passage to change the register to suit a specific audience. For example, have students rewrite a compliment so that it is suitable for a four-year-old sister; a priest, rabbi, or other clergyperson; a policeman; a best friend.

Essays

Have each student select a topic and develop a thesis statement for it. Then have the students draft, edit, and produce final versions of their essays.

List 9.7. Tests for Assessing English Language Learners

Selecting tests for use in your classroom, school, or school district is an important professional decision. To make appropriate choices, be clear about how you plan to use the test (placement, language dominance, ability, progress, and so on), then look for a test constructed for that use. Be sure that the test matches your population (age, grade, L1/L2) and check its published statements of validity and reliability. Ask whether the results correlate to other standardized tests you already use in your district. Most of these answers are available online at the publishers' Web sites and listed under technical information. The following tests are commonly used for identification, diagnosis, placement, and progress measurement of ELL students in K–12 settings. Some, as noted, are also appropriate for use with adults.

Bilingual Oral Language Test (BOLT), 1977

Bilingual Media Productions, Inc., P.O. Box 9337, North Berkeley Station, Berkeley, CA 94709. Formerly called the Bahia Oral Language Test, BOLT has independent English and Spanish measures in the same instrument. It measures syntax use in simple to complex oral sentence patterns and classifies students as non-English speaking, limited English speaking, and English speaking. Administration takes under ten minutes. Use in grades intermediate and above.

Basic English Skills Test (BEST), 1984

Center for Applied Linguistics, 4646 40th Street NW, Washington, DC 20016-1859. http://www.cal.org. The BEST is a criterion-referenced test for adults who have studied English. It tests elementary English language proficiency in listening comprehension, speaking, reading, and writing. The test takes about ninety minutes and is used for placement and to assess proficiency.

Basic Elementary Skills Test—Spanish (BEST-Spanish), 1984

Los Amigos Research Associates, 7035 Galewood Street, San Diego, CA 92120. The BEST-Spanish is a multiple-choice achievement test of reading, writing, spelling, and math in Spanish. It can be used in grades K to 9 for placement, progress, and program assessment. It is untimed, and approximate grade-level scores are derived from the number of correct answers. The test is also available in other languages, including Arabic, Chinese, Farsi, and Vietnamese.

Bilingual Syntax Measure I (BSM I), 1980

The Psychological Corporation, Harcourt Assessment, Inc., 19500 Bulverde Road, San Antonio, TX 78259. http://www.harcourtassessment.com. The BSM I assesses speaking and listening proficiency in English and Spanish in children in grades K to 2. It is untimed and discriminates proficiency at five levels. It is used for identifying language dominance, for placement, for assessing proficiency, and for program assessment.

Bilingual Syntax Measure II (BSM II), 1980

The Psychological Corporation, Harcourt Assessment, Inc., 19500 Bulverde Road, San Antonio, TX 78259. http://www.harcourtassessment.com. The BSM II is similar to BSM I and assesses speaking and listening proficiency in English and Spanish. It is appropriate for students in grades 3 to 12. In addition to the five elementary proficiency levels of BSM I, there is a sixth level representing intermediate language skills. It is untimed and is used for identifying language dominance, for placement, for assessing proficiency, and for program assessment.

Boehm Test of Basic Concepts, Third Edition (Boehm-3), 2000

Harcourt Assessment, Inc., P.O. Box 599700, San Antonio, TX 78259. http://www. harcourtassessment.com. Boehm-3 is a group-administered test of fifty spatial and other concepts considered necessary for school achievement in grades K to 2. There are provisions for administration in Spanish and English, and two forms are available if you are planning for pre- and posttest comparison. Test administration takes between thirty and thirty-five minutes.

Brigance Assessment of Basic Skills—Revised, Spanish Edition, 2007

Curriculum Associates, Inc., 153 Rangeway Road, North Billerica, MA 01862. http:// www.curriculumassociates.com. The Brigance Assessment of Basic Skills is an individual test used to assess academic performance in K to 6 students for whom Spanish is their native language. The test has ten sections on readiness, speech, functional word recognition, oral reading, reading comprehension, word analysis, listening, writing and alphabetizing, numbers and computation, and measurement. The test is begun at a level believed to be one year below the student's actual performance level, so not all sections of the test are used for each student. The test is criterion-referenced, untimed, and scored while the testing is in progress. Scores can be used for placement, performance, progress, and program assessment.

Degrees of Reading Power (DRP), 1989

Questar Assessment, Inc., 4 Hardscrabble Heights, Brewster, NY 10509-0382. http://www. questarai.com. The DRP tests are standardized group-administered cloze tests of prose reading comprehension for students in grades 4 to 12. Scores reported as DRP units are converted to percentile ranks and stanine scores, and can be used to identify readability levels of materials that students would be likely to read and understand at the independent, instructional, and frustration levels. DRP tests are usually scored by the publisher rather than locally.

IDEA Language Proficiency Test—English (IPT), 1994

Ballard & Tighe, Publishers, 480 Atlas Street, Brea, CA 92821. http://www.ballard-tighe.com. The three levels of the IDEA proficiency tests measure the language proficiency of students in preschool through secondary school. Oral and written tests are used to assess overall language ability, although the oral proficiency test may be used for the placement of ELLs in ESL programs. The tests are administered to individuals and progress through levels until examinees reach their proficiency ceiling. Test results place students in one of three categories: non-English speaking, limited English speaking, or fluent English speaking. The reading and written tests consist of multiple-choice items for vocabulary, comprehension, syntax, verbal expression, and writing. The three levels of oral proficiency tests are pre-ITP (for ages 3 to 5), ITP I (for grades K to 6), and ITP II (for grades 7 to 12).

IDEA Oral Language Proficiency Test—Spanish (IPT I–Spanish), 1987

Ballard & Tighe, Publishers, 480 Atlas Street, Brea, CA 92821. http://www.ballard-tighe. com. The IPT I–Spanish provides information on native Spanish-speakers' use of syntax, morphological structure, lexical items, phonological structure, comprehension, and oral production. Results categorize students as non-, limited, or fluent Spanish speakers. It is used for placement of Spanish-speaking students in grades K to 6. It is an individual test in which examinees move through levels of difficulty until they reach their proficiency ceiling. It takes about fifteen minutes.

Language Assessment Scales (LAS R/W), 1990

CTB/McGraw Hill, 20 Ryan Ranch Road, Monterey, CA 93940. http://www.ctb.com. The LAS R/W has three levels. Level 1 is used for grades 2 to 3, level 2 is used for grades 4 to 6, and level 3 is used for grades 7 to 9. The LAS R/W has subtests in vocabulary, fluency, reading for information, mechanics and usage, comprehension, oral production, and writing. It is used to assess reading and writing competency and has two forms to facilitate use for pre- and postinstruction. It is used in conjunction with the Language Assessment Scales Oral for a complete language assessment. Scoring can be done locally or by the publisher. Results categorize students as nonreaders, limited readers, or competent readers. *Competent* is considered at or above the 40th percentile on a nationally normed test for mainstream students.

Language Assessment Scales Oral (LAS-O)—English, 1990

CTB/McGraw Hill, 20 Ryan Ranch Road, Monterey, CA 93940. http://www.ctb.com. LAS-O has two levels and categorizes students as non-English speakers, limited English speakers, or fluent English speakers. Level 1 is used in grades 1 to 6 and level 2 is used in grades 7 to 12. As with LAS R/W, the test has two forms that can be used for pre- and posttesting. LAS-O has an oral language subtest of vocabulary, listening comprehension, and story retelling, and a pronunciation subtest of minimal sound pairs and phonemes.

Language Proficiency Test (LPT), 1981

Academic Therapy Publications, 20 Commercial Boulevard, Novato, CA 94947. http://www.academictherapy.com. The LPT measures the aural and oral language, reading, and writing ability of ELLs in grades 7 to 12 and adults. It is a criterion-referenced test and seven of the nine subtests can be administered in a group setting. In the aural/oral component, students respond to commands, questions about home and school, and questions about a paragraph that is read to them. The reading component has students choose words to complete sentences and answer comprehension questions about text samples from the first grade to sixth grade level of difficulty. The writing component has a grammar subtest, an open-ended short-answer writing test, and a paragraph-writing subtest. Results categorize students as having no proficiency or elementary, intermediate, or advanced proficiency.

The Maculaitis Assessment of Competencies (MAC), 2001

Touchstone Applied Science Associates, Inc., 4 Hardscrabble Heights, Brewster, NY 10509. http://www.questarai.com. The MAC has five levels and is used in grades K to 12 to identify students for placement, progress, and proficiency as ELLs and for ESL program evaluation. The graded test levels are K–1, 2–3, 4–5, 6–8, and 9–12. MAC addresses five areas: oral expression, listening comprehension, vocabulary knowledge, reading comprehension, and writing ability. A readiness level for K–3 is also available. There are two forms that can be used as pre- and posttests. Scoring is reported in percentiles, stanines, and normal curve equivalents. Although some parts can be administered to groups, others require individual administration.

Test of English as a Foreign Language (TOEFL), 2005

Educational Testing Service (ETS), P.O. Box 6155, Princeton, NJ 08541. http://www.ets.org. The TOEFL has been a mainstay of college and adult English proficiency and is commonly required for entrance to a U.S. college or university or for employment with a government agency. Since 2005, ETS has been phasing in its Internet-based (iBT) version of the test and phasing out the paper-based version. TOEFL assesses reading, listening, speaking, and writing skills for success in academic settings. It is based on a vocabulary database of nearly three million words collected from classes, labs, office interactions, study groups, and campus service interactions at U.S. educational institutions. Scores are reported for each of the four components and as a total score. Additional information about the examinee's strengths and weaknesses as identified by test-item responses are also reported.

Woodcock Munoz Language Survey—Revised (WMLS-R), 2006

Riverside Publishing, 3800 Golf Road, Suite 100, Rolling Meadows, IL 60008. http://www. riverpub.com. The WMLS-R is a standardized assessment of reading, writing, listening, and comprehension with grade norms from kindergarten to graduate school. It focuses on cognitive-academic language proficiency and includes seven individually administered tests on picture vocabulary, verbal analogies, letter-word identification, dictation, understanding directions, story recall, and passage comprehension. It has an English and a Spanish form, and when both are administered a comparative score can be calculated. Scores are derived for the individual tests, and results for the seven tests are combined into eleven clusters (oral expression; listening; oral language; reading; writing; reading-writing; language comprehension; applied language proficiency; broad English ability; broad English ability, total; and oral language, total) using the WMLS-R scoring and reporting program. The program also generates a narrative report of the student's language competence, including the identification of the student's cognitive-academic language proficiency at one of six levels from negligible to advanced.

Universal Nonverbal Intelligence Test (UNIT), 1996

Riverside Publishing, 3800 Golf Road, Suite 100, Rolling Meadows, IL 60008. http://www. riverpub.com. The UNIT can be used with students between the ages of five and seventeen years, eleven months. There are three test options—abbreviated, standard, and extended, and administration takes between fifteen and forty-five minutes, depending on the option selected. It uses hand and body gestures, paper and pencil activities, pointing, and manipulatives for stimulus-response and is entirely nonverbal. Scores include age equivalents, intelligence quotients, and other derived scales. The nonverbal format is considered to reduce sources of test bias.

Section Ten

Helpful Resources and References

List 10.1. ESL/ELL Virtual Reference Library

Every ESL/ELL classroom (and every ESL/ELL teacher) is just a click or two away from a world-class reference library. The following sites and their links provide information and answers for just about every question. Create a hotlist, or bookmark individual sites to make browsing and using them easy.

Dictionaries

Little Explorers Picture Dictionary	http://www.LittleExplorers.com/dictionary.html
Multilingual Picture Dictionary	http://www.EnchantedLearning.com/Dictionary.html
The Internet Picture Dictionary	http://www.pdictionary.com
One Look Dictionary	http://www.onelook.com
A Web of On-Line Dictionaries	http://ling.kgw.tu-berlin.de/call/webofdic/diction4.html
Spanish-English Dictionary	http://www.spanishdict.com
Spanish-English Dictionary	http://www.wordreference.com
Chinese-English Dictionary	http://www.chinese-tools.com/tools/dictionary.html
Chinese-English Dictionary	http://www.lexiconer.com
French-English Dictionary	http://www.wordreference.com

French-English Dictionary	http://machaut.uchicago.edu/?resource=frengdict
French-English Dictionary	http://www.french-linguistics.co.uk/dictionary
Portuguese-English Dictionary	http://www.freedict.com/onldict/por.html
Portuguese-English Dictionary	http://www.wordreference.com
Italian-English Dictionary	http://www.freedict.com/onldict/ita.html
Italian-English Dictionary	http://www.wordreference.com/enit
Vietnamese-English Dictionary	http://vdict.com
German-English Dictionary	http://dict.tu-chemnitz.de
German-English Dictionary	http://www.ieee.et.tu-dresden.de/cgi-bin/cgiwrap/warnerr/search.sh
Hmong-English Dictionary	http://ww2.saturn.stpaul.k12.mn.us/hmong.sathmong.html
Pashto-English Dictionary	http://www.yorku.ca/twainweb/troberts/pashto/pashlex1.html
Swahili-English Dictionary	http://www.freedict.com/onldict/swa.html
English Homophone Dictionary	http://www.earlham.edu/~peters/writing/homofone.htm
Merriam-Webster Dictionary	http://www.m-w.com
refdesk.com Dictionaries and Language Resources	http://www.refdesk.com/factdict.html
Cambridge Dictionaries	http://dictionary.cambridge.org
Online Dictionaries	http://www.dict.org
Online Dictionaries	http://www.dictionary.com
I Love Languages (formerly Human Languages Page)	http://www.ilovelanguages.com

Multilingual Language Tools

Multilingual language tools for searching the Web across languages, translating text, and translating Web pages	http://www.google.com/language_tools?hl=en

Almanacs, Encyclopedias, and Specialized References

Fact Monster	http://www.factmonster.com
Information Please Almanac	http://www.infoplease.com/almanacs.html
My Virtual Reference Desk	http://www.refdesk.com

The Old Farmers Almanac	http://www.almanac.com
Roget's New Millennium Thesaurus	http://www.thesaurus.com
Wikipedia	http://en.wikipedia.org/wiki/Main_Page
Events and Calendars of the Day	http://www.sldirectory.com/cal.html
Encyclopedia Smithsonian	http://www.si.edu/resource/faq/start.htm
KidSpace @ the Internet Public Library	http://www.ipl.org/youth
Bartleby.com Great Books Online	http://www.bartleby.com
Franklin Institute Educational Hotlists	http://sln.fi.edu/tfi/hotlists/hotlists.html

Countries, Maps, and Culture

CIA World Factbook	http://www.odci.gov/cia/publications/factbook
Google Maps	http://maps.google.com
Google Earth	http://www.earth.google.com
MapQuest	http://www.mapquest.com
United Nations Cyberschoolbus	http://cyberschoolbus.un.org/index.asp
NASA Earth Images	http://modis.gsfc.nasa.gov/gallery/index.php
National Geographic Homework Help	http://www.nationalgeographic.com/education/homework
United Nations Education, Scientific, and Cultural Organization (UNESCO)	http://portal.unesco.org/culture
Perry-Castañeda Library Map Collection	http://www.lib.utexas.edu/maps/index.html
World Cultures	http://members.aol.com/bowermanb/culture.html
Internet Public Library Culture Quest World Tour	http://www.ipl.org/div/cquest
Library of Congress Global Gateway	http://international.loc.gov/intldl/intldlhome.html
U.S. and Worldwide Newspapers	http://www.refdesk.com/paper.html
World Clock	http://eslus.com/Gizmos/worldclock.html

Graphics, Photos, Clip Art, and Video Sources

AOL Photo of the Day	http://reference.aol.com/photooftheday
Kodak Picture of the Day	http://www.kodak.com
Google Images	http://images.google.com
YouTube videos	http://www.youtube.com

Google Video	http://video.google.com
Classroom Clip Art	http://classroomclipart.com
Clip Art	http://www.clip-art.com/index.php
Microsoft Clip Art	http://office.microsoft.com/en-us/clipart/default.aspx
Dover Clip Art	http://www.doverpublications.com/dspa023
Discovery Education Clip Art	http://school.discoveryeducation.com/clipart

List 10.2. Web Sites for ESL/ELL Teachers

Looking for professional information? Language research? Lesson plan ideas? Teaching resources? Language games? Puzzle makers? Worksheets? Everything you need for teaching ESL/ELL can be found on the following Web sites. Be sure to bookmark your personal favorites. Note: only *free* resources are listed.

Associations and Resource Centers

Teachers of English to Speakers of Other Languages (TESOL)	http://www.tesol.org
National Association for Bilingual Education	http://www.nabe.org
National Clearinghouse for English Language Acquisition and Language Instruction Educational Programs	http://www.ncela.gwu.edu
Institute of Education Sciences Regional Education Laboratories	http://ies.ed.gov/ncee/edlabs
National Council of Teachers of English	http://www.ncte.org
Center for Applied Linguistics	http://www.cal.org

Journals and Magazines

ESL Magazine	http://www.eslmag.com
English Teaching Forum	http://exchanges.state.gov/forum
Bilingual Research Journal	http://brj.asu.edu
Language Magazine	http://www.languagemagazine.com
The Internet TESL Journal	http://iteslj.org
Teaching English as a Second or Foreign Language	http://tesl-ej.org/ej42/toc.html
Language Learning and Technology	http://llt.msu.edu
Reading in a Foreign Language	http://nflrc.hawaii.edu/rfl

Teaching Resources

1-Language: alphabet practice, games	http://www.1-language.com
Activities for ESL: podcasts, puzzles, conversation starters, quizzes	http://a4esl.org
Apples 4 the Teacher: interactive games, music, math, science, and more	http://www.apples4theteacher.com/index.html
Ben's Guide to U.S. Government for Kids: graded materials for social studies	http://bensguide.gpo.gov/3-5/games/print.html

Bilingual/ESL/Multicultural Education Resources: links and resources for ESL, bilingual, and multicultural education

http://www-bcf.usc.edu/~cmmr/ BEResources.html

Breaking News English: current events reading and audio files for intermediate ESL students

http://www.breakingnewsenglish.com

Common Errors in English: practice and lessons for grammar

http://www.wsu.edu:8080/~brians/ errors/errors.html

Daily ESL: short readings with discussion and study questions to encourage development of context-appropriate language and range of conversational skills

http://www.dailyesl.com

Dave's ESL Cafe: wide variety of teacher and student materials; lots of links

http://www.eslcafe.com/search/ index.html

ESL EFL Resources for Teachers of Young Children

http://www.mes-english.com

ESL Flow: teaching materials, printables, games, and more for elementary through adult students

http://www.eslflow.com

ESL Independent Study Lab: leveled material for listening, games, vocabulary, reading, and more

http://www.lclark.edu/~krauss/ toppicks/toppicks.html

ESL Mania: lessons, vocabulary, accent reduction, resources, and more for teachers and secondary to adult students

http://www.eslmania.com

ESL Partyland: lesson plans, interactive games, links, and other resources for teachers and students

http://www.eslpartyland.com/teachers/ Tinitial.htm

Everything ESL: lesson plans, discussions, downloads

http://www.everythingesl.net

Exam English: practice for TOEFL and other English proficiency tests

http://www.examenglish.com/ default.php

Fun Spelling Facts: humorous poems and facts about English spelling

http://www.espindle.org/fun_facts.html

Games and Activities for the ESL/ELL Classroom: more than one hundred games and activities

http://iteslj.org/c/games.html

Gamequarium: loads of games and interactives for grades K to 6

http://www.gamequarium.com

Graphic Organizers: printable; many types	http://gotoscience.com/Graphic_Organizers.html
Interesting Things for ESL Students: podcasts, games, puzzles, vocabulary, lessons	http://www.manythings.org
Karin's ESL Partyland: interactive lessons, games, links, discussion forums, quizzes	http://www.eslpartyland.com
Lanternfish: ESL lesson plans, printables, science, vocabulary, games, seasonal activities, and more	http://bogglesworldesl.com
Learning Vocabulary Fun: games to support vocabulary development	http://www.vocabulary.co.il/index_main.php
Mes English: games, flashcards, and other printables for elementary grades	http://www.mes-english.com
Randall's ESL Cyber Listening Lab: recorded graded conversations for listening practice	http://www.esl-lab.com
Sing-Along Songs: midis and lyrics	http://kids.niehs.nih.gov/musicchild.htm
Spelling Wizard: uses your vocabulary list to make word searches	http://www.scholastic.com/kids/homework/spelling.htm
States and Capitals: Information on all fifty states	http://www.50states.com
Teaching Tips: ESL, reading, lesson plans, classroom management	http://www.teachingtips.com
Using English: worksheets, lesson plans for grammar	http://www.usingenglish.com/handouts

List 10.3. Glossary of ESL/ELL Language Learning Terms

Abstract noun.   A word that names a quality or idea. Examples: *beauty, trust, fear, patience.*

Academic communicative competence.   The ability to use appropriate school and subject area vocabulary to express concepts and ideas at a level consonant with the age or grade of the learner.

Accent.   The relative stress, emphasis, or degree of loudness placed on a syllable. Examples: *a*-ble, in-*struct.* Accent also refers to the pronunciation style associated with speakers of a region. Examples: *a French accent, a Southern accent.*

Accommodations.   Changes in order to make something more usable or understandable to someone with a special language, learning, or physical need. In assessment, accommodations may be made to the presentation, response method, setting, timing, or scheduling of the test.

Action series.   In language learning, a sequence of statements about actions being performed.

Active vocabulary.   Vocabulary an individual understands and uses independently.

Active voice.   When the subject of a verb is the doer or agent of the action. Example: *Kathy baked the pie.*

Adapted program.   Allows students with special language, learning, or physical needs to participate in an existing curriculum by making changes to format (for example, Braille and Books on Tape), strategies (such as visual aids and models), presentation (for example, using a sign language interpreter, transcriptions, or closed captioning), and assessment practices (such as use of a computer, extended time, oral exams, written exams, and taped responses).

Additive bilingualism.   A second language is learned but does not replace an individual's first language. The individual becomes literate in two languages.

Adjective.   A word that describes a noun or a pronoun and tells what kind, how many, or which one. Examples: *lazy, beautiful, three, that.*

Adverb.   A word that describes a verb, an adjective, or another adverb by providing information about where, when, how, how much, or to what extent. Examples: *outside, later, seriously, few.*

Affective filter.   An unconscious change, distortion, or blocking of information that occurs because an individual reacts to its emotional or psychological content.

Allophone.   The variations of sounds associated with a single phoneme. Allophones are the result of the phoneme's juxtaposition to other phonemes. Allophones do not change meaning. Example: the variation of the /p/ sound in pick/cup.

Alternative assessment.   Approaches that differ from the traditional format for measuring students' knowledge and skills. Example: having a debate on causes for the Civil War rather than giving a multiple-choice test.

AMAO.   Annual measurable achievement objectives, or expected gain, in English language proficiency (reading, writing, speaking, listening, and comprehension) for children served under Title III programs.

Analogy.   A correspondence between two things on the basis of a similar feature or application of a rule. In language learning, grammatical structures are often applied and practiced using analogy. Example: *set/setting, get/_____.*

Appositive. A noun or phrase placed immediately after the noun it explains and that has the same grammatical function. Examples: My sister *Nancy* is the youngest. The HighTops, *a local band*, are going to play at the picnic.

Aprenda achievement test. A Spanish-language achievement test similar to the Stanford Achievement Test. Aprenda has several forms, including preschool, primary, and intermediate grades, and measures reading, language arts, and mathematics.

Articles. Adjectives that precede and identify nouns; also called *determiners*. A definite article (*the*) points to a particular item; an indefinite article (*a, an, some*) points to a class of items; a partitive article (*a few, some, a lot of, many, a little, much*) points to a portion of the class of items. Examples: *the ticket, a box, a few raisins*.

Articulation. The purposeful production of sounds by the vocal organs.

Audiolingual method. In language teaching, a method in which the student listens to the spoken message and then repeats it. This instructional process is also called the aural-oral method. It is based on the theory that making certain sounds and using correct grammar is an automatic, unconscious act that is developed through vocabulary and sentence pattern repetition.

Audiologist. Measures hearing ability and provides services for auditory training; offers advice on hearing aids.

Aural learner. One who learns best by processing auditory information.

Auxiliary verb. Used with the main verb for verb forms that show tense and mood; also called a helping verb. Examples: *will* go, *has been* crying, *had* gone.

Backward buildup. A language-teaching strategy in which a word or sentence is broken into components and reconstructed in a series of repetitions, beginning with the end followed by the next to the end plus the end, and so on. This strategy is particularly useful in practicing stress and intonation patterns. (See *Right-to-left strings*.)

Baseline data. Performance data (such as test scores) collected at the beginning of instruction for comparison after teaching and learning have taken place.

Basic interpersonal communication skills (BICS). Language necessary to participate in everyday conversations and in which context provides clues to meaning. BICS may be acquired in less than two years. See *CALP* for contrasting skill.

Bicultural. Identifying with two cultures and exhibiting their characteristics. A person who is bicultural may or may not be bilingual.

Bidialectal. Able to speak and understand two dialects of a single language.

Bilingual education. Instruction using both the native language (L1) and the target language (L2) of the students.

Bilingual. Having the ability to speak and understand two languages.

Biliterate. Able to understand and communicate effectively using two languages' vocabulary, writing, and syntax systems.

Blending. Fusing discrete sounds or phonemes into recognizable words.

CALP. Cognitive academic language proficiency. Language skill needed for academic learning. More advanced than BICS. New information is presented formally in books, lectures, and other media, unsupported by gestures or social cues. Example: new information in social studies or science texts.

Chained dialogue.   In language teaching, a practice exercise in which the first speaker makes a statement or asks a question, the second speaker responds to the first, the third speaker responds to the second, and so on.

Chants.   Short, repetitive songs or rhymes that have distinctive rhythms. Chants are often used in group work to introduce a concept or words, or to teach English intonation.

Choral response.   A response by a group speaking the same words in unison.

Chunk.   To divide a long word into smaller, pronounceable parts. Usually suffixes, prefixes, and roots, or component words of a compound word. Example: *un-luck-y.*

Clause.   A group of words containing a subject and predicate (noun and verb) that expresses a thought. An independent clause can stand alone as a sentence. Example: *It's time for lunch.* A dependent clause cannot stand alone as a sentence. Example: *When John rings the bell,* it's time for lunch.

Cloze passage.   A sentence or paragraph from which specific words (nouns, adjectives, verbs, and so on) or words in a pattern (such as every fifth word) are deleted. Students fill in the missing words using context to construct meaning.

Cluster.   A group of letters or sounds that frequently occur together. Example: *–ble, spr–.*

Code.   A system of symbols, letters, or words used to transmit meaning. Also, the total language system of a community.

Code switching.   Changing from one language to another in a conversation or writing.

Cognate.   Words in different languages that came from the same root and have similar spellings and meanings. Example: *admiration/admiracion* (English/Spanish).

Cognitive code theory.   A theory of language acquisition that suggests language is learned by repeated exposure to examples of the rules of the language.

Collective noun.   A word that names a group or collection of people or things. Examples: *family, army, group, flock, band, herd.*

Collocations.   Words that occur together to convey a meaning. Example: *commit a crime, take a peek.*

Common noun.   A word that names one of a class or group of persons, places, or things. Common nouns are not capitalized. Examples: *state, sea, building.*

Common underlying proficiency (CUP).   Theory that two languages may integrate into one central system and that underlying skills not directly related to language—such as art, Internet searching, and mathematics—may be transferred from one language to another once the skill is acquired.

Communicative competence.   Ability to communicate effectively and appropriately in a variety of social and academic contexts by knowing when to speak, whom to address, what to say, and how to say it.

Compound noun.   A noun made up of two or more words. Examples: *seatbelt, brothers-in-law, sunshine.*

Concrete noun.   Something that can be perceived by one or more of the senses. Examples: *book, snow, steam, child.*

Conditional.   A word part, word, phrase, or other language expressing a condition. Example: *If it snows tomorrow,* school will be canceled.

Conjunction.   A word used to join words, phrases, or clauses. Examples: *and, or, because, however, but.*

Connotation.   Meaning of a word or phrase based on context or usage rather than on the literal definition of the word or words.

Constituent.   In language, the smallest structural unit carrying meaning. Example: town/*s*, carry/*ing*.

Content words.   The words that name things, actions, and qualities.

Content-based ESL.   Teaching method that uses instructional materials and strategies related to subject areas to teach English and to teach and reinforce content and study skills.

Continuant.   A sound that can be extended or prolonged. Example: /*m*/, /*s*/.

Contrastive analysis.   Comparison of the features of two or more languages. A contrastive analysis of a student's native language and English is often used as an instructional tool.

Correlation.   A positive or negative relationship between two things, in which change in one thing will result in a change in the other.

Countable noun.   A noun that can be modified by a numeral and that has both singular and plural forms. Examples: *one pillow, five pillows; one bed, two beds.*

Criterion-referenced test.   A test that determines whether the test taker has mastered a particular skill sufficiently by comparing the performance of the test taker to a fixed standard or criterion. Criterion-referenced tests are often used as placement or promotion tests.

Critical period hypothesis.   The idea that the brain is most receptive to language learning in the years before puberty.

Cue.   A stimulus used to elicit or provoke a response. Cues can be verbal or nonverbal. For example, a question cues an answer, and raised eyebrows cue an explanation.

Cultural pluralism.   Two or more ethnic groups coexisting in a community.

Culturally and linguistically diverse (CLD).   Individuals or groups whose culture and language are different from the dominant culture or language. This term is gaining in prevalence in the literature and government references and is considered more cross-culturally respectful than terms such as *limited English proficient* (LEP) and *language minority student* (LMS).

Culturally biased material.   Material that relies on cultural knowledge that cannot be assumed to be common to all.

Culture shock.   Emotional and psychological reaction to a sudden change in environment to one in which the signs and rules are unknown or not readily discernable, and in which those of the previous environment are not effective.

Curriculum-based assessment.   Method of measuring the level of achievement of students in terms of what they are taught in the classroom.

Dangling participle.   A grammar error caused by the association of the subject of the -*ing* verb with the subject of the sentence. Example: *Running,* Jason's coffee spilled.

Decode.   To get meaning from language or other symbols.

Demonstrative pronoun.   Pronoun that identifies or points out a noun. Examples: *that, this, these, those, such.*

Denotation.   The literal meaning or dictionary definition of a word.

Dental sound.   A sound produced using the teeth in articulation.

Derived.   Produced by applying a transformation rule to a basic word, phrase, or sentence. For example, *biker, biking,* and *bikes* are derived from the basic word *bike.*

Descriptive adjective.   An adjective that tells some quality of the noun. Examples: *pretty* girl, *soft* pillow.

Determiner.   In grammar, a word that signals a noun. Examples: articles *(a, the)*, demonstrative adjectives *(these, that)*, partitives *(some, each)*.

Diagnostic test.   A test that determines a student's current strengths and weaknesses in relation to part of the curriculum. Diagnostic test results answer the question, *Which of these skills or understandings does the student possess?*

Dialect.   Variant of a language, spoken by people of a particular geographic region.

Dictation.   Writing down what another person says. In ELL instruction, students explain what happened in a story or what they experienced and the teacher writes it down. This practice enables students to express what they might not be able to write independently. Also, teachers may dictate words, sentences, and short prose as students write them down. This exercise tests students' listening, vocabulary, spelling, and grammar skills.

Diphthong.   A sound created by combining two vowel sounds. Example: *long i.*

Dominant language.   The language in which the speaker is more proficient and/or that he or she uses more often.

English as a Foreign Language (EFL).   The teaching of English in non-English-speaking countries as a subject rather than using it as a primary vehicle of personal communication.

English Language Learners (ELLs).   Students whose first language is not English and who are in the process of learning English.

Encode.   To represent something in an agreed-upon form using a pattern or system of representation that has meaning for others. Examples: American Sign Language, Morse code, English.

Endangered language.   A language with a decreasing number of speakers that is being replaced by the majority language of the region. For example, some Native American languages are endangered.

Equivalent.   A word or expression that conveys the same meaning as another word or expression.

English for specific purposes (ESP).   English language instruction focused on the vocabulary and language needs of a specific career, vocation, or profession.

False cognate.   Words in different languages that have similar spellings but very different meanings.

Fluency.   Ability to read or use language with speed, accuracy, and proper expression.

Formative assessment.   Ongoing collection of data used to determine whether expectations are achieved. Examples: anecdotal records, checklists, learning logs, portfolios, student self-evaluation, and so on.

Formula.   A common expression of greeting, leave taking, and so on that is used almost automatically. Examples: *See you later. God bless you. How are you?*

Frame.   An exercise in which students insert, in various positions or slots in the sentence, a word or words that will form a semantically and grammatically correct sentence.

Fricative.   See *Continuant.*

Frustration level.   The level at which the student reads with less than 90 percent accuracy in decoding or less than 60 percent accuracy in comprehension.

Function words.   Words that convey little meaning by themselves but are used to show relationships among content words. Examples: articles, prepositions, conjunctions.

Gerund.   A noun formed by adding *-ing* to a verb. Example: *Drawing* is my hobby.

Grade-equivalent score.   A statistically estimated grade level for which a test score is the presumed average score. For example, a student achieving a grade-equivalent score of 6.5 performed as well on the test as the average student midway through sixth grade would have performed on the same test.

Grapheme.   Printed letters or groups of letters that represent the sounds (phonemes) that make up words in a spoken language.

Graphic organizer.   A visual representation of key concepts or information, such as a chart or diagram. Such a visual may be used to support the comprehension of new content being learned or to help students organize and present or record data.

Guided reading.   An explicit reading-instruction strategy in which the teacher works with a group of students who are at the same reading level to develop and practice reading strategies for carefully selected text, providing direction in pre-reading vocabulary and prediction activities, during reading word recognition and context clue use, and after reading-comprehension activities.

Heritage language.   The language a person regards as their native, home, or ancestral language.

Idiom.   A word or expression whose meaning is not derived from the literal meaning of the word or words.

Immersion.   Approach to teaching language in which the target language is used exclusively.

Inclusion.   The education of students with special learning needs in regular classes.

Indefinite pronoun.   A general rather than specific person or thing. Examples: *one, some, no one, anybody, several, both, many, few, all.*

Individual education plan (IEP).   A written plan developed for a student that describes learning goals and the program modifications and services to be provided to enable the student to achieve the goals. A collaborative planning tool for the school, the parents, the student, and other school personnel.

Inflection.   Change in pitch in spoken language. Also, the form of a word used to indicate number, tense, mood, voice, or person.

Informal assessment.   An evaluation based on teachers' observations and interactions with students using checklists, anecdotal recordkeeping, and notes.

Instructional reading level.   The level at which the student can decode a text with 90 to 94 percent word-recognition accuracy, and comprehend with 60 to 90 percent accuracy.

Interjection.   A word used alone to express strong emotion. Examples: *Oh! Congratulations! Damn! Bravo!*

Interrogative pronoun.   Used to ask a question. Examples: *who, what, whom, whose, which.*

Intonation.   The relative levels of pitch in a sentence; the variation of the four usual speech pitches (below normal, normal, somewhat above normal, very much above normal).

Intransitive verb.   A verb that does not have an object. Example: The baby *cried.*

Idea Proficiency Test (IPT). A standardized inventory assessment of oral, reading, and writing skills published by Ballard & Tighe. The IPT is often used to place students in ELL instructional classes.

Irregular verb. A verb that does not form its past tense and past participle by adding -*d* or -*ed* to the verb base. The past and past participle forms do not follow a pattern. Examples: *go, went, gone; see, saw, seen.*

Juncture. The separation or space between sounds that demarks the words. Examples: I/ *scream ice/cream; solo so/low.*

Kernel sentence. The basic sentence, containing a noun phrase and a verb phrase.

Key visual. A graphic organizer, such as a chart or form that organizes and represents key, or important, information in a visual format. Example: sound cards mounted above the chalkboard that show a key word for each sound or letter.

Knowledge framework approach. An approach to integrating the instruction of language and content that focuses on clusters of thinking skills (description, classification, sequence, principles, choice, evaluation). The approach links language, thinking, and content via learning activities.

L1. First language.

L2. Second language.

Labial sound. A sound that uses the lips in its articulation.

Language acquisition. The psycholinguistic process by which individuals gain fluent knowledge and use of a system of communication (language).

Language attrition. The gradual loss of a language by an individual or group.

Language experience approach. A literacy development approach that begins with students dictating to the teacher a story based on a common experience. The story is then used as the material for learning to read. This approach shows that what students can think they can say. What they can say can be written in words. What can be written in words can be read.

Language majority. A person or language community that is associated with the dominant language of the country.

Language minority students. Students whose primary or home language is other than English.

Language proficiency. Language fluency skills acquired in one or more languages.

Language Assessment Scales—Reading and Writing Test (LAS R/W). A standardized assessment of English or Spanish proficiency in reading and writing published by CTB/ McGraw-Hill. Used to place students, track growth, and exit students from ELL programs.

Language Assessment Scales, Oral Test (LAS-O). An individual standardized assessment of oral English or oral Spanish proficiency published by CTB/McGraw-Hill.

Lau Remedies. Guidelines for the education of limited English proficient students for school district compliance with the civil rights requirements of Title VI, based on the Supreme Court rulings in *Lau* v. *Nichols.*

Lau *v.* Nichols. A 1974 lawsuit filed by Chinese parents in San Francisco that led to a landmark Supreme Court ruling that identical education does not constitute equal education under the Civil Rights Act of 1964. As a result, schools were required to act to help non-English speakers learn.

Limited English proficiency (LEP).   The term used by the federal government, most states, and local school districts to identify those students who have insufficient English to succeed in English-only classrooms. Increasingly, English Language Learner (ELL) is used in place of LEP.

Lexical approach.   An approach to developing students' language proficiency by focusing on common phrases learned as wholes or "chunks" of language that are later used to extract patterns of grammar. Example: Watch where you're going. I'm sorry. I didn't mean to run into you.

Lexicon.   The words of the language.

Limiting adjective.   An adjective that narrows the noun or concept being discussed; possessive adjectives, demonstrative adjectives, and interrogative adjectives limit nouns. Examples: *his* sweater, *several* chairs, *whose* sandwich.

Linguistics.   The descriptive, analytic science of languages.

Linking verb.   A verb that connects the subject and the complement that describes or relates back to the subject.

Literacy.   The ability to function socially, academically, and culturally in a language. In reading instruction the term may be used strictly to refer to the ability to read and write.

Local norms.   Performance standards established using school or district results on a test or other performance indicator.

Manipulatives.   Concrete objects used to demonstrate learning concepts. Manipulatives enhance instruction by providing the opportunity to experience the concept through more than one sense.

Marker.   A word or word part that identifies the grammatical function of a word. For example, the words *a* and *the* are noun markers.

Mass noun.   See *noncountable noun.*

Metacognition.   Recognition and regulation of one's own thought processes. During reading, the reader monitors progress and adjusts strategies for understanding and purpose.

Metalinguistic skills.   The ability to think about language, talk about it, separate it from context, analyze it, and judge it. Metalinguistic skills, such as phonemic awareness and sound-symbol correspondence, have been shown to predict reading achievement.

Mimicry.   In language learning, mimicry is the repetition of a speech model for the purpose of memorizing it.

Minimal pair.   Two words that differ by one sound. Examples: *beg/peg, spool/spell, kid/kit.*

Miscue analysis.   An analysis of the types of errors a student makes in reading to determine the underlying cause. The results are used to plan instruction for individual students. See *running record.*

Modal auxiliary verb.   A verb that indicates possibility, need, ability, willingness, or obligation. Modals include *can, could, should, may, might, must, ought, shall, will,* and *would.* Examples: You *may* stay out late. I *ought* to call home.

Modal Score.   The score most frequently earned by the test takers.

Modeling.   Demonstrating a learning activity. Frequently the teacher demonstrates an action, then students do it with him, then students do it alone.

Modification.   Changes made to a student's program or instruction that reflect an individualized education plan.

Modified program.   A program that has learning outcomes different from those of the prescribed curriculum and that are specifically selected to meet the student's special needs.

Morpheme.   The smallest unit of speech that conveys meaning. Bound morphemes cannot stand alone (*-ed,* for instance, designates past tense); free morphemes can stand alone (for example, *toy*).

Multisensory activities.   Lesson activities that use more than one sense (seeing, hearing, touching, smelling, moving, tasting).

Nasal sound.   A sound that requires the flow of air through the nose for articulation.

National norms.   Performance standards established by administering a test or other performance indicator to a group of people representative of the national population.

Native language.   The language a person acquires first in life or identifies with as a member of an ethnic group.

Natural order hypothesis.   The assumption that language elements are learned in a reasonably fixed order by all language groups.

Newcomer program.   A program for recent immigrant students, often at middle or high school level, that includes beginning English language skills, basic academic skills, and acculturation to school and the community.

Noncountable noun.   Something that cannot be counted. Examples: *justice, trouble, air, gold, juice, tea, water, paper, electricity, work*.

Non–English proficient (NEP).   Having virtually no command of English in the communicative skills areas of speaking, listening, reading, or writing.

Norm-referenced test.   A test that compares the performance of the test taker to the performance of similar individuals who have previously taken the test. See *norming population*.

Normal distribution.   A statistical distribution of performance scores in which the mean, mode, and median scores are the same and the proportion of performance scores declines as performance moves away from the mean.

Norming population.   The group of people used to establish performance standards for age or grade levels on a test or other performance indicator. The composition of the norming population must be similar to that of the population of interest for a standardized test to be appropriate.

Noun.   A word that names or points out a person, place, thing, or idea. It can act or be acted upon. Examples: *teacher, home, bike, democracy*.

Numeracy.   A term used to refer to the world of numbers and their application to everyday life. It suggests a person's fluency in mathematical operations and the application of mathematical concepts.

Observational data.   Data gathered through teacher monitoring of a student to determine the level of performance.

Office of English Language Acquisition (OELA).   A U.S. Department of Education office with responsibility to support school districts' efforts to provide an equal education opportunity to ELLs. See http://www.ed.gov/offices/oela.

Passive vocabulary.   What a learner can recognize or understand in both oral and print contexts. Also *receptive vocabulary*. (See *active vocabulary* to compare.)

Passive voice.   When the subject of a verb is the receiver of the action. Example: The pie was baked by Marie.

Past participle.   A verbal that is based on a verb and acts like an adjective. Past participles end in *-ed, -en, -d, -t,* or *-n,* as in *wanted, stolen, saved, felt,* and *seen.*

Patterned practice.   The repetition of structured sentence patterns; includes the substitution of elements in the sentence, and modifications to other parts of the sentence to retain correct syntax. Example: I have a rose. I have two roses.

Percentile rank.   The comparison of the test taker's score with the scores of others; reported as the percentage of all test takers who scored equal to or below the test taker's score. For example, a percentile rank of 94 means the test taker's score was equal to or above the score of 94 percent of the total group of test takers.

Performance assessment.   An activity that requires students to accomplish a complete complex task, integrating both past and recently acquired knowledge and skills that are relevant to the task.

Performance indicators.   A specific description of an outcome in terms of observable and assessable behaviors. Example: All fourth graders will achieve a minimum of 82 percent on the district test of frequently used words.

Performance standards.   Established levels of achievement, quality of performance, or degree of proficiency.

Personal pronoun.   A pronoun that refers to one or more individuals or things. Personal pronouns have three cases: nominative (*I, he, we*), possessive (*my, his, our*), and objective (*me, him, us*).

Primary home language other than English (PHLOTE).   Identifies the language spoken at home.

Phonemes.   Small, discrete spoken sounds of a language that help to distinguish one word from another. They affect meaning but do not have meaning in and of themselves.

Phonemic awareness.   The awareness that sounds make up spoken words, and the ability to discriminate the individual sounds.

Phonemics.   The study of the sounds of a language.

Phonetics.   The study of the sounds of speech and their production.

Phonics instruction.   A way of teaching reading that focuses on teaching children to understand the relationships between the sounds of the spoken words they hear and the letters of the written words they see in print.

Phonics.   The predictable relationship between the sounds (phonemes) of spoken language and the letters and spellings (graphemes) that represent those sounds in written language. Also the study of sound and spelling correspondences in a language.

Phonological awareness.   The oral language ability to segment and analyze spoken words in several different ways. Examples: *syllables, onsets,* and *rhymes.*

Phrasal verb.   A verb plus a preposition or adverb that together create a meaning different from the original verb. Examples: *hand over, look up, run into.* Can be separable (*Hand it over.*) or inseparable (*When did you run into Tom?*).

Pitch.   The lowness or highness of a sound or tone.

Plosive sound.   A sound that requires a burst of air through the lips for articulation.

Possessive pronoun.   A pronoun that shows ownership when used with a noun. Examples: *my* hat, *our* tickets, *their* dog.

Preposition.   A word used to show the relationship of a noun or pronoun to another word. Examples: *to, on, across, below, of, at, from.*

Present participle.   A verbal based on a verb that acts like an adjective. Ends in *-ing.* Examples: *flying, leaking, smoking.*

Preview-Review Method.   A bilingual instructional approach in which content areas are previewed in one language, presented in another, and reviewed in the first.

Primary language.   The language in which the speakers are most fluent or that they prefer to use. Not necessarily their first language.

Productive language.   The language a learner is able to produce independently. (See also *receptive language.*)

Proficiency test.   A standardized test that compares the performance of the student with a standard or criterion used to describe a condition of proficiency or competence. (See also *criterion-referenced test.*)

Pronoun.   A word used in place of a noun. Can be personal, interrogative, relative, indefinite, demonstrative, or reflexive. Examples: *it, my, I, them, who, that.*

Proper adjective.   An adjective derived from a proper noun. Always capitalized. Examples: *Italian* bread, *Irish* coffee.

Proper noun.   A noun that names a specific person, place, or thing. Always capitalized. Examples: *Jennifer, New Jersey, North Sea, Eiffel Tower, Central Park.*

Read alouds.   A literacy instruction strategy in which the teacher first discusses the pictures and key words of a story with the students, who have the opportunity to make predictions about the story and to think about what they already know about the subject (prior knowledge). Then the teacher reads a section of the story, followed by the students reading the same section with the teacher. Next the students read the story aloud as a group without the teacher. Later, in a small group, students have the opportunity to read sections independently, either silently or aloud.

Readability.   The level of difficulty of a written passage. Depends on factors such as length of words, length of sentences, grammatical complexity, and word frequency.

Reading inventory.   A checklist or questionnaire for gathering information about a student's reading ability, interests, behaviors, and so on.

Reading recovery.   An early-intervention reading program developed by Marie Clay that provides highly structured, intensive daily reading instruction for students at risk in reading. See http://www.readingrecovery.org.

Realia.   Objects from real life used in classroom instruction. Examples: *coins, buttons, measuring spoons, measuring cups, articles of clothing.*

Receptive language.   The language a learner can understand but not yet produce effectively. (See also *productive language.*)

Redundancy.   The presence of multiple signals of linguistic information. For example, in *The actress opened her suitcase, -ess* and *her* indicate that the subject is female.

Referent.   A referent is the actual thing, action, quality, or idea to which a word refers.

Reflexive pronoun.   A pronoun that refers to a noun and provides emphasis or shows distinction from others. Formed with the suffix *-self* or *-selves*. Examples: Gloria told me *herself*. The boys fixed the car by *themselves*.

Register.   A systematic variation—including select vocabulary, sentence structure, and tone—associated with a particular communication environment. For example, different registers are used for ceremonial language than for dialogue among friends, and explanations given to adults have different registers than explanations given to young children.

Regular verb.   A verb that forms its past tense and past participle by adding the suffix *-d* or *-ed* to the verb base.

Rejoinder.   A response to a reply.

Relative pronoun.   A pronoun that relates groups of words to nouns or other pronouns. Examples: *who, which, that.*

Rhythm.   The regular pattern in speech sequences caused by the position of accented and unaccented syllables.

Right-to-Left Strings.   Strings of letters or words used to teach intonation patterns in oral language. In a right-to-left string, the last sound or word is pronounced first, then the next to the last plus the last, and so on, until the entire word or sentence is constructed from right to left and pronounced. Example: *ball. The ball. Hit the ball. Jill hit the ball.*

Rubric.   A set of general criteria used to evaluate a student's performance in a given outcome area. A rubric consists of a fixed measurement scale (for example, four-point) and a list of criteria that describe the characteristics of products or performances for each score point.

Running record.   A tool for coding, scoring, and analyzing a student's miscues while reading aloud. The analysis can inform instruction, evaluation, reporting, and grouping.

Scaffolding.   Support for students' learning and use of knowledge or a skill by providing just enough instruction, modeling, graphic organizers, context clues, questioning, and feedback to accomplish the task. Based on Vygotzsky's theory that learning takes place in the "zone of proximal development."

Second language.   The second language an individual learned, or the individual's less frequently used, weaker language.

Segmental phonemes.   Vowels and consonants.

Segmentation.   The phonological processing ability to break words into their component phonemes or sound parts.

Semantics.   The study of word meanings and communication.

Silent period.   An early stage of second language acquisition in which students listen and begin to recognize sounds, rhythms, and some words in the new language but are not ready to produce language.

Skimming.   A rapid reading strategy that focuses on getting the main idea or gist of the material by reading headings, bold text, first sentences of paragraphs, and some content words (nouns, verbs, adjectives).

Slot.   The position of a word or group of words in a sentence. (See also *frame.*)

Social communicative competence.   The ability to use natural speech communication in a variety of social situations, including the classroom. (See also *academic communicative competence.*)

Spanish Assessment of Basic Education (SABE).   A series of norm-referenced tests published by CTB/McGraw-Hill for grades 1 through 8. Designed to measure achievement in the basic skills of reading, mathematics, spelling, language, and study skills. Statistically linked with the Comprehensive Tests of Basic Skills (CTBS) and the California Achievement Tests (CAT).

Speech language pathologist (SLP).   A communication professional, sometimes called a *speech therapist,* who is educated and trained to assess, diagnose, treat, and help prevent speech, language, cognitive-communication, voice, fluency, and related speech and language disorders.

Standard English.   The variety of English used in textbooks and by most educated English speakers, though they may speak another variety or dialect in social and community contexts.

Standardized test.   A test for which norms or standards have been established using a select population of test takers under set conditions.

Stanford Achievement Test, Ninth Edition (SAT 9).   A widely used norm-referenced assessment of English reading vocabulary, reading comprehension, mathematics problem solving and procedures, and language (prewriting, composing, and editing). Published by Harcourt Assessment.

Stanine score.   A score from 1 to 9 assigned to a raw score for performance on a test or other performance indicator. Stanine scores have a mean of 5 and a standard deviation of 2.

Stop.   A consonant that requires a stoppage of breath to articulate. Examples: /p/, /t/.

Stress.   See *accent* and *rhythm.*

String.   A sequence of letters or words.

Structure.   The grammatical forms of a language.

Subtractive bilingualism.   A second language learned with the expectation that it will replace the first language. Immersion and English-only programs may have this outcome.

Summative assessment.   The use of a collection of data to make a judgment about a student's achievements in relation to a standard or to a body of knowledge.

Suprasegmental phonemes.   Language features such as pitch, stress, and juncture that are added to the sounds of vowels or consonants.

Syntax.   The acceptable pattern of the parts of speech in a language; common grammatical patterns.

Tagmeme.   A word and the position it fills in a sentence. (See also *frame* and *slot.*)

Target language.   The language a child is learning as a second language.

Tense.   The form of a word that indicates the relative position in time of the action or state of being referred to in the sentence. The three simple tenses are *present, past,* and *future.* The progressive form of the tenses is used to show continuing action.

Teachers of English to Speakers of Other Languages (TESOL).   An international professional organization for teachers, administrators, and others concerned with teaching English to speakers of other languages. For additional information, visit their Web site at http://www.tesol.org.

Total physical response (TPR).   An instructional strategy that uses students' physical movements to enhance learning. In a TPR lesson, the teacher gives a set of commands and students act them out. For example, the teacher says, "Touch your right ear," and the students touch their right ears. The strategy allows all students to practice responding at the same time.

Transfer.   A person's use of knowledge of his or her native language in the study of a new language.

Transitive verb.   A verb that relates an action that has an object. Example: Ellen *baked* the bread.

Universal Design for Learning (UDL).   An approach that takes into account learner diversity and identifies and removes barriers to learning present in materials and instructional activities so that each student can be engaged and progress. Uses media to provide multiple means of representation to give learners various ways of acquiring information and knowledge; multiple means of expression to provide learners with alternatives for demonstrating what they know; and multiple means of engagement to tap into learners' interests, offer appropriate challenges, and increase motivation.

Validity.   The measure of the extent to which a test measures what it purports to measure.

Verb.   A word that shows a physical or mental action, or the state of being of a subject. Examples: *sit, think, appear, know.*

Visual imagery.   The process of forming mental images while reading, writing, listening to a story, or recalling an event.

Voiced sound.   A sound produced with the vocal cords vibrating. Examples: *these, butter.*

Voiceless sound.   A sound produced without the vocal cords vibrating. Examples: *thin, pat.*